**This book is to be returned on or before
the last date stamped below.**

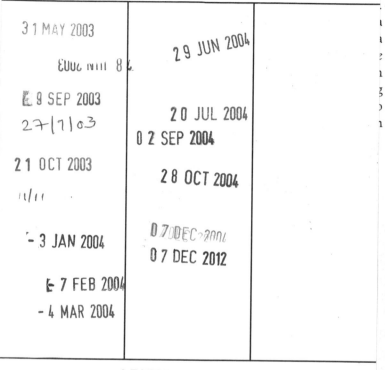

LEARNING FOR LIFE
LONDON BOROUGH OF SUTTON LIBRARIES

RENEWALS   Please quote: date of return, your ticket number
and computer label number for each item.

Consider the Lilies

AUBERON WAUGH

HOUSE OF
STRATUS

Copyright © 1968 Auberon Waugh

This edition published in 2001 by House of Stratus, an imprint of Stratus Holdings plc, 24c Old Burlington Street, London, W1X 1RL, UK.

www.houseofstratus.com

Typeset, printed and bound by House of Stratus.

A catalogue record for this book is available from the British Library.

ISBN 0-7551-0551-6

For Alistair MacColl

CHAPTER ONE

'Interviews always make me nervous. When I presented myself at CACTM to be accepted as a candidate, the first question they asked me was why I wanted to become a priest. I replied: 'Because I like meeting people.'

This was the most acceptable answer, but it could not be further from the truth. I am an intensely shy person, and find any communication with other people a nervous strain, particularly when it exceeds the minimum required to impart essential information. Meetings involve endless, tedious obligations: people expect to be remembered and recognised; they even expect that one should attach some sort of importance to their identity. Yet it is my experience that other people differ from each other in only the minutest detail. They all seek freedom from discomfort, but I have never been able to see anything admirable or holy in their quest, nor any reason why I should assist them. When one balances the supreme importance we attach to our concerns against the fact that we are all destined to an absurdly short life-span, we appear to be mildly ridiculous. Gillian, of course, does not agree. Neither would a common field-mouse. Indeed, with such a weight of opinion against me, I could well be wrong.

Gillian has very little sense of humour, and I suspect – although the distinction is unimportant – that she has an inferior intelligence to my own. No worth attaches to possession of a high intelligence, and it is possible that her opinions are as valid as mine. Nothing is so unimportant as an opinion. It is just, as I sometimes try to explain to her, that her opinions are liable to be more boring.

Gillian will have none of this. I am not sure that she knows the meaning of boredom. She judges everything by the sterner criterion of moral worth. As a clergyman I could scarcely argue with that, except that her morality is defective. One of the great messages of the New Testament, it seems to me, is that boredom is also a sin. Half of Jesus' remarks seem prompted by a conscious desire to say the unexpected. I mentioned this once to the Bishop, Dr Toplass, and he agreed enthusiastically. If we are right, then Gillian is the most offending soul alive and will probably go to Hell. I would have mentioned this to her if she had not been driving, but nothing would make such a bad impression at an interview as a corpse.

Of course, Jesus' example is no good at interviews. Questions and answers there do not have the purpose of eliciting information. They are merely a catechism to ensure that candidates know the right answers. Deviations are not encouraged. I very much doubt whether Jesus would have been accepted for training in the priesthood of the Church of England.

In fact, I am being irresponsible. So great is the shortage of priests that almost anybody is accepted nowadays. The one candidate to be turned down at my CACTM was semi-literate – he could write only in capital letters – and gave as his reason for wishing to become a priest that he had been visited in his sleep by an Angel who revealed that the end of the world was at hand. Even then he might have passed if he had not seemed at one stage to be advocating the death penalty for sinners. The Church has its image to consider.

But even if Jesus had scraped through His CACTM and suffered the outrageous indignities of a theological college, I doubt very much whether He would have made the right impression when He came to apply for the presentation of a living. Only a few are still in private hands, but both Gillian and myself felt it most unjust that we should have to motor fifty miles to a rich man's house and answer whatever impertinent and uninformed questions he might choose to ask. Neither of us had ever heard of Mr Eugene Boissaens, nor he of us. He might have High Church leanings, in which case I could assure him of my firm belief in the efficacy of the sacraments. Or he might be an evangelical, in which case I could quote extensively from the Old Testament and refer to it as the Good Book. In neither case did it matter much, as there were unlikely to be any other applicants for the living, but I detest uncertainty.

Gillian is often shocked by my acquiescence in opinions I do not hold. Unlike her, I am seldom guilty of conscious deception over ascertainable fact. Neither she nor I attach any importance to other people's opinions, but, unlike me, she attaches considerable importance to her own. She is both wrong and illogical, of course. In the days when we used to discuss these things, I frequently accused her of solipsism, but she never knew what it meant and was much too lazy to look it up.

Since the Church accepted me for the ministry on the strength of my assurance that I enjoyed meeting people – when in fact I do not – it might be argued that my Orders are invalid. In idle moments, it amuses me to speculate along these lines. But the only other acceptable answer to the question of why a candidate wishes to become a priest is even more ridiculous:

'Because I feel it a challenge.'

I tried rehearsing this answer to myself, and even in front of a mirror, but I could never say it with a straight face. Of course, I had little to lose. The life of a chartered accountant is tedious, and undignified, but it is a long way short of ultimate humiliation. In any case, many candidates who replied that they felt the ministry a challenge became involved in an interminable discussion about how they were to meet this challenge. It hinted at restless, radical zeal, an urge to uproot and change. Hours of time were spent in assuring the panel that they had no such intentions. My own interview was much easier.

'You are aware that some of these people will not belong to the same social class as yourself?'

I replied that my pleasure would be undiminished.

'Have you in fact much experience of mixing with ordinary sort of people?'

I replied that I engaged them in conversation at every opportunity, in railway carriages or in the Street. This was not true, of course, but the question was a silly one. It is almost impossible to escape contact nowadays, even if it is only on the level of inane smiles.

'But you must be aware of your position. People like to look up to their vicar.'

I assured them that I would strike the balance between condescension and over-familiarity.

Of all human relationships, that between interviewer and interviewed is the least satisfactory. Many people rejoice in it as a means of talking about themselves and making new discoveries about their own fascinating personalities. I have never had the slightest interest in my own personality, and would never enquire about anyone else's. But this interview with Mr Boissaens was really most important, ridiculous as it may sound. Anybody who has spent six years as an assistant curate in Swindon, bearing the Christian message among the shiftiest and stupidest people on earth, will have decided that any additional advantages which might accrue in the after-life cannot possibly justify the outlay of risk-capital investment in this one. It is almost impossible to believe that the inhabitants of Swindon have immortal souls. If, as I suspect, they have not, then it is probable that I have none. By applying for a country parish, I had at least hoped to cut my losses. But everything depended on the goodwill of a total stranger.

We drove through Reading in silence, broken only by the noise of Gillian chewing a barley-sugar. She is recklessly self-indulgent with other people's money. Before we reached Twyford, my hatred of the patronage system in the Church of England, my loathing of the rich and my especial contempt for Mr Eugene Boissaens had resolved themselves into a single, nervous ache.

'If you see a Gentlemen's lavatory, we might stop for a moment,' I said.

'Certainly not,' said Gillian. 'If you can't control yourself at the age of thirty four you should be back at school again.'

I glared at the back of her head with loathing. She often insisted on driving, and I always insisted on sitting in the back seat, as it was my only way of annoying her. I could have pointed out that no schools offer this sort of learning as part of the curriculum, but it would have been a waste of time. She would have answered: 'Then it is high time they did.'

I could have pointed out that her statement, which represented an opinion, offered no solution to my present troubles, but Gillian is as illogical as she is spiteful, and would have thought that she had won the argument. As it was, she continued to chew barley-sugar.

We arrived at the gates of Middlewalk Hall fifteen minutes before my appointment, so we stopped the car and lit cigarettes. I got out and walked behind a rhododendron bush.

'Just like a little schoolboy, piddling behind a tree,' said Gillian when I returned. 'What will your parishioners say when they see you?'

Relief had made me light-hearted. 'I expect they will say: "There goes Vicar piddling"', I said.

Humour was never a good idea with Gillian. She returned to the attack.

'I'm glad you think so. They'll probably be delighted to have a dirty little boy as their vicar. I suppose you hope that someone will go sniffing around after you, like a dog.'

'Oh, shut up,' I said.

'Why should I?' she began, but I had blocked my ears.

Occasional noises came through. '...Piddle...puddle...dirty... wee-wee...smelly.'

When it was over, I said: 'I'm sorry if I was short–tempered, but I am a little nervous about this interview.' All conversation between us had to end with an apology from me. It was one of the conventions which had supported our married life for seven years. A clergyman has to have a wife, and I never supposed that Gillian was much worse than any of the others.

From scolding her little boy, Gillian hastened to uphold him. 'Who is Mr Boissaens, anyway?'

'I believe he's very rich.'

'Fancy being famous just for being rich. I wouldn't be very proud of myself. Don't go sucking up to him.'

'He isn't even famous for that. Nobody in Swindon had heard of him and he isn't in *Who's Who*. Probably some dim little squire who wants to find out if I'm a gentleman.'

'Do you think you'll pass?'

'I don't know. We can only do our best. You'd better stay in the car.'

But when we drove up to the Hall, it was obvious that Mr Boissaens was no impoverished landowner. Enormous lawns stretched in every direction, three huge American cars were drawn up on the gravel and the whole house, a Georgian pile of crippling elegance, smelled unmistakably of money.

I climbed the winding stone steps. Before I could ring, the door swung open, and a plump man stood wringing his hands in front of me.

'Mr Boissaens?' I said.

The plump man grinned and nodded. A thinner man behind the door grinned and pointed. I followed the plump man over a marble floor, through two rooms smelling of pot-pourri and hot-house lilies into a small white drawing-room where the panelling had been picked out in gilt and a huge painting by Stubbs stood over the white marble fireplace. I was left alone, and started reading an old copy of *Country Life*, perched awkwardly on the sofa. Perhaps Mr Boissaens was a particularly successful dentist, and this was his waiting room. Jade objects were strewn about on every flat surface, and at one end an urn which looked as if it must have been a baptismal font, made of bluejohn, held the kind of flower display you normally see only at very fashionable weddings in London.

Presently, I was joined by a large, handsome woman who held a pair of secateurs.

'Mr Trumpeter, I am terribly sorry to have kept you waiting. You're the new vicar, aren't you?'

'My appointment is not official yet. I came to see Mr Boissaens,' I said pompously.

She laughed as if she were genuinely amused.

'Eugene has no interest in village affairs, and I don't think he's been to church since we were married. He only wants to hear what you have to say, and probably to see if he can fluster you. Don't worry about him. I'm the one you'll have to deal with.'

She was exactly like the matron of a large hospital, large and friendly, but strangely formidable. At least she was a recognisable type. I was beginning to feel uneasy in the presence of such wealth.

'Can I assume that I've got the job?'

'You'll have to ask Eugene. Unless he takes a violent dislike to you, it should be all right. Do you feel strongly about South Africa?'

'I'm not sure. What does he feel?'

'That's all right then. Oh, and don't make any jokes about suicides. People always do. If you can keep him off the subject of religion, you'll be a lot happier.'

'I see. Has he any particular topics which he enjoys discussing?'

Again Mrs Boissaens laughed.

'Nothing bores him, except politeness. You can tell him about the sea-shell industry in Antigua or Portuguese weaving or the problems of negro workers in Halifax and he will be utterly absorbed. He is nearly blind, you see, and can't read. He has just finished talking to a lot of men about business, and he will probably be very pleased to hear you. Remember to answer him straight. He likes that. Afterwards, I will show you the Rectory where you may be going to live. Come along and I'll introduce you.'

I was led through two more rooms and a circular hall. Mrs Boissaens walked in a slightly disjointed way, as if trying to make me feel at home amid such splendour. I followed her carefully, afraid of slipping on the marble or tripping over some priceless Chippendale footstool. Eventually she knocked on a polished mahogany door, smiling at me as if to apologise.

'We never know what we may find him doing,' she whispered.

'Come in,' said a voice. 'Why are you whispering outside my door?'

'This is Mr Trumpeter, the new vicar. I was telling him not to be frightened of you.'

'You are quite wrong. There is no new vicar until I have appointed one. How do you do, Mr Trumpeter? You will forgive my not getting up. I am unable to do so without assistance.'

'My husband is an invalid,' explained Mrs Boissaens. I looked compassionate.

'It is kind of you to point it out,' said Mr Boissaens. 'But, no doubt your friend is capable of rational deduction. Finding me in an invalid chair covered with blankets, he must have decided either that I was constrained to appear like this or that I was mad. The term "invalid" embraces either affliction, nowadays. Perhaps you would be kind enough to leave me alone with Mr Trumpeter. You will understand that the appointment of a vicar is a heavy responsibility, and I am afraid you will only distract us both.'

After Mrs Boissaens had withdrawn, with a conspiratorial smile at me, I was left in a large, white-painted room completely devoid of furniture, facing Mr Boissaens across twenty feet of marble flooring. He was a small man with a thin, wasted face. Under some orderly white hair, his appearance was intelligent but not kindly. A pair of gold–framed spectacles could only be worn as an ornament, or to stop people looking into his eyes.

'I would ask you to sit, but as you may have noticed there are no chairs, and I fear you might find the floor rather hard.'

'That is all right,' I murmured. They were the first words I had spoken.

'I am sorry, I did not catch what you said.'

'Nothing. I just said that it was all right. I have no objection to standing.'

Mr Boissaens weighed my words carefully.

'Good,' he said eventually. 'Of course it would be a grave handicap in your profession if you did have objections to standing, or if, as in my case, you were able to stand only with the greatest difficulty. My wife may have told you that I am not a religious man, but I understand that the celebrant at your religious gatherings almost invariably stands. In weighing up your suitability for my parish, I shall bear in mind your readiness to stand as a definite point in your favour.'

I began to suspect that the old man was baiting me. There was nothing facetious about his manner. I gave a noncommittal giggle and muttered, 'Thank you'.

'But there are other considerations. I have no quarrel with the content of such remarks as you have so far addressed to me, but your manner of delivery leaves much to be desired. I should have thought that clarity of enunciation was vital for a parson. Is that how they teach clergymen to talk nowadays? Perhaps modern churchgoers like to hear a stream of unrecognisable noises, and find it more conducive to prayer than words which, however well delivered, are equally meaningless.'

'I am sorry if I have not been speaking clearly. So far, I have had very little to say, because you have asked me no questions. If there is anything you would like to know about me, I shall be happy to answer.' It was difficult to be polite, but I would have been prepared to lick him from head to foot if it ensured that I should never return to Swindon.

'That is much better. I am not hard of hearing, and I enjoy conversation. It is one of the few means I have of communicating with other people. Increasingly, I find that conversation takes the form of a monologue from me and indeterminate grunts from my companion. Three men who came to lunch had flown all the way from Cape Town to see me, and a fourth had come from Canada. Yet all they had to contribute when they arrived were a few grunts and some titters. Is that how businessmen communicate? Clearly the secret is to ask questions.'

'I was ordained priest in 1961, and spent six years as curate in an industrial parish in Swindon,' I said.

'How fascinating. Was your ordination accompanied by great festivity, or was it gloomy and decorous? Were you Anointed with Holy Oil, or did you just receive a contract through the post? Are the industrial workers of Swindon any less stupid than the farm labourers of my village? How has prosperity affected them? Are their coarse appetites refined by affluence, or has it brutalised them still further?'

'Definitely the latter,' I said. 'But few of them ever come to church, so we only see them at a distance. Many of the workers in pressed steel earn £30 a week, and I think they despised us for our poverty. I should like to think they feel ashamed. None of them is remotely interested in religion and many feel a conscious antipathy.'

'I very much doubt whether they feel ashamed of being richer. I do not know your private circumstances, and it would be impertinent to ask, but I would be prepared to hazard that I am slightly the richer. I feel no shame, merely a keen sense of enjoyment in the disparity. But perhaps I am exceptional. Poor people such as yourself never realise the extent to which you are hated by the well-to-do. What did you talk about with my wife?'

'She was very kind, and offered to show me over the Rectory.'

'That was wrong of her, as I had not agreed to present you with the living. Nor have I yet. No doubt you thought she was charming?'

'She seemed very kind.'

'Angela loathes and detests you. No matter what you do, she will always hold you in the greatest contempt. She will patronise you and be infinitely kind. She may even accept you as her lover. But you will always be an inferior animal, because you are poor and she is rich. Are you married?'

'Yes.'

'Where is your wife?'

'I left her in the car.'

The springs on Mr Boissaens' black steel chair creaked as he shook with delighted, silent laughter.

'How wonderful. Was she not considered an advantage? Perhaps she is coloured? No, I fear it simply means she is a neurotic, and not suitable for civilised company. Mr Trumpeter, I shall be delighted to give you the living. The stipend is not large – £1,200 a year. In New York, that would be considered beneath the poverty line. But I propose to add £500 a year of my own, on condition that you come up and see me occasionally while I am in England. Do you play chess?'

'A little.'

'Piquet, Bezique, Draughts, Gin Rummy, Dominoes? Never mind, I shall teach you them all. I tried the same arrangement with your predecessor, but he was an infinitely dull man and insisted on bringing his wife. Words cannot describe the tedium of that woman. I believe she has now been locked up. Let me congratulate you on your appointment as the new incumbent of Middlewalk, Berkshire.'

'Thank you very much.'

'Eh?'

'I said that I can see no reason why you should ever meet my wife, if you do not wish to. She is not very sociable by nature.'

'That's better. I think you will make a fine upstanding parson. Of course, I have asked you none of the right questions. My eyesight is poor, you know. I should have asked if you have a plump, red face. Have you greedy little eyes? Do you constantly lick your lips with a thin, brown tongue? These are the tests by

which you can tell the genuine Anglican parson from any
imposter. But I was interested in what you said about the
industrial working class of Swindon. I share their antipathy to
religion, I think, but not their lack of interest.'

'In that case,' I said coyly, 'there is still hope that I shall be able
to light a candle.'

For the first time, Mr Boissaens looked annoyed. 'You
misunderstand me. I have no interest in the claims of your
Church, or those of any other. I have already investigated them,
and they seem too ridiculous to merit rational discussion. What
interests me is why so many people should choose to acquiesce
in these preposterous suggestions. Why did you decide to
become a priest in the Church of England?'

'Because I felt it a challenge,' I replied, looking him full in his
gold-rimmed spectacles.

Once again the black steel chair rocked as Mr Boissaens
laughed. I laughed too. After all, I had made a very good joke.

Mrs Boissaens was just a shade more patronising to Gillian than
to me. Her manner suggested a constant, valiant struggle not to
be patronising. But I think she was genuinely interested in us
both, in so far as such a woman can ever be interested in anyone
except herself.

'I hope you'll both call me Angela,' she said. 'Mrs Boissaens
makes me sound so terribly old.' Gillian, being a simpleton,
immediately did as she was told, but I wasn't going to give the
great lady any cheap, egalitarian thrills. Mrs Boissaens was old
enough to be my mother, but she was strikingly handsome.
Although it would be inaccurate to describe her plump, jerky
great body as voluptuous, there was something about her manner
which suggested that she liked a good time.

'Here is the Rectory. You'll find there is plenty of room inside
it. It's a pity, really, you haven't any children, but you'll probably
be able to keep it a good deal tidier without them.'

Gillian bridled. She had decided some time before our wedding that in deference to the hunger of the underdeveloped world and our own acute housing shortage in England, it would be most irresponsible to burden the economy with further hungry mouths. This decision was communicated to me in a series of lengthy harangues which helped to pass the tedious hours of courtship. It was a matter of complete indifference to me. I find very little pleasure in the company of children, and have no desire to procreate my species or perpetuate my name.

Our Rectory was vast. 'You'll find it nearly as big as Middlewalk,' said Mrs Boissaens, immensely tickled that any poor parson's dwelling could be compared to her own luxurious abode. 'The garden is in a bit of a mess. Poor Mr Mandarill was never much of a gardener, and when his wife was taken ill, he rather let things go. Perhaps I can come down and give you a hand sometimes.' If she wished, she could have sent half a dozen gardeners from the Hall who would have cleared it up in a single day. But she was far too tactful even to contemplate such a course of action. 'Tell me, Gillian, you do like gardening, don't you?'

'No,' said Gillian. 'Not much.'

'Such a pity,' said Mrs Boissaens. 'You could have such a lovely garden here. There must be at least four acres of it, not counting the orchard. It looks as if Nicholas and I will have to do it all. You wait here and I will get the keys from Mr Swinger.'

We sat in the car, staring at the gaunt façade of what was to be our new home. I counted fourteen windows in a row on each floor. The house had been built in a variety of styles around the turn of the century, but Byzantine predominated. Two small onion-shaped domes at each end had turned blue, but the centre dome, a huge protuberance reminding us both of Madame Tussaud's Planetarium, had been skimped, and was covered with asbestos.

'Home, sweet home,' I said merrily.

'I hate that woman. She worries me,' said Gillian.

'Why? She seems rather amusing,' I said, purely to annoy her. 'I don't know how she discovered my Christian name.'

'How on earth are we going to furnish the place?' asked Gillian, ever practical when there was a chance to be disagreeable.

'It looks as if I shall have to sell some of my shares.' When my father died, I received £10,000. It was just after the war, and my trustee patriotically invested it all in 3½% undated gilt edged securities. They are now worth £4,000 in theory, but of course that sum represents only about a quarter of what it would have bought originally. In effect, I have lost nine tenths of my patrimony through the exercise of thrift and patriotism. Neither virtue has ever appealed to me much in any case.

'Here we are,' said Mrs Boissaens. 'We have been invited to tea by Mrs Swinger afterwards. Isn't that sweet of her? You will find the Swingers invaluable. They practically run the village. Here is the great hall. Mrs Mandarill used to use it for jumble sales before her illness, and the village always use it for carol singing and junior First Aid practice. On the left here is the old library, but as you can see that is full of British Legion things. The Boy Scouts used to meet here before the troop was merged. In the corner are decorations left over from the last Coronation. You could throw them out now if you wanted to, but the village spent so many hours' work on them that it might be kinder to keep them somewhere. This room is full of the Mandarill's clothes and things, and I think it would be better if you didn't go in there. Through here is the conservatory. In this little room the Mandarills used to keep their pets. The RSPCA had to come and clean it out after poor Mr Mandarill's accident.'

'What happened?' said Gillian breathlessly. We had walked down two long corridors, through rooms smelling of damp, and dogs, and an indefinable odour, probably vegetable, reminiscent of flower water which has not been thrown out. Nearly all the rooms were furnished after a fashion.

'Haven't you heard? It was in the spring, and the poor old boy had not been seeing many people in the last few months. The milkman stopped delivering years ago, when he said it wasn't worth the journey. A few people noticed that he hadn't turned up to conduct the services for two weeks, but nobody paid much attention because he often got the days wrong. Then somebody in the village started getting up a petition to the Rural District Council for an Old People's Dance Hall, and they always go to the vicar for his signature. Mr Swinger climbed in one of the windows, and when lie noticed something funny he sent for the police. The old boy had been dead for nearly three weeks.'

'How awful,' said Gillian, much affected.

'Now here's the kitchen, where Gillian can cook all her little dishes.' An enormous iron range took up one wall. On another, the dresser held congealed pots of marmalade, peanut butter, chocolate spread and some Nescafé. 'Of course all this technically belongs to Mrs Mandarill, who is in hospital, but she doesn't take in much, and I should use anything you want. There is a married daughter who lives in Slough. She came down and removed all the silver and any furniture which was worth having. I should treat everything else as your own.'

'How did he die?'

'Mandarill? He fell down and broke his leg. He died of exhaustion and shock. It was in the big drawing-room – beyond the billiard room before you get to the old gunroom.'

'How charming,' said Gillian, her voice a mixture of sarcasm and self-pity.

'It was probably the best thing for him, really,' said Mrs Boissaens. 'In the last few years, the village had begun to suspect that their vicar had no *joie de vivre*, and they don't like that.'

I chuckled merrily to show that I was not deficient in this important quality. Gillian shivered. Somewhere in that huge building a door slammed. Mrs Boissaens took my hand in an impulsive, maternal way which had just enough of the little girl in it to make the gesture inoffensive.

'Come upstairs. I will show you the bedrooms.'

Mr Swinger had little to say, but he enjoyed staring. The only guarantee of animation in his long, sad face was supplied by a pair of yellow, red-rimmed eyes which peered through the steam from a pint mug of tea. They never closed. Mrs Swinger took her duties as hostess very seriously. The duties of a guest were simply to eat as many damp sweet biscuits as possible without being sick. Mrs Swinger supplied the conversation.

'You'll find we're all completely mad in this village. Some of the things which go on here are nobody's business. One day we'll have the newspapers down here, and then the lid will be off. Quite honestly, I wouldn't like to be the vicar here, not for all the money. There's too much competition.'

We laughed politely. Mrs Swinger had shown us to the front room, obviously reserved for great occasions such as this. The mantelpiece was decorated by hundreds of photographs of children and babies. We were clearly expected to ask about them, but neither I nor Mrs Boissaens was interested, and Gillian disapproved of babies.

'Have you told him about Mrs Hallowes and the White Circle?' said Mrs Boissaens.

'He'll learn about that soon enough,' said Mrs Swinger. 'One thing I will tell him though. Ted Mullins is seeing a great deal too much of his younger sister. We thought she'd be all right when we got her away from Willum – that's the father – but now she has to fasten on young Ted. George saw them climbing up the loft above the Flitcroft's cowshed, didn't you, George?'

'Yes,' said George. 'I saw them.'

'She didn't have any knickers on, did she, George?'

'Didn't look like it,' said George.

'It's quite surprising, some of the things George sees,' said Mrs Swinger with pride.

'What do you think the vicar should know before he comes to take up his appointment next month?' said Mrs Boissaens.

'There isn't much he can know. I don't suppose he'll be much help getting us the Dance Hall. I told you last time I saw you, Mrs

Boissaens, about how we all think the village needs a dance hall, especially for the elderly folk and the old age pensioners. I expect you didn't have time to mention it to your husband.'

'You know how busy he is,' said Mrs Boissaens.

'So are we all nowadays,' said Mrs Swinger. 'Especially the elderly folk and the old age pensioners. A lot of them are not so well off as they were, and they can't be expected to provide everything for themselves. Did you mention that to him?'

'I did. He wasn't too helpful, I'm afraid. He seemed to think that if the old age pensioners wanted to dance together, they should do it in the privacy of their own homes.'

For a moment, Mrs Swinger looked extremely disapproving. After a shocked silence, she relaxed a little. 'That would be from the religious viewpoint, I expect. I thought religion says how you've got to look after the old age pensioners. What do you think, Vicar?'

She was wrong, of course. Provision of unnecessary luxuries for the aged is a very small part of the Christian message. On the other hand, concern for old age pensioners is so widespread in England nowadays that it might set itself up as a rival religion if we made no efforts to accommodate it. Personally, I have never been able to share in the general enthusiasm. People are poor through no virtue of their own, but because they lack the qualities to be otherwise, and if they are to be extravagantly rewarded in the after-life simply for being poor in this one, it strikes me as an obvious injustice

Gillian often accuses me of being a money snob, and she is right to the extent that I would sooner be bored by a rich bore than by a poor bore. The poor seldom have much originality, whatever one reads to the contrary. Heaven, if it exists at all along the lines suggested in the New Testament, must be an ineffably tedious place, like a North Country Working Man's Club on Sunday morning.

'I was asking for your opinions about our new dance hall,' said Mrs Swinger, with a dangerous edge on her voice.

'It sounds most interesting. I shall certainly enquire about the matter,' I said humbly. Mrs Swinger thought she had won a point. Foolish woman! It is not those with an income somewhere in the lower reaches of the national average who will inherit the earth. It is the *meek*.

'I must go back to the Hall and prepare my husband's tea,' said Mrs Boissaens, meaning she had to tinkle a silver bell for the tea to be brought.

'We, too, must drive back to Swindon,' I said.

'But won't you stay for a drink?' Once again, she had seized my hand impulsively. I felt the watery, yellow eyes of George Swinger on us, and shook myself free.

'No, I must return to my duties.'

'Whatever happens,' said Mrs Swinger, 'don't let Miss Honeycomb get hold of you. She will poison your mind.'

'Oh really?' I said.

'There are a lot of troublemakers in this village,' said Mrs Swinger. 'They will all try and get hold of you. Mrs Lackey is no better, but her husband drinks. They may even try and foist Arthur Long on you as People's Warden. Well, he was in trouble about five years ago. I won't tell you what I know about him but George knows, don't you George?'

'He were indecent,' said George, his eyes never wavering from me and Mrs Boissaens. 'In the Bag of Corn.'

'I expect you'll be appointing George as the Rector's Warden again,' said Mrs Swinger. 'He only likes to help.'

'No doubt. I shall arrange these things after my induction,' I said. Nobody had addressed a word to Gillian. Even through the mists of their limited understanding, it was apparent to everybody that she was a nonentity. My last impression on leaving the dismal cottage was of George Swinger's fixed unwinking stare – those same eyes which had seen Sylvia Mullins climb the ladder to Mr Flitcroft's barn without any knickers on.

CHAPTER TWO

'Reverend Father in God,' said Mrs Boissaens. 'I present unto you Nicholas Trumpeter, clerk, to be admitted to the cure of souls in this Parish.'

'Hullo, Nicky,' said Dr Toplass. 'I'm glad you cleared all the hurdles. Where is the Patron of the living?'

'He was unable to attend,' I said. 'His wife is taking his place.'

'Ah well,' said Dr Toplass. 'I suppose we'd better get on with the service.' He very much enjoyed introducing a note of informality, and was for ever winking at people in the congregation. When originally consecrated as Suffragan Bishop of Slough, Feltham and London Airport he used a magnificent seventeenth-century crozier of silver gilt, encrusted with amethyst, topaz and tourmaline. Now, translated to the ancient see of Silchester, he had somehow acquired a wooden object of hideous Scandinavian design.

'Beloved in the Lord, we accept this your presentation praying that God's blessing may rest thereon,' he intoned in a curious nasal sing-song. 'Let the declaration and oaths be made, subscribed and taken according to law.'

After I had made them, I was required to kneel in front of this preposterous clown for his blessing:

'The God of peace, who brought again from the dead Our Lord Jesus Christ, the great Shepherd of the sheep, through the blood of the everlasting covenant, make thee perfect in every good work to do His will, working in thee that which is pleasing in His sight…'

None of which indignity I would have minded if Dr Toplass had not insisted on ruffling my hair. Or if Mrs Boissaens, leading me down the aisle in front of the Rural Dean, two Churchwardens and the Archdeacon, had not insisted on holding my hand. Once again, there was something half maternal and half flirtatious in her gesture, which irritated me intensely, particularly as Gillian was watching the whole proceedings with a priggish, disapproving air. Gillian, I should mention, is a convinced atheist. It is probably the only thing which preserves my semblance of Christian belief. Her arguments are so futile, her reasoning so illogical that it is very difficult to believe, against all the evidence, that she is not wrong. For my own part, I keep an open mind about religion, which, I am sure, is the sanest and most mature approach. It is impossible to be completely dispassionate. Possibly my occasional anti-religious frenzies derive from having too much religion forced down my throat at the theological college. Nobody, least of all people intending to become clergymen, should be given too much religion. It stretches credulity and encourages cynicism.

The most important moment of the service arrived – for me, at any rate – when the Archdeacon handed me the key of the church: 'By virtue of this mandate of the Lord Bishop, I, Thomas Good-Buller, Archdeacon of Silchester, do induct you, Nicholas Trumpeter, clerk, into the real, actual and corporeal possession of the Church of St Swithin, Middlewalk, with all the rights, members and appurtenances thereto belonging, and may the Lord preserve thy going out and thy coming in from this time forth and for evermore.'

I clutched the key to my chest, and went to toll the bell seven times, signifying to those parishioners who were too idle to turn up that I was in control now. Then, red-faced and puffing, I waddled up the aisle for the rest of the charade.

'I will diligently admonish the people that they defer not the baptism of their children; and will seek out any unbaptised persons,' I said. 'I will be diligent in the saying of public and private prayers. I will be diligent in the study of God's holy word.'

The congregation joined in with various encouraging sentiments:

> We love the place, O God
> Wherein thine honour dwells;
> The joy of thine abode
> All earthly joy excels.

It was not a bad turn-out at all. Of a congregation numbering some two hundred and fifty, about three quarters came from the county or professional classes. The exceptions were easily recognisable by their dull, serious faces and obsequious attention to their prayers.

> We love the sacred font
> For there the Holy Dove
> To pour is ever wont
> His blessings from above.

Eventually, all the kneelings and curtseyings were over, and the Bishop arose to make his address. I sat back in the Rector's stall, shut out the noise of his peevish, excitable little voice and allowed my eye to wander over the congregation. Gillian sat alone, looking sour and priggish with a closed prayer book in her hand. In front of her was a gaggle of clergymen from neighbouring parishes whom I would shortly be meeting. I would have to talk to them and flatter their sense of importance, and recognise them again, and pretend to be interested in them. Worst of all, I would have to meet their ridiculous wives. At the very front sat Mrs Boissaens, her eyes completely blank, her face that study of polite inattention which I knew so well from preaching in the pulpit myself. Next to her sat a swarthy, thick-lipped girl of about 25.

It was while I was glancing at her that the disturbing thing occurred. Our eyes met. In that half-second, our souls opened to each other. As unmistakably as if she had shouted the words, I read intense passion and naked sexual curiosity. Goodness knows what she read in my eyes. Startled, we both looked away, but the struggle was too much, and throughout the sermon our eyes kept creeping back to each other's faces. Finally the Bishop, Dr Toplass, in order to make some imbecile point of his own, beat the pulpit with his hand and shouted, 'Blimey'. After the first shock of embarrassment, a few people tittered. The girl and I laughed outright. We laughed longer and louder than anyone else, because we knew that we were not laughing at Dr Toplass' antics, but at our private joke.

'The life of a clergyman is not easy. It is dedicated to God's service and to the service of every one of you in this church today. The Church of England enshrines everything that makes England a worthwhile place to live in, and I know that all of you in your heart of hearts agree, whether you are frequent churchgoers or whether you only attend for an exciting occasion like the present one. Follow me, said Jesus, and I will give you greater peace of mind, greater self-confidence, greater ability in your job, and before very long a better job with better prospects. You will have greater powers of concentration, you will make friends more easily. All this is in the Gospel, if only you take the trouble to read it. Follow Nicky Trumpeter, and he will show you the way out of your present state of despair into a new life – fuller, happier and more enjoyable than ever before. This is because, by coming to church, you will not only be doing yourselves good, but others as well. All it needs to fill the churches is for a few good people who aren't afraid of being thought "reactionary" or "old-fashioned" to set the ball rolling. Jesus always refers to us as His sheep, and of course He's absolutely right. But even the best sheep need a good shepherd, so now I'm going to ask you all to pray for your new vicar.'

In the silence, I wondered what the swarthy girl was thinking.

After my induction, we were all asked to lunch at the Hall. I was taken in charge by Mr Tuck, the Rural Dean, who introduced me to my fellow clergy:

'Mr Plimsoll.'

'How do you do.'

'Mr Jackson.'

'How do you do.'

'Mr Heifer.'

'How do you do.'

'Do you know the Archdeacon, Father Good-Buller?'

'Father Thomas,' said Mr Good-Buller. 'There are many things about which Mr Tuck and I disagree, but we remain the best of friends.'

'Oh really?' I said. Why should I be interested in that?

'Yes, indeed,' said Mr Good-Buller, who clearly found the topic absorbing. 'We have known each other for nearly twelve years, and have never had a kind word to say for each other.'

'Ha, ha.'

'Ha, ha.'

'Ha, ha, ha.'

'I say, this sherry really is most exceptionally good, don't you think?'

It had seemed much the same as any other sherry to me. No doubt the remark was intended to draw my attention to the comfort of our surroundings, about which I had no editorial comment to offer. It was hard to believe that such luxury still existed in England. In the painted salon, where we gathered, we stood on a beautiful faded pink Aubusson carpet. An enormous log fire blazed at each end of the room. Four gilt Chippendale mirrors stretched from ceiling to floor against the lime silk wall-covering. Two menservants of South European extraction carried trays, and when we moved into the dining room I counted another three menservants hovering behind the chairs. Could Mr Boissaens afford all this out of his taxed income, and pay Selective Employment Tax, too? But Middlewalk, I had been told, was only the tip of the iceberg. They had an enormous farm in Cape Province, a flat in Amsterdam, a large estate in Kenya and permanent hotel suites in Toronto and at the Dorchester. Yet the name Boissaens never appears in legends of the very rich. Perhaps there are hundreds of families like them, but it was all a revelation to me.

I sat between Mrs Boissaens and – so help me – Mrs Tuck. To spare embarrassment, I avoided talking to her as much as possible. She was nervous and shy and her little pedestrian mind was matched only by her little pedestrian stomach which gave up after the first two courses. She said that everything was very nice, and then gave up that effort, too. On the other side of Mrs Boissaens sat Dr Toplass, who seemed quite at home. Beyond him, Gillian looked disapproving and superior as course after course of exquisitely prepared food was put in front of her. At the far end of the table, between Mr Heifer and a strange man, sat my sultry raven-haired beauty. We had not exchanged a glance since leaving church. Perhaps she had forgotten our moment of intimacy. Perhaps, like me, she was shy. Mr Heifer spoke to her in an animated way, waving his knife and fork in the air. He managed to consume a huge amount of food and drink besides what he spilt down his front. Before lunch was over, he had left the room twice, red faced and sweating. On the second occasion, he walked straight into the door without taking the precaution of opening it first, and collapsed like a hippopotamus on the floor. No doubt he was trying to draw attention to himself.

Mrs Boissaens was at her most charming and poised. As she shepherded the women out of the room, she gave my hand a squeeze. 'Don't be long. I want to take you and the Bishop to see my husband before you go. Mr Orison will look after you. He is my husband's manager in Quebec.'

'This is very old-fashioned,' said Mr Heifer, when the men were left alone. 'I didn't realise they still did it. Do you know that in olden times the reason for separating the sexes after a meal was to allow everyone to release springs.'

'What, again?' said Archdeacon Good-Buller,

'I have no wish to do anything of the sort,' replied Mr Heifer stiffly, as if the idea of his ever having indulged himself in this way was in poor taste. 'I was merely remarking how habits outlive their historical context.' He helped himself to some more port, murmuring: 'Perhaps a drop.'

'Such a beautiful service,' said the Archdeacon. 'Of no liturgical significance, but of great beauty. I hope they never get round to messing it about. What do you think, Mr Orison?'

'I am afraid I know nothing. Both my parents were Catholics.'

'Roman,' murmured the Archdeacon automatically. 'But don't you think some of the words have profound significance, Mr Tuck?'

'Tommy's riding his hobby-horse,' said Dr Toplass.

'Which words?' said Mr Tuck cautiously.

'When the incumbent promises diligently and frequently to celebrate the Holy Communion of the Body and Blood of Christ, and to prepare the people for receiving the same according to their need. No doubt you made the same promise when you were inducted, Mr Tuck.'

'Symbolically speaking, of course,' said the Rural Dean.

'Where do you stand, Mr Trumpeter, on the vexed question of transubstantiation? Mr Tuck will tell you it's rubbish, Mr Jackson will say it depends what you mean, which he thinks a very clever answer, Mr Plimsoll has no interest in religious matters and Mr Heifer will say: Rather, he believes in anything which is going around.'

My own attitude was an amalgam of all four. It has always seemed to me exceedingly unlikely that by uttering some words over a few wafers and some inferior British-made wine I can change them into the Body and Blood of Christ. On the other hand I have no quarrel with those who believe that I am capable of it. Nobody would have endowed me with these miraculous abilities if I had decided to become an accountant in the City of London. Whenever anybody assures me that I possess these powers, I feel flattered and slightly grateful.

'I believe in keeping an open mind,' I said.

Good-Buller muttered something sarcastic about 'the essence of middle churchmanship,' but Dr Toplass beat the table with his jewelled hand and cried:

'Hear, hear. That is by far the most sensible answer I have heard today. It is what I would like all my clergy to say when asked these tiresome questions. People only want to make trouble. Jesus detested nobody so much as those with closed minds. Look at the Scribes and Pharisees.'

'Rotten crowd of people,' agreed Mr Heifer. But I was left with the impression that I had made an enemy of Father Archdeacon.

Mr Boissaens was sitting just as I had left him two months ago.

'I am sorry not to get up, but I am unable to do so without assistance. I should like to ask you to sit down, but as you can see there are no chairs.'

'Eugene, this is Dr Toplass, Bishop of Silchester, who has come to see you.'

'What about?'

'No particular purpose. I wished to present your new vicar to you, Mr Nicholas Trumpeter,' said the Bishop.

'I have already met him.'

'Well, that's all right then.' His bland pseudo-vulgarian manner was no protection against the rich man's malice.

'And I should like to thank you for our lunch. I was sorry not to see you there, and thought perhaps you were not well.'

'I am perfectly well. That is to say I suffer from no indisposition which might have prevented me from lunching with you. I lunched separately because I feared I might be bored.'

'Eugene tires very easily,' explained Mrs Boissaens sympathetically. It was not until I had seen them together half a dozen times that I began to suspect she enjoyed egging him on.

'That is true, but it is not relevant to the Bishop's speculation about my absence from lunch. You are misleading him. My only motive was to avoid the company of people I might find tedious.'

'I am afraid that some of my junior clergy are not very polished socialites,' said the Bishop. I noticed that he excluded himself from this category.

'Indeed not,' said Mr Boissaens. 'No doubt their minds are on higher matters. It is my experience of the clergy that they are severely limited in their topics of conversation and even in their own field they are seldom well-informed or amusing. It is very kind of you to come and talk to me, Dr Toplass. You can mark among your charitable works of the day that you have given comfort to the afflicted but not, I insist, that you have visited the sick. I hope I am not keeping you from your episcopal duties?'

'No, indeed not,' said the Bishop, who had a very thick skin. 'It is a pleasure to be in such a charming house.'

'Nor from the exercise of other charitable works among people in greater need than myself?'

'In the eyes of the Lord we are all equal.'

For the first time, Mr Boissaens dropped his pretences. No longer the sardonic host, he became just another anti-religious maniac. 'I find it hard to believe there are not many people whose need of your attention is greater than my own, and who will consequently welcome it more. You have delighted us enough. If you will allow Angela to show you where you have left your hat, or mitre, I have some important matters to discuss with Mr Trumpeter.'

As Mrs Boissaens led him from the room, we both heard her say in a stage whisper: 'You see how easily he becomes tired.'

Mr Boissaens laughed to himself.

'Angela is more intelligent than you might suppose. That little visit was her revenge on me for having asked Mr Orison to stay.

She can't stand Canadians. Paradoxically, I find them less troublesome than English people who come to see me. No doubt you thought I was rude to your Bishop.'

'You might have hurt his feelings,' I said.

'He has no feelings. Otherwise it would have given me the greatest pleasure to hurt them. He is a pompous, conceited brute. Perhaps I am shocking you?'

'Not at all. He is not such a fool as you suppose.'

'In that case, he is a villain – and a thoroughly incompetent one. He could earn more money stealing motor-cars in the West End of London. What is his stipend – £4,000 a year?'

'If that. But there are many perks, and it is not an unpleasant life.'

'You may be right. I expect he enjoys dressing up in absurd clothes and prancing in front of a congregation. I wish my pleasures were so simple.'

'What are they?'

'A few things amuse me. Angela tells me that you wish to solicit money for an Old Folk's Palais de Danse in the village. You must come and discuss it tomorrow after dinner. I wish to know your reasons for supposing that I might be inclined to give you any.'

'Your wife has misinformed you. I gave her no such message. The village hall is no concern of mine.'

Mr Boissaens looked put out. For the first time I had scored a point.

'I misjudged you. Of course not. You are trying to rob me of my pleasures, Mr Trumpeter. Is that kind? In any case, come to my house after dinner tomorrow and we will play chess or Scrabble. Will you come?'

'Of course.'

'Good, now I have kept you too long. No doubt your little wife is waiting for you in the drawing room, pining for such comforts as only you can bring. Is she very passionate?'

'No,' I said. Gillian reserved her passions for discussion – invariably on such trite and uninteresting subjects as the death penalty, the negro problem and abortion.

'You don't know how lucky you are. There is no spectacle so terrifying as voracious, unsatisfied womanhood.'

When I returned to the drawing-room, it seemed to me that Mr Boissaens was sorry to see me go. Perhaps he liked me. Few people do. I am too shy, and too much on the defensive to make friends easily. But then, there are few people whom I like or wish to know any better. It seemed to me that from time to time he lifted a corner of his lonely and embittered heart. As often as not, I snubbed him for it. He certainly snubbed me whenever he saw the opportunity, or thought it necessary. But we were two of a kind, and tacitly recognised each other's failings. When I overcome my shyness, I often become bumptious. When Mr Boissaens overcame his, he became sad.

In the drawing-room, Mr Heifer was holding forth. The Heifers were the last to go, and Mrs Heifer looked uneasy.

'Come in, my dear fellow. We have been discussing the reorganisation of your parish. Miss Boissaens says that you need a special mission to the youth, and I agree. Youth has always been my especial interest. If ever we reorganise the Chapter into a Group Ministry I hope I will be given charge of youth. Miss Boissaens would like to be put in charge of a youth committee, to work with you and co-ordinate youth studies in the parish. What do you think?'

So the identity of my dusky charmer was revealed. She was the daughter of the house. As she came towards me with a provocative smile, hand extended, Mrs Boissaens said:

'I don't know if you've met my step-daughter, Danae. She has just discovered an absorbing interest in Church affairs. It is most encouraging for us all, I must say. Personally, I wouldn't let her anywhere near the impressionable young. But I am all for widening her horizons.'

As we shook hands – she held mine with unnecessary firmness – Danae looked into my eyes, and behind the truculent effrontery I read genuine pride. She wanted to be congratulated.

'I think that an excellent idea. We must discuss it.'

'Of course you must,' said Gillian vehemently. She had been sitting quiet and mouselike in a corner, exuding uneasiness like an unpleasant smell. 'If you believe in anything at all, you must believe in your duty to the young. They are the ones who matter, not these complacent, middle-aged windbags.'

An awkward silence followed her violent outburst. She made things much worse by adding: 'I don't mean any of you, of course.'

Mr Heifer clearly thought she meant him. None of us knew it, but he was famous in the Rural Chapter, and many miles outside it, for having bad control of his wind.

'Well then, Mr Trumpeter and Miss Boissaens will be able to work together,' he said. I loved him, then. 'My own feeling is that it is impossible to work too closely with youth. Lose touch with the young, and you have lost touch with life. Eh, Emily?'

As vicars' wives go, Mrs Heifer was a comfortable, well-rounded woman, but she could not hope to aspire to her husband's greatness, nor to his sublime generosity of spirit.

'They're all right, so long as they don't get you into trouble,' she said. 'Now we must go back. I have a Mothers' Union tea party and knitting group at four.'

'Mothers' Union,' said Mr Heifer humorously. 'The greatest collection of malicious gossips and middle-aged windbags in the country. I shall never understand how such an organisation came to flourish under the auspices of the Church. Lose touch with youth, Mr Trumpeter, and you are left with the Mothers' Union. Oh, fate worse than death,' he rocked on the sofa, covering his face. 'The unbearable torment of Mrs Green-Partridge.'

'That will do, Cyril. You always go too far. There is nothing wrong with Mrs Partridge. It is just her name which gets my husband so excited.'

'You can go home to your chicken's tea-party. I am not going to move off this sofa. It is a long time since I had such a good lunch, or in such amusing company.'

'Won't you have another glass of brandy?' said Danae.

'I'm afraid the servants have removed it,' said Mrs Boissaens.

'We can easily get it back again,' said Danae.

'Come along, Cyril. You will be in no fit condition for the Boys' Club meeting tonight.'

'I am always in fit condition for the Boys' Club,' said Mr Heifer with dignity.

In the excitement of coaxing him through the door, Danae and I bumped into each other. She turned to me with a ravishing smile, and seemed to thrust her breasts at me. I am not an exceptionally attractive man, but I have often noticed that a clergyman's cloth has this effect on women. Her step-mother was little different at our first meeting. Normally, however, our fans are respectable and deeply unattractive matrons in the change of life. Danae was young, beautiful and intelligent. Although we had hardly spoken, we had looked into each other's souls. On the spur of the moment, I put my hand on her jersey and gave her a gentle push. Perhaps it was a gauche way to endear myself, but we understood each other. Both of us were a little taken aback by my boldness. Then she beamed at me gratefully.

Either nobody had noticed, or they were all pretending not to have noticed. Struck by uncertainty, I felt awkward in the silence which followed the Heifers' departure, imagining it to be pregnant with inner tensions. Mrs Boissaens saved the situation.

'I do declare the Reverend has had an accident,' she exclaimed.

There could be no doubt about it. There was a large, irregular patch of damp on the cushion where Mr Heifer had been sitting.

'Poor man,' said Mrs Boissaens. 'It's such a shame he had to choose the red sofa. It makes it look worse.'

Danae and I laughed uproariously. Gillian looked disapproving.

'He ought to have learned self-control by now,' she said with a threatening glance at me. 'We'll have to put rubber sheets over all the furniture if ever he comes to the Rectory.'

'Not at all,' I said, anxious to be loyal to my new friend. 'I shan't mind in the least.'

'You won't be expected to clean up,' said Gillian. I honestly think that nothing could ever have made her happy. She held the secret of the Philosophers' Stone in reverse. The crucible of her mundane, humourless mind turned everything to lead.

I also thought it in bad taste to remind the company of our comparative indigence. When with the rich, I always assume that I am as rich as they. Nobody is ever deceived, of course.

'I only hope Eugene never gets to hear of this,' said Mrs Boissaens holding the cushion in front of the fire. 'He tends to be a trifle rigid in his views on religious subjects. Thank you, I am quite capable of holding the cushion myself.' The last remark was addressed to Mr Orison who was trying to be gallant in an incompetent, gigolo-like way.

'You know that Daddy will be delighted,' said Danae. 'It will make the week for him.'

'I know,' said Mrs Boissaens. 'And that is why I propose to tell him nothing. He has quite enough unhealthy amusements as it is. Mr Trumpeter, if you have important things to do in the village, I will not keep you. Gillian must come up and discuss her garden one day. It is so nice to have seen you both, and I am so glad the Bishop was able to come. Such an amusing man.'

'He was a dreadful man. Conceited, boring and second-rate,' said Danae. Something had made her very truculent. I would have liked to think she was showing off to me.

'Danae becomes over-excited very easily. Perhaps it is her new-found religious fervour. I must admit, I wish I knew exactly what you two are going to get up to.'

We giggled like schoolchildren, Danae and I.

' When are you going to come down and discuss things?' I said.

'Any time.' Wide open.

'What about tomorrow morning. Tennish?' It was the time Gillian went shopping in Twyford.

'Ten o'clock tomorrow morning then. We will discuss plans for capturing the youth of Middlewalk.'

As Gillian climbed into our Morris Minor – I bought it secondhand in Swindon for £125, and was cheated – we all shook hands again. Mrs Boissaens dropped my hand like a damp sponge.

The Rectory offered no welcoming hearth when we returned. Rather than hasten the moment when we would find ourselves in its vast, damp spaces, Gillian and I sat in the car and smoked cigarettes. Conversation with Gillian was not easy. Editorial comment always preceded the news, and readers' letters in the form of encouraging noises were expected the whole time.

'I think it intolerable, don't you?'

'Yes, indeed.'

'And totally irresponsible.'

'Most irresponsible.'

'One could understand it if he was a two-year-old, but it puts one in such a difficult position.'

'Yes, doesn't it.' My mind was far away, dreaming about Danae, but after a while I began to suspect that Gillian was insulting my dear friend Cyril Heifer. It was a long time since I had given up pretending to be interested in anything Gillian might have to say, but sometimes, just to ring the changes, I registered disagreement.

'No,' I said, at the end of her next harangue. 'I disagree.' Under normal circumstances, I could sit back at this point while Gillian's voice rose to a frenzy, accusing me of anti-socialist tendencies, hatred of the poor, snobbery, religious obscurantism, intellectual pretensiousness, ignorance, sexual incompetence, misogyny and wife-beating, or any combination of these defects. Then I would apologise meekly, saying that I was worried about something, and she would go away, in a highly emotional state, to prepare the food or to read a woman's magazine in her bedroom.

On this occasion, however, there was a shocked silence.

'Nicholas, I don't think you have been listening to a word I was saying.'

'Perhaps not,' I admitted, handsomely enough.

'If you'd been prepared to wait a moment, I was going to tell you that I saw someone staring in at me while I was having my bath this morning. I didn't tell you earlier, because you had already gone to dress up when I came down.'

'Robe myself,' I said automatically. It was a sure way of annoying her.

'But don't you find it odd?' said Gillian.

'Yes I do,' I said. Who on earth could possibly be interested in seeing Gillian naked? Her pinched little body was no more erotic than a corpse. It was true that her grey, sickly legs were still capable of movement and her bowels operated, with monotonous regularity, but apart from these manifestations she might well have been a corpse. Sex, when it occurred, was treated as a slightly childish bore. When it did not occur, she was being deprived of her rights as a woman. Within five years, I think, she would have made me completely impotent. Perhaps that was her purpose.

'Who do you think it was?'

'I don't know, but I think it might have been George Swinger.'

'It probably was. I asked him to clear some of the gutters this morning. There is water coming in through the roof of Bethlehem.' All the bedrooms – there were eight of them on the first floor – were named after places in the Bible. Gillian resented this enormously, but as they were inscribed in Gothic on heavy brass plates, and as she lacked the invention to think of other names, they remained.

'It must be cascading through the attic above.'

'I am not in the least bit worried about your plumbing arrangements. What I do feel concerned about is that your Vicar's Warden is a sex maniac.'

'I should not worry. He has a wretched life, and these people have to have some consolations.'

'It's me he's staring at, not you. What would happen if he murdered me?'

An interesting field of speculation. The most obvious consequence was that Gillian would be dead. After that, she would be no responsibility of mine.

'It is most unlikely. The working classes have lost all spirit of initiative. They expect to have everything done for them. I very much doubt whether George Swinger is capable of any independent action of that sort. He would not do it for money, because he can earn as much as he needs more easily in other ways, and he would be unlikely to undertake it as a leisure activity, because he lacks the imagination to think of any enjoyment greater than watching television. Talking of which, I think the first programme will be starting at 4.15.' It was an educational programme, designed to teach Pakistani immigrants the rudiments of English. I watched it every day, riveted. The demands of office take up a very small time in the day of an Anglican clergyman. Children's Hour, which followed the Pakistani programme every day, was more of a trial. But then I never supposed the ministry would be all beer and skittles. Essentially, it is a challenge.

'But supposing that Swinger went mad?' said Gillian.

'Mr Swinger. We are not living in seventeenth-century Russia.'

'Mr Swinger then. What would happen if he went mad?'

'He would be most unlikely to harm you. Even in madness, the working class person is essentially timid. Under those circumstances, they usually murder their wives or children. They only attack a comparative stranger in numbers, and then it is usually something to do with football.'

'But you read of sex murders.'

'The English sex murderer confines himself to children. Only American airmen attack mature women in this country.'

'That's nonsense, Nicholas.'

Perhaps it was, but I had become bored by the conversation and wanted to get to the television set. Before either of us could move, another car had driven down our short drive, and stopped with a cheeky little honk of the horn in front of the main door. Without looking inside, I immediately knew that our visitor was Danae Boissaens.

'Who is it?' said Gillian.

'How on earth can I know?' I said. 'I suggest you go and ask it who it is.'

'Perhaps it is the doctor,' said Gillian. She expected frequent attendance from her medical advisers, always with the concealed purpose of being reassured that she had not contracted a malignant tumour. This was another of her obsessions. Three times since marriage she had been tested for cervical cancer. As I remarked on each occasion, every married woman should have a hobby.

'Before exposing your private parts to him, it might be as well to make sure,' I said.

Her answer was a stinging slap in the face. 'Shut up, you cold-blooded, dirty-minded hypocrite,' she said. I knew if I kept going I would have her in tears.

'I'm sorry if I'm interrupting anything,' said a pert young voice. 'Are you the Reverend Nicholas Trumpeter?' Unbelievably, it was not Danae but a brash, complacent young man with a horrible wave in his hair.

'Yes, who are you?'

'I'm from the Press. Can I come in and see you?'

'Into the car?'

'If that's where you see people.'

'What do you wish to see me about?'

'I'm freelance, actually. Most of my work is done for the nationals, covering local stories, but I also do occasional pieces for the local newspaper. They like to have a profile whenever a new vicar is appointed. Don't ask my why. I suppose they think people like to read it. They've got to fill up the newspaper somehow.'

'Very well, I suppose you had better come in,' I said in a bored voice. In fact, I was wildly excited by the idea. Anything for a change; but it would be bad for the young man's character to show too much eagerness.

'In that case, you won't mind if I let my photographer out.'

'Please do.'

A strange, shaggy creature emerged from the back of the car, which was a van, and blinked in the dim light of the late afternoon.

'This is Cliff,' said the man from the Press. We shook hands.

'Not bad. Not bad at all,' said Cliff, eyeing me. 'I like your collar.'

'We all wear them,' I said. 'You may not have noticed.'

'I like it,' said Cliff. 'We must try and bring that out if possible.'

'Don't worry about Cliff,' said the man from the Press. 'He suffers from the Leonardo da Vinci complex. Not a bad sort of place you've got here, Vicar.'

'Do you like it?'

'I've been here before, of course. One of the best stories we had for years when your predecessor passed on. Made the front page of the *Daily Mail*. Body must have lain there for nearly three weeks. Still, I suppose you're used to that sort of thing in your profession. How long have you been living here?'

'We moved in last week.'

'Find it comfy?'

'No.'

'Still, you get the money. That's the important thing. I never know what my income's going to be from one week to the next.'

'Would you like some tea?' said Gillian. Nobody had paid any attention to her, and I saw no reason to make introductions.

'No, thank you, ma'am,' said the man from the Press. 'I'm a hard liquor man, myself. We might have a drop of whisky afterwards.'

'I'm afraid we haven't any.'

'That doesn't matter. We can go to the Bag of Corn. To entertaining Vicar of Middlewalk, £3. Scandalous how much these clerical gentlemen drink.'

'I don't know your name,' said Gillian. Neither did I, but there was no reason why I should ever wish to know it. The interesting thing about this cocky young man was that he came from the Press. Trust Gillian to find something boring in an exciting situation.

'Hutton,' said the man from the Press. 'Mr Hutton.'

'Oh, really?' I said, trying to sound interested.

'Aren't you going to ask them in?' said Gillian.

'Ah, yes,' I said. 'Where shall we sit? The house is still in a bit of a mess, I am afraid.'

We sat in the library facing each other across Mr Mandarill's desk. Its drawers were still full of letters, Christmas cards, bills and receipts belonging to the previous incumbent.

Mr Hutton tried to intimidate me by switching the desk lamp on and off, but I thought I knew all the answers.

'What changes do you hope to bring about in this parish, Mr Trumpeter?'

Absolutely none, of course. I said: 'We must all move with the times.'

'In what way, particularly?'

'I would like to make Christianity more relevant in the lives of everyday people. I should like them to feel the Church as the centre of the community, a vital force in all their lives. Particularly, of course, the man in the street.' Splendid stuff. I could keep this up for hours on end.

'How are you going to achieve this end?'

'Oh, in various ways. Before coming down here, I worked for six years in an industrial parish. I think it gave me some idea of the contemporary reality.'

'What sort of thing?'

He was an extremely tiresome young man. I began to think of the television programmes I was missing. 'Prostitutes. Teenage drug addicts. Meths drinkers. You know the sort of thing.' In fact, I had seen none of these in Swindon. But that was what industrial parishes were supposed to be about.

'Good. I like that,' said Mr Hutton. 'Of course, there isn't much opportunity for this sort of thing in Middlewalk. The place is a dump. You have to go to Maidenhead or Reading for any life.'

'I have plans for a youth committee in the village. We hope to buy a juke box later in the year.'

'Quite a swinging vicar,' said Mr Hutton.

'Then we're going to build a dance hall for the old people. An important function of the Church nowadays is to give the old people a good time. When they are not using it, the hall will be free for the young people. There is nothing wrong with young people today. It is just that they have never been instructed properly. A lot of young girls go to London without any money, and before they know it they are appearing in the strip clubs. The same is true about sex. They just let one thing follow another, until suddenly they find themselves with babies.'

'Are you against sex?' There was an aggressive note in his voice.

'Of course not. Sex in itself is a very good thing indeed. That is the great Christian message of our time. But it must be approached with responsibility. The Church believes very strongly in responsible sexual intercourse. We have produced a booklet teaching couples ways to enjoy it more thoroughly. When Jesus gave us sexual intercourse, he intended us to make use of it. Please do not misunderstand me. There is nothing wrong with sex, but the Church is anxious to combat the things which sex can lead to. I mentioned prostitution, drugs and meths drinking, but they are only a few. Much unhappiness results from unwanted pregnancies, and our first thoughts must always be for the child. With good sense and instruction, all these things can be avoided. Now, if you have got all you want, I am afraid that I am rather busy.'

'There is a television programme he likes to watch,' said Gillian.

'Just a minute. Did you say you were going to give sex instruction to the village?'

'No I didn't, but of course if they ask me for advice, I can't refuse them. That is what I am here for.'

'Thanks. I think we'll be able to make quite a nice story out of all this. The last vicar I did was Mr Plimsoll down at Hatch Bottom. He thought the most important thing was to cut down on Church Services. One a year is all people want, he said. Anything else just makes a lot of work. Vicars were overworked, he said, and under-valued. But I got a beautiful quote out of him. "They don't like me in this village, and I don't like any of them." Quite a character.'

'Wait a minute,' said Cliff. 'There's the pictures. Will you just hold the telephone in your hand for a minute. No, it's not quite what I'm after. Perhaps we could have you in front of the television set, to add the modern touch. Switch it on. That's right.'

'Does your husband always watch Children's Hour?' said Hutton.

'Nearly always,' said Gillian. 'When there's nothing else.'

'I wished to see the earlier programme,' I said with dignity. 'It is in Pakistani. I am particularly concerned about the colour problem. Those are the three things the man in the street is interested in nowadays – the colour problem, sex and compassion for old age pensioners. At least, I suppose a few of them are interested in other things, but that is how they associate religion.'

A bore and a hypocrite in Swindon once suggested that the main purpose of the Church was to urge people to give more money to Oxfam. I pointed out that the income of the Church

Commissioners from interest-yielding investments alone was more than forty times that of Oxfam. If this ignorant prig had been right, we would have been the most inefficient fundraisers in the world.

It is true that the role of the Church has changed. We used to provide comfort to people living wretched, undernourished lives, and we fulfilled a useful social purpose: by assuring them of a real or imaginary paradise ahead we accustomed them to accepting a miserable existence in this world without creating further unhappiness for themselves by trying to change it. Nowadays, in the age of affluence, we are just one more luxury offered in the already glutted consumer market. So, of course, is Oxfam. People actually derive more satisfaction from giving sixpence to Oxfam than from buying an extra packet of chocolate-flavoured potato crisps. The Church teaches you why it is better to give the sixpence to the starving millions. Oxfam merely knows what people like, and caters for their tastes, like a cynical prostitute. We still have a purpose – to fill that aching void left in the consciousness of even the most affluent which might be called spiritual and aesthetic awareness. Oxfam has none. People might as well eat their revolting potato crisps and die with a nasty taste in their mouths.

'I am particularly interested in the work of Oxfam,' I said. 'If we in this village can do something, however small, to relieve the suffering of our many millions of brothers in Africa and Asia, then my time here will not have been wasted.' One should never deliberately offend the religious susceptibilities of other people.

'I know,' said Hutton. 'They all say that.'

'Do you think we could have one of you with your collar off, staring at it in your hand,' said Cliff.

'All right,' I said, and removed my clerical collar. Few people realise that they look much the same as any other collar when off. We wear them back to front, as it were.

'In your shirt sleeves,' said Cliff. 'Roll up your sleeves as if for action. We can't have braces. Take them off and put them out of sight. Now, what can we have you doing? You wouldn't have a dustpan and brush, Mrs Trumpeter?'

'This is most unrepresentative,' said Gillian. 'He's never done any housework in his life.'

'We're only trying to be symbolic,' said Cliff. 'Perhaps we could have him at the kitchen sink. That's quite modern.'

Eventually I knelt down on the carpet and pretended to be brushing away something disgusting which had fallen there. It was not hard to imagine. The carpet was covered with stains and smelled of cats.

'Hold it while I set up the floods. We will need two spots behind. Stay down there, Vicar.'

After ten minutes, I began to feel uncomfortable. The dog collar, clutched in my left hand, began to melt. Finally, the great artist was ready.

'No,' he said. 'It won't do. I am sorry. It just isn't a picture. As soon as I see a picture, it jumps out at me. We couldn't have you in bed with the wife, could we? That would tie in with what we've got in copy about sex and responsibility.'

I was quite game, but Gillian looked shocked. 'Certainly not. What will you be asking us to do next?'

'Not that, madam. They wouldn't print it. Even between a vicar and his wife. That's censorship for you.'

I laughed pleasantly. The thought of Gillian immortalised in one of her most uncharacteristic poses tickled me.

'Take a broom,' said Cliff 'You know, a new broom sweeps clean. Start sweeping the carpet.'

It certainly had not been swept for twenty years. In the clouds of evil-smelling dust I sweated away. Cliff actually deigned to take a few photographs.

'Sterling work, Vicar. Now would you like to come down to the pub?

'I hardly think it suitable.'

'Come off it. Mr Heifer at Silvercombe is seldom out of his pub. They like the vicar to be human.'

'Do you think so? I don't believe they care in the least. But it will give them something to gossip about. That is one of the most important functions of a vicar.'

'That's right, Rev. I always say, there's no smoke without fire. We're none of us completely human.'

George Swinger was sitting alone in the bar, his watery yellow eyes blinking over a pint mug of beer. I knew I had something to say to him, but I had forgotten what it was.

'What's yours, Cliff?'

'Double Diamond.'

'If that's all you want. Double Scotch for the vicar. What's yours, George?'

Swinger's eyes never left me, but he indicated his mug.

'Glad we got that interview over. By the way, my name's Lennie. No relation to *the* Sir Leonard Hutton.'

The name sounded vaguely familiar. 'Who's he?' I said.

'Blimey. Doesn't know who Sir Leonard Hutton is. You've got a lot to learn, if I may say so. Never mind, you gave me some good copy for *The Globe*. Was it true what you said about starting a youth club in the village, or was that just for the mugs?'

'No, indeed. Danae Boissaens is going to organise it.'

'She's the daughter of the blind one, isn't she? I've lived in the village for five years, and I've only seen her twice. Do you know them?'

'He knows Mrs Boissaens all right. She was in the house with him. I sawed her with my own eyes,' said George Swinger.

'She showed us round the house. It was very kind of her,' I said.

'Kind was it?' said Swinger. 'I wondered what it was. I sawed you both.'

'I think I may look in at this youth club of yours,' said Lennie. 'Not on business, though. For some reason we're not allowed to mention the Boissaens family in the newspaper. I expect he's a big shareholder. But I'd like to have a look at this Danae Boissaens.'

'It's Mrs Boissaens the vicar likes,' said Swinger. 'Holding hands they was like two little children, ever so dainty. I told Mildred, but she didn't believe me. She won't believe nothing unless you shove it under her nose. Where's Mrs Trumpeter this evening, Vicar?'

'She stayed at home. She's not feeling any too well.' Nobody had thought of asking her.

On the way out, I remembered what I had to say to Swinger. 'You did a very good job with the gutter, George. If you can think of anything else needs doing at the Rectory, just come straight up. I'm out a lot of the time, but you might like to keep Mrs Trumpeter company. She likes to have a man around the house.'

CHAPTER THREE

After breakfast, I retired to my study to work. Gillian usually enjoyed making as much noise as possible outside the study door with a vacuum cleaner. Of all noises, I find it the most detestable. Occasionally, she would come into the room and announce that the mechanism was faulty.

'Why should that interest me? I am not an electrician.'

'You are supposed to be a man.'

'Even if that supposition is correct, it would scarcely help me to mend your machine.'

'You are only reading a book, in any case.'

'Reading is an unfortunate necessity of my job.' In fact, I was half way through an excellent novel by Erle Stanley Gardner – *The Case of the Footloose Doll* – which I was reading while I waited for Danae to arrive. I had just reached the point where the girl, having assumed the identity of another girl who was killed in a car-crash, accidentally stabs the other girl's blackmailer with an icepick, and looks like being arraigned on a First Degree Murder charge. No wonder I was impatient with Gillian's trivialities. It was intolerable to be interrupted in the middle of my work.

'And it is an unfortunate necessity that I have to do the housework,' said Gillian. She was a pompous bully, like Hamilton Burger, the district attorney. I longed to shout at her: 'That is incompetent, irrelevant and immaterial,' but there was no judge to rule 'Objection sustained', and Gillian always enjoyed a row.

Instead, I said: 'You should not do so much, darling. You only stir up a lot of dust, and scientists nowadays think that dust is definitely a contributory factor in certain diseases.'

'Who told you?'

'I read it in the *British Medical Journal*. Three cases out of four of patients suffering from cancer of the lung, rectum and lower intestine in a California hospital turned out to have been living in a dusty environment.'

'That is why I sweep up the dust.'

'You only succeed in reactivating it.'

'Sometimes I think you are trying to frighten me.'

'Don't be childish. Haven't you any shopping to do?' It was true, there would have been a poetic justice at work if Gillian had contracted cancer, having bored me about it for seven years. But I had no idea how such poetic justice could be engineered. Nor did I think that it would have been morally defensible. *'Thou must not kill but need not strive officiously to keep alive'*. It is true that I assiduously kept her supplied with cigarettes. In a month-long discussion at the time of the last scare, I succeeded in convincing her that the whole thing was a Left Wing plot. Too much Government revenue came from the tobacco tax, I explained, and so from the pockets of the poorer classes. By discouraging people from smoking – even, in the last resort, by passing a law against it – the Government would force itself to make up the revenue from increased income-tax and supertax, thereby bringing about a more egalitarian society. Gillian heartily approved of all these aims and smoked away happily, thinking, in her muddle-headed way, that she was hastening the age of the Common Man and smoking for victory. Women are incapable of the simplest logical progressions.

'Yes. Unlike your smart friends up at the Hall, I have to do my own shopping.'

'Remember that I'm out to dinner.'

'Dining with Mr Boissaens, I suppose? I am beginning to think I am not grand enough for you.'

When Gillian left the house, an entirely new spirit descended on it. It became homely, welcoming and kind. I walked round the rooms sniffing delightedly at the variety of musty odours. The Mandarills had left behind all the properties of an older, happier culture: unfinished patchwork quilts, scrap albums, commonplace books, Indian ivory counters, two incomplete Mah-Jong sets, broken croquet mallets, paper knives of strange, oriental design, a quantity of dried, aromatic herbs in linen bags, eight walking sticks, a family photograph album dating from the 1880s, some unframed water colours of Florence and a faded, Florentine leather spectacle case, a necklace of jet and a Spanish silver filigree brooch, tresses of Mandarill hair preserved in lockets, bracelets and ear-rings, a paste-pot, the remains of a stamp collection, a butterfly collection and a further collection of interesting mineral specimens – everything the heart could desire. We were the cuckoos in the nest. I had already found a quantity of clothing which fitted me well. Some of it had gravy stains down the front, but that was a small price to pay. Everything which had ever made England a civilised country was preserved in my Rectory, and I loved the place.

Gillian, of course, hated it and saw disease lurking in every corner. I tried to re-assure her that Mr Mandarill had not died of cancer; Mrs Mandarill had merely suffered a nervous collapse, no rare occurrence in clerical circles, where the pressure of work was so intense. But Gillian was adamant, and refused even to eat Mrs Mandarill's home-made gooseberry jam or crab-apple jelly, which was a pity. Although it might easily have done her no harm, it could not conceivably have done her any good.

Gillian was absolutely right, of course. She was not nearly grand enough for me. At one time, in the cloistered world of my theological college, it seemed quite a feather in my cap to marry the Principal's daughter. He was a dull, unimaginative man, and his wife was peculiarly horrible by any standards. But at St Anselm's College, Faringdon, he appeared to possess infinite power and prestige. The other students became quite sentimental when discussing Gillian's charms, but she was the only woman in the place. So, for the first time in my life, I allowed myself to be influenced by other people's judgements rather than by my own. It had been an appalling error.

The front door bell rang. It was of an old-fashioned design, and made a lugubrious sound which echoed through the passages. At a quarter to ten, it was too early for Danae, but my heart beat a little faster as I walked through the great domed hall.

'I have come to see you about my old age pension,' said Mrs Morelli, looking sentimental. I don't know what it is about old age pensions that makes the English look sentimental.

'Oh really?' I said, trying to appear compassionate.

'You may not know, but I am an old age pensioner,' said Mrs Morelli. As if anybody could fail to know it. Every time she sniffed she proclaimed the dismal fact, as if her receipt of a totally unearned and undeserved weekly allowance somehow made her an object of pity.

'I would never have believed it,' I said gallantly.

'Yes, I manage to keep going, in spite of all I put up with,' said Mrs Morelli. There followed a speech of such excruciating boredom that I did not even pretend to listen. It seemed that she had been exposed in some minor fraud against the National Assistance Board, claiming money to which she was not entitled, and wished me to perpetuate the fraud by testifying to the truth of some obviously false proposition.

'I can't do that, Mrs Morelli. You forget that I am a man of religion.'

'The last vicar used to. He once swore I had three children under the age of sixteen so I could get family allowances. I am only asking for my rights, not for anything extra.'

'Have you any children?'

'Of course not. When my husband was alive we decided we didn't want any, being so poor, as we all were in those days. Then when things got a bit better, he'd lost interest. After that he was dead, and I was glad we'd never had any. I'm badly enough off as it is.'

'Oh dear,' I said. The door-bell rang again. Mrs Morelli was immovable. 'I'll sign it this time,' I said.

'Good. When are we going to get our dance hall?'

'I am seeing Mr Boissaens tonight.'

'Oh, so he doesn't mind then, about you and Mrs Boissaens? I expect he's past it. I hear your wife's been taken poorly.'

'Gillian has never been very well,' I said.

'No. I expect it was the shock when she discovered what was going on. I don't mind of course. I'm quite broadminded. Funny, though, that Mrs Boissaens should have fancied you. I would have thought she would have preferred the heavier sort, like my late husband. But you never can tell. Mrs Swinger was telling me she thought there was something funny about the way Mrs Trumpeter walked. We wondered if there was anything wrong with her legs or if it was, well, higher up.'

'We don't know what it is. We are frightened that it might be cervical cancer,' I said. 'But I know you won't tell anything about it until we are sure.'

'Of course not, Mr Trumpeter. Fancy that. Poor dear, how does she feel? I could tell there was something wrong with her in the church service, but Mrs Hallowes said it was just emotion.'

'Not at all. She often experiences strange sensations, as of something growing inside her. But for Heaven's sake, don't tell anyone.'

'Of course I won't. Willum Mullins had his first wife die of cancer. Never got over it. Cries to this day if you mention her name. And his second wife, too. He's a very passionate man, Mr Mullins. Once he drove his tractor straight through the wall of Mr Flitcroft's barn. Said he was upset about the Rhodesian situation, and all those poor coloured boys being sold down the river.'

'Ah yes,' I said. 'The colour question. Mrs Morelli, I am afraid I have another caller. I hope you don't have any difficulty with your children's allowances, maternity grants and war disability increment. If ever you want any help, please come back.' By now we were standing at the front door. Danae, in black jersey and skirt, stood in the porch.

'Why, it's Miss Boissaens. I expect you've brought a message to the vicar from your mother. How's everybody keeping?'

'Very well, thank you.'

'So glad to hear it, Miss. Everything going all right? Perhaps they don't discuss things much. And Mr Boissaens? Is he feeling at all disturbed?'

'No.'

'So glad to hear it, Miss. Well, I must be on my way. Can't spend the whole day gossiping about, can we?'

'I suppose not.'

'Not if you're just a poor old age pensioner. Too many things to be done.'

'I suppose there are.'

'Not that you'd know anything about it of course, being young and well looked after. But you may come to it yet. There's no point in being envious of other people's possessions, my husband used to say. Not that it did him much good. Look after yourself in this world, because no one else is going to look after you. That and kindness. Always be kind to everyone else and everybody else will be kind to you. There's many an old saying has some truth in it.'

'Goodbye, Mrs Morelli,' I said.

'A leap in time saves nine. Too many cooks spoil the broth. It's easier for a rich man to get to Heaven, than it is for him to climb through the eye of a needle.'

'Goodbye,' said Danae.

'Goodbye, Miss. So pleased to see you in such good health. Give my regards to your parents.'

'What on earth was she talking about?' said Danae, when the door had closed behind the stupid old woman.

'Everybody in the village is terribly over-excited because they think I am the lover of your step-mother.'

Danae threw back her head and laughed helplessly, staggering around the hall. 'Is that what it was? All those crafty quotations and sly glances. You should be ashamed of yourself. She's old enough to be your mother.'

'They have nothing else to live for, the poor dears. Vicars are an absolute godsend to them.'

'Every rolling stone has a silver lining,' said Danae, giggling fatuously.

'She is rather a sweet old thing, really,' I said.

'Men in glass houses are worth two in the bush,' said Danae, still giggling. 'She is a silly, malicious old hypocrite. How many beans make five?'

'Shall we go into the library and start discussing our youth programme?'

'One and a half and a half of one and one and two halves and two halves of one. You'll never get on with the villagers if you don't know that. It's the sort of joke they tell each other for hours on end, only they've usually had too much beer to drink and get it wrong. Then they spend the rest of the evening cackling over the mistake. It must be lovely to be so easily pleased. I shall tell Angela what they're saying in the village about her.'

'Angela?'

'My step-mother.'

'Please don't. She won't like it.'

'Of course she won't like it. She was hot on your tracks the minute you arrived. "Such a sweet little vicar," she said. "I'm sure he'll be good for the village. And I really believe he's going to get on rather well with Eugene. The young man seems to have quite a sense of humour, and you know how much store your father sets by that, Danae darling".'

'Did she say that to you?'

'You were her only topic of conversation for a month. "I do hope that nice young couple like their house. Of course, it's much too big for them." I'm surprised she hasn't been round already, trying to hook you into her bed.'

'She's made no overtures.'

'When she does it will be in the form of an order. You don't know my step-mother. Even when you're making love to her, one half of her mind will be enjoying it and the other will refuse to admit that it's happening. She could go into a witness box next day and swear she had never let you touch her – and believe it. She is a complete schizophrenic. Where is Gillian?'

'Out shopping. Don't you think we ought to get on with our youth?'

'Is there any youth in the village? I have never seen it. They all seem to be old age pensioners. We could dress them up, I suppose, in jerseys and jeans and give them karate lessons and lectures on Zen Buddhism.' Danae wandered round the great hall, picking up odd objects which lay strewn around – a broken fishing rod, some curtain rings, an old fountain pen, prayer books, a pipe. Eventually, she found a black homburg hat which my predecessor wore to make his daily rounds, always arriving at the houses of the well-to-do at drinks time. She put it on her head.

'I think this rather becomes me. Can I keep it?'

'It doesn't fit,' I said.

Danae giggled wickedly. 'As the Bishop said to the actress.'

I thought we were wasting time. She was quite right, the hat gave her a most striking appearance. She stood looking provocative and infinitely appealing, like a Wild West moll. I walked through the fishing rods, canvas satchels and Wellington boots on the floor and kissed her impulsively where she stood.

For seven years, I had kissed only Gillian and Gillian's unspeakable mother. It was as if a deep sea diver who had spent his life underwater with cold fishy things suddenly found himself in contact with a warm-blooded creature. There was eagerness and excitement in Danae's kiss. Most miraculous of all, there was affection.

'Is that how the Church teaches you to do it?' she said. 'I've never been kissed by a vicar before.'

'If you shut up for a moment,' I said, 'you will have the experience for a second time.'

She kept quiet.

'Do you kiss all your callers like that?' she asked. 'I begin to understand how the Church of England has survived for so long.'

'You are being cheap and irreverent.'

'I am sorry.'

As we stood face to face, our bodies squeezed together, I began to understand what was the matter with Gillian. She was dead. Goodness knows when she had died – certainly long before I met her. She was probably strangled at birth by her mother. Death was not a subject for compassion. Let the dead bury their dead. For seven years I had been moribund. My hands, clumsy and useless through many dutiful embraces, quickened to purpose.

'We can't stay here,' said Danae. 'Where can we go?'

In Bethlehem, the bed was unmade. Gethsemane had mildew on the ceiling and Nazareth was almost certain to be overlooked by George Swinger, as it was next door to the Sea of Galilee where Gillian took her bath. Jerusalem was too large. Canaan would have been suitable for a marriage feast, but it smelled of rats. Eventually, I took her up to Calvary, a small circular room in the eastern dome, where a bed was made up which could not have been slept in for twelve years.

'Don't you think we ought to take any precautions,' I asked, when our intentions became unmistakable.

Danae giggled. Even in moments of great excitement she found life irresistibly comic. 'I love parsons. It looks as if we shall have to risk it. Don't take your shirt and dog-collar off. They suit you.'

Gillian returned in a state of high indignation. 'They are saying in the village that you drink. Mrs Allsopp told me that when her husband started drinking she put turpentine in his beer. He never noticed the difference but drank less and less until he died. That's how she got her widow's pension, although she was never married to him. She advised me to do the same. I think it's disgusting the way these old women talk.'

'Pay no attention,' I said. 'It's all they have to do.'

'How do you think I feel, being labelled the wife of a drunken husband? They will all say that I have failed as a wife.'

Gillian's failings as a wife were too obvious to remark. I was feeling exhausted.

'I have no objection to being cast as a drunken husband. You should not mind being the innocent sufferer. It might even win you a little sympathy.'

'They have no sympathy for anyone but themselves and I can't blame them. With the new Government freeze it looks as if none of their pensions are going to be increased. Some of them are talking about going on strike.'

'A strike is the withdrawal of labour. Since none of them work, they have no labour to withdraw.' If there were any justice or humanity inside the Welfare State, it would allow me to put Gillian in a dustbin and have her removed by smiling, black-faced workmen to the municipal tip.

Gillian looked at me in a manner which was supposed to convey mature appraisal. It made her seem cross-eyed. 'I sometimes wish you had a heart behind all your cleverness. What are you going to do about the pensioners?'

What did she expect me to do? Nothing whatever, of course, merely to show compassion. Compassion is the base currency of second-rate minds, a substitute for thought. It is possible to feel compassionate for an individual person, or even for a class of people who have sufferings in common. But it cannot be produced on the slot-machine principle. A catalogue of woes is merely comical unless it is applied to a person one likes, or is prepared to like in the absence of any reason for disliking. But I had seen too many old age pensioners to feel any liking for them as a class. Many of them should have been dead years ago. Stuffed with life-preserving chemicals at the public expense their only function was to cast a gloom over the entire community.

Existence had no meaning for them, unless to exist is to touch, feel, see, smell, perform the essential bodily functions with ever diminishing competence and to feel sorry for yourself. Do not misunderstand me. I am not suggesting that they should be sent to the gas-chambers, or even that they should be denied those chemicals necessary to prolong their vegetable existence, merely that we should not waste the brief period when such faculties as we possess are at their most active in feeling sorry for them. Before long, their problems will be our own, but sufficient unto the day is the evil thereof. Like the dead, the old must look after themselves.

'As you know, Gillian,' I said, 'I am deeply concerned about the elderly, and am trying to have a dance hall constructed for them. Old age pensioners have had a very raw deal in the past, particularly during the hunger strikes of the 1930s and in the early days of the Industrial Revolution. It is a problem with roots deep in human nature. In primitive tribes, the custom varies between an absurd and exaggerated respect for elders to negligence and geriophagy. More civilised societies have accepted that the elderly stay on in the home, usually in a menial capacity, until death. Nowadays the process of dying has been infinitely prolonged, and the State has taken over the responsibility which formerly belonged to the family of caring for people in this condition. However, human nature has not kept in step with social and scientific advance. If you wish the young to spend a greater period of time preparing for old age and the joys which await them there you must educate them to the task. My own education was deficient in this respect. We were taught that the consummation of life on this earth, far from being a large old age pension was to be found after death in the joys – possibly illusory – of the Heavenly Kingdom. But even if the promise of Heaven is illusory, it seems to me that you can live a saner, happier life in this world being deluded than you can planning for a prosperous old age, when your sensibilities are blunted and you have no appetite for enjoyment. Which is why I am busily engaged in forming a Youth Committee for the redemption of the youth of Middlewalk.'

'I can never understand a word you say. You talk too quickly and half of it makes no sense. You know it makes me feel sick to have you talk of the Heavenly Kingdom so piously. I don't think you believe a word of it.'

'I never said I did.'

'How hypocritical can you get?'

This was Gillian's unfailing rejoinder whenever I mentioned religion. Only self-deception is hypocritical, and Gillian was surely the most hypocritical person alive.

'There is nothing hypocritical about trying to rescue young people and give them a chance in life,' I said, with as much sincerity as I could muster.

Gillian had to admit that she could find no fault in my work for the young. Even she could not condone prostitution, backstreet abortions and drug addiction, although she claimed they were more often the result of housing conditions than faulty education.

'How did your meeting with Danae go?' she asked.

'Very well. We arranged to co-opt a second, co-ordinative committee as soon as we have enough people interested. How is your throat?'

'You mean my stomach?' It was hard to keep track of the malignant outbreaks on Gillian's body. 'The pains are not so bad, but I suspect there may be a lump forming. Do you think it could be anything serious?'

'I shouldn't think so.' It was too much to hope for. Lumps were an extremely commonplace phenomenon on Gillian's body. Her breasts produced them in rotation. Once we even found a surgeon prepared to cut one of them off, although he said there was nothing wrong with it. After that, she developed cancer of the spine, which is inoperable. 'Definitely, we should leave it for three months or so, in case it gets any worse.'

'Then it will be too late,' said Gillian, with a brave, patient smile.

'I know, but the latest theory is that these things are probably better left alone, since you can't do anything about them.'

'But you can,' said Gillian. 'In the early stages.'

It was inconceivable that any disease Gillian might be suffering from should be in its early stages. She had been ravaged by every known disease for at least seven years.

'That's another thing we can do with the youth club when we get it going,' I said. 'Have them all X-rayed and tested for cancer. People enjoy that.'

'Not when they are young,' said Gillian. Obviously, these pleasures were restricted to grown-ups. 'The latest theory is that too many X-rays can cause exactly what they are trying to prevent.'

'In that case, you are in some danger. I should go and be X-rayed again immediately to see if you have caught it.'

'Children don't mind about that sort of thing. It is only when you grow older that you learn a sense of responsibility.' Gillian was two years older than me, a grave mistake in any marriage. 'You might teach them that neglect of personal hygiene is sinful, if you think that would encourage them to be any cleaner.'

'I doubt if it is true.'

'Of course it is true. Illness flourishes wherever there is dirt. Having caught a disease, they might infect other people, which is selfish.'

'Illness is not sinful. The contagiousness of disease fulfils a very useful social function, and is certainly part of God's plan, if there is any God to have devised such a plan. If there is not a God, there is no possible excuse for failing to encourage disease. The world is bursting at its seams for want of a plague. Somebody has got to start it, somewhere. I doubt if anyone has gone to Hell for being dirty.'

'Hell,' cried Gillian in malicious delight. 'I suppose you are going to pretend you believe in Hell.'

I gave her a long, hard stare.

'I don't know whether or not it exists, but I sincerely hope it does,' I replied.

The evening was cool and bright with a magnificent night sky, reminding all who cared to reflect of the almost infinite insignificance of the human condition. I decided to walk the half mile to the Hall. Gillian was not feeling well, and had retired to bed, or at any rate I assumed she had. I lacked the curiosity to enquire.

On the way out, I noticed a glint of metal in the rhododendron bushes beside the gate. Investigating, I found myself staring into the great yellow eyes of George Swinger. He held a scythe in his hand, and stared at me unblinkingly.

'Good evening, George,' I said cheerily. 'Putting in some useful work in the garden? I am going out and will not be back until quite late. Mrs Trumpeter is not feeling very well and has gone to bed. She is all alone in there. Quite, utterly alone. In the bedroom, I think.'

It was a mistake to arrive at the Hall on foot. The mechanism of the house was not adjusted to it. The two footmen, or male domestic helps – however they like to be described – were probably watching from an upstairs window for the arrival of a car. I rattled the door and rang the bell for some time. Eventually a man came up behind me with two large Alsatians held on a tight lead, and a torch in his other hand.

'What do you want?'

'I have been asked to dinner by Mr Boissaens. There seems nobody to open the door.'

'If they were expecting anybody, the door would be opened by now. Would you like to come round the back and see the Steward?'

'I have no wish to see the Steward, or anyone else.' My hunger was not so insatiable as he seemed to imagine. If nobody wished to open the door, I should return home and find myself a tin of baked beans in the larder.

'I am sorry, sir, Instructions are that anyone found wandering in the grounds at night should be taken to the Steward's office. I expect he'll fix you up with something.'

I made my third entrance to Middlewalk Hall through the back regions, a well-lit area of plastic tiles and huge, white-painted pipes, like a ship's engine room. I had imagined stone-flagged floors, flaking paint and the smell of vegetables. A great noise of washing up, innumerable electric engines and the babble of latin voices came from one end of a long corridor. In the kitchen, two men in chef's hats stood over the range while a third made adjustments to a mixing machine. The slight hum of a smell-extractor and the roar of an oil-fired central heating plant added to the impression that we were in an ocean liner. All this to keep three people in comfort and idleness.

Nothing could ever turn me into a socialist. My place is unmistakably at the top table, and I have always entertained the warmest feelings of class solidarity with the very rich even if they are seldom reciprocated. But something told me that the Boissaens household went too far. I began to suspect that Mr Boissaens was not really a gentleman. No gentleman kept a steward. In these distressing times, the rich should learn to lie low. It was one thing to resent the forcible redistribution of wealth to satisfy the brutal appetites of the working class, quite another to see it hoarded on this scale. None of which would have occurred to me if someone had been present to open the front door. There was no excuse for the very rich. They existed on the sufferance of such intelligent people as myself, and should learn to be ingratiating.

The Steward's office was decorated with time charts and work sheets. A map of the estate showed that Mr Boissaens owned the entire village, except the Rectory, the church and a small area described as War Memorial Park which I knew as a scrap heap.

His land extended to the Great Bath Road and almost into Twyford.

'Mr Trumpeter, I am afraid there has been some sort of mistake. Nobody is expected to dinner, and you are marked as coming after dinner to see Mr Boissaens.' The Steward was a dapper, grey-haired little man with a handsome face which was almost too mature and kindly. I immediately suspected that he was a homosexual. His voice was accentless.

'How most unfortunate. Perhaps you are right. I have a distinct impression of being asked to dinner.'

'It is often very difficult, when you are talking with Mr Boissaens, to know exactly what he is saying. He speaks quite clearly, but a great deal seems to be going on in his mind. Many people are so frightened of him they can't take in a word he says.'

'I am not at all frightened of him. He distinctly asked me to dinner, and Miss Danae confirmed it when I saw her this morning.'

'I'm afraid you're wrong about Mr Boissaens. He never makes a mistake of that sort. He is far too meticulous. Danae is another matter. Never believe a word she says until you've checked it up in the *Encyclopaedia Britannica*. She's always been a wicked little liar, but she's a warm-hearted girl and I know that Mr Boissaens is very fond of her. Of course, she's all he's got nowadays.'

All? The great house vibrated with activity around us. Two telephones sat on the Steward's desk between a vase of hothouse flowers.

'…Now you're here, we'd better give you something to eat. Another time you're in doubt as to what Mr Boissaens has said, ring me up and find out. Ask for Mr Perrins, the Steward. Of course, you'll always be welcome to drop in and have a meal with me, if you like. It gets quite lonely living among all these foreigners, although they're not a bad bunch this time. Last year we had two Italians chasing each other round the kitchen table with a knife. We had to get Father O'Toole to settle it. He sprayed them all with Holy Water, or whatever it is, and they seemed quite happy. Simple, ignorant people of course, but they knew which side their bread was buttered when it came to money. I've never seen people so greedy for it. Always quarrelling among themselves about their wives. I expect you get lots of that sort of thing in your calling?'

Happily, Anglicans seldom chase each other round the table with a kitchen knife. When they do, they usually send for the police, or a probation officer. The usefulness of Anglican clergymen is more subtle than that.

Our food was brought on a tray.

'I'm sorry about the tin plates,' said Mr Perrins. 'We had so many breakages that it didn't seem worthwhile to provide more china. Will you have a glass of wine? Not as good as you'd get in the dining-room, but they don't treat us too badly.'

Two lamb chops, some mashed potato and cabbage were already served on the plates. I accepted a glass of red wine from an unlabelled bottle in the cocktail cupboard. The food was much better than anything Gillian ever served, and the wine seemed perfectly all right. I have no pretensions to being a connoisseur.

'Mr Boissaens must be quite a wealthy man,' I said.

'He's tremendous,' said Mr Perrins with enthusiasm. 'You've only seen the tip of the iceberg. I know more about it than I should because he always asks me to witness documents. He doesn't mind me reading them first. I think it rather amuses him.'

'Where does it all come from?' I asked.

'That's a very big question,' said Mr Perrins. Obviously, the subject was his hobby. 'Basically, the Boissaens fortune is a South African one – diamonds and asbestos, but long before South Africa became important they had tobacco in New Guinea, oil in Dutch Shell, real estate in Canada and Winston Salem, North Carolina. He owns two railroads in America and the greater part of a domestic airline. Then I know he's got interests in Zambia and Katanga and I think you'd find he owns a sizeable chunk of the City of Melbourne which was bought by his great-uncle. But really you can't say where it all is. South Africa could blow up tomorrow and it wouldn't really make the smallest difference. Just like New Guinea. We lost everything there when they invented Indonesia, but Mr Boissaens just laughed. He knew the whole place would disintegrate when it was left in the hands of the natives, and he likes to think of people who are sure of themselves being absolutely wrong. It would need a world war to upset him, and even then he'd probably be all right. He's got a big farm in Kenya where he goes sometimes, just to laugh at the natives. I don't approve of that sort of thing, of course, but they all worship him out there. He's a wonderful man to work for. Would you like a glass of crème de menthe while we're waiting for them to finish?'

'Have you anything else?'

'I'm afraid not. I always like a glass of crème de menthe when I have company. It settles the digestion.'

We sat facing each other over the desk, each with a ridiculously small glass of green liquid held daintily in his fingers.

'Why does he live in England?'

'He's only here three or four months in the year. Never more than six. We make it quite comfortable for him, and his second wife is English. As a matter of fact, he went to school here, at Wellington. He always says he comes here to get away from his relations on the Continent. But he won't keep any of his money in England. Doesn't trust the English with money. Worse than negroes, he says, and more cunning. Another reason he won't keep money here is death duties, and because he doesn't want his wife to have too much. By English law, a widow must receive at least the interest on half your estate. "Much too much for a woman of Angela's simple tastes," he said to me once. The daughter's going to get every penny of it.'

'Oh, really?' I said.

'I witnessed the will,' said Mr Perrins. 'It won't be easy for her. The old man has more nationalities than there are skins to an onion. He started off Dutch and American and English, now he's given up English and become South African and then he discovered that if he wanted to keep his Kenyan property he'd have to become a Kenyan.'

One of his telephones rang. 'Oh-ho. Trouble. Perrins speaking.' He listened attentively. I recognised the voice of Mr Boissaens. 'Very good, sir. Straight away, or when you see him?' He winked at me. 'We'll have it brought up in about half an hour, then.'

He put down the receiver. 'They're doing you proud. Champagne and smoked salmon sandwiches in the study. What sort of champagne would you like?'

'What is best?'

'Many people like the Dom Perignon, but I don't think you can do much better than the Krug '52, myself. He must have taken quite a fancy to you. Shall I have some put on ice?'

'What happened to Danae's mother?'

'There was an accident. I'm surprised nobody's told you. They had a son, you see. He was a lovely boy – handsome, kind, intelligent, cheerful. I never heard a word against him from anyone. Then something went wrong – he fell in with bad company at Cape Town, where he went to university. Next thing we heard, he'd shot himself. Nobody knows why – it might have been a girl or some other trouble. Mr Boissaens was in Kenya at the time with his first wife, who was a Belgian. They charter an aeroplane to take them down to the Cape, and before they get into the air from Nairobi Airport, what happens? Bang, whoomph, there you are with an aeroplane upside down blazing away, a dead pilot and a wife strapped in by her seat belt with the seat on top of her who might be dead or alive. He stays for ten minutes trying to get her out of that seat, then the ambulance people drag him away, an awful mess, swearing blue murder. He can't see out of either of his eyes, and his spine's got a great chip out of it, so that his legs fold under him if he tries to walk. Now he's only got his daughter.'

'What about Mrs Boissaens?'

'Oh, he picked her up somewhere. Crumpets are two a penny when you are as rich as that, if you'll excuse the expression. It was the first wife he was keen on. He's never even set eyes on the second. He'd probably drop her like a ton of bricks if he did, too.'

'I didn't think she was too bad.'

'Well, you're wrong. I'd stick to your little wife back home, Mr Parson.' Somehow there was nothing impertinent about this piece of advice. It was just a friendly tip. 'They say in the village she's taken a fancy to you. If it's true, the best thing you can do is lock yourself up in your church and pretend to be a corpse awaiting burial. There are some months of the year when her husband's away and she stays here. Then she's on the prowl. I wouldn't be telling you all these stories if you weren't a Man of God, and I was pretty sure they wouldn't get any farther.'

'Quite right.'

'When those two Italians were chasing each other round the kitchen table, it wasn't anything to do with their wives, as I told Father O'Toole. It was Mrs Boissaens they were squabbling over. I'm only thankful that I'm removed from it all,' said Mr Perrins. 'Owing to my position.'

'It's the daughter I prefer,' I said, in a man-to-man sort of way.

'Danae's a lovely girl. She's wild, of course, but there's no real malice in her. It's a pity you're married – she needs a man to steady her, and you couldn't do much better than a Church of England parson. And think of all those lovely millions she'll have.'

'Yes,' I said. 'It's a pity, really, I'm married.'

Danae greeted me with imprudent warmth. 'How's my favourite clergyman?' she cried, kissing me warmly on the cheek. Mrs Boissaens concentrated viciously on her patchwork. Her husband smiled benignly from the corner. It was the first time I had seen him in the drawing-room, or anywhere except in his terrifying, empty study. He looked mellower with the soft light and warm carpets.

'I am sorry not to get up to greet you,' he said.

'Here it comes again,' said Danae. 'But unfortunately I am unable to do so without the greatest difficulty.'

Mr Boissaens smiled indulgently. 'Danae likes to mock me for my infirmity. It is true, of course, that I revel in other people's pity. But I think I could have chosen a less inconvenient way of drawing attention to myself if I had been given the choice.'

'Your father has a lot to put up with, and I don't think we would any of us be as patient or uncomplaining as he is,' said Mrs Boissaens. It was exactly the wrong thing to say. In the resentful silence which followed only her husband chuckled to himself, but his reaction came too late to stop her thinking she had won a victory.

'Now tell me about parish affairs. And how's your charming little wife?'

'Gillian is very well,' I replied automatically. 'That is to say she is not well at all. She has retired to bed for the evening.'

'Oh dear, I wonder what is wrong.' I could not possibly remember which of Gillian's illnesses was afflicting her this evening. 'I expect it is some periodical trouble. Many women do not feel at all well at this time of year. There is no need to worry about it,' said Mrs Boissaens.

'I imagine Mr Trumpeter is well acquainted with the type of affliction you describe,' said Mr Boissaens. 'He has been married for seven years.'

'Indeed I am. Female parishioners nowadays seem to equate religion with sex, and they always expect me to discuss their monthly troubles. That and their husbands' performance.'

'I often wondered what you found to discuss with your parishioners,' said Mr Boissaens. 'I find they have very little conversation.'

'Daddy frightens them. It is no good talking to them as if you were really interested in what they were going to say. You have to simper and complain about the weather first. Eventually, if you're very gentle and very obsequious, they will tell you that they are expecting the curse in about a week. Nicholas must be an expert by now. When Angela or I are expecting the curse, we can come and talk to you about it.'

'Danae always goes too far,' said Mrs Boissaens.

'I would much sooner you didn't come and tell me,' I said. 'Everybody else does and there is really nothing I can do about it.'

'Oh, isn't there?' said Danae, with a huge, conspiratorial grin.

Very few things embarrass me. In seven years with Gillian, I have acquired a fairly thick skin. But in the tense silence which followed Danae's remark, I felt myself blushing. Mrs Boissaens cut in with deadly tact: 'Perhaps we women ought to go to bed. The men probably want to talk business.'

'I have arranged that everything should be laid out in the study,' said Mr Boissaens. 'It seems a shame to call Miguel. Perhaps one of you would be kind enough to push me there.'

I found the idea embarrassing. He would certainly turn the situation to his advantage somehow. Mrs Boissaens came forward with an odiously tender look.

'Perhaps we ought to arrange the next meeting of the Youth Committee,' I said, avoiding her eye. 'I am rather busy this week, and I am afraid I won't be seeing you again tonight.'

'You will,' said Danae.

'What are those children whispering about?' Mr Boissaens was just being pushed out of the door.

'No doubt it's some little secret of their own,' said his wife cattily. 'It doesn't do to pry too much into the secrets of the young.'

As soon as they were out of the room, Danae put both her arms round my neck and we kissed.

'Don't be too long. I'll be left alone with Angela.'

'I cannot remember what it is you wished to talk to me about. Perhaps you would be kind enough to remind me.' Mr Boissaens was less friendly now. He made no movement towards the champagne or smoked salmon sandwiches which had been laid out on a trestle table.

'You told me you wished to speak to me.'

'I think it was about some money you wanted.'

'I can't remember asking you for any. Of course, the parish is always in need of funds.'

'Could it have been about a dance hall or something like that?'

'Conceivably.'

He wearied of trying to bait me. 'Well, I have decided to give you the money. Not because I have any particular wish to ingratiate myself with the old people in the village, and even less because I feel it important or desirable that they should have somewhere to dance. You could call it a friendly gesture to yourself, if you liked.'

Even that was not going to embarrass me.

'Thank you very much,' I said. 'It is extremely kind.'

'Here is a letter to Lillibet & Sprigman, my solicitors in Reading. The total sum required, I understand, is fifteen hundred pounds. It will have to be paid in a covenant, so that you receive a tax rebate from the Government. Then I suggest you raise a loan with an insurance company, so that you receive, over a twelve month period, tax concessions on the capital repayments as well as the interest. While my contribution is waiting to service the loan, I suggest you invest it in a building society, with tax-free interest at four per cent. In that way the Government will make a significant contribution, as is only right, since all politicians feel particularly tender to old age pensioners. If you build it without a lavatory, I think you may be able to get a local authority grant to cover the cost of one. All that dancing is bound to have an unfortunate effect. The District Council is very keen on lavatories. Ask for Mr Kitchen at Lillibet and Sprigman's. He is not particularly efficient, or even particularly likeable, but I think he is the best man in Reading. He will also arrange for the payment of my own contribution to your salary, which we discussed the first time we met. How is the village reacting to your Christian message?'

'My first sermon comes tomorrow.'

'Have you thought of a subject?'

'There was something in the newspapers today about the scandal of inflammable nighties. I thought I might draw attention to that.'

'You think they don't read the newspapers?'

'Even if they do, they much prefer hearing the same thing said twice. If I were to talk about the dangers of inflammable bed socks, or underwear, they would think I had gone mad. The greatest single danger to health in the village is probably the main road. Then all those sweets they eat. They stuff the children with sweets and iced lollies every morning in the village shop until their teeth fall out, but that doesn't worry them. They get new ones for practically nothing, and I think dentures are something of a status symbol in the village. There's one girl of fifteen with two sets of false teeth. Even Gillian finds that excessive.'

'Does she think the girl ought to be made to go toothless?'

'It is hard to know what she thinks. She has no capacity for sustained thought.'

'Why don't you preach against the dangers of sweets?'

'They would complain to the Bishop. You begin to learn, after a time, the sort of thing you can get away with. At Christmas I always preach a sermon about keeping death off the roads, but it has to be directed against drunken drivers. Everybody knows that by far the greatest proportion of deaths is among completely sober pedestrians who don't look where they're going. But you can't mention that inside the religious context. People come to church to be flattered, not insulted.'

'Is that why they go? I have often wondered.'

If I came to the Hall twice a week during Mr Boissaens' occupancy, his allowance of five hundred pounds a year worked out at about twenty guineas a time. One might as well try to give him his money's worth.

'It is obviously no longer true to say that we fill an emotional or spiritual need in mankind as a whole. But we still satisfy one rather specialised consumer demand. If we closed down all the churches, turned away such congregations as survive and sold all property which does not yield income, we would be much better off. It would also be less trouble for everybody, and most of' the clergymen would be much happier. But they lack both the logic and the honesty to do that. They prefer occupying themselves with trivial, unnecessary things to doing nothing. A few mislead themselves into believing that they really are of use, and that they add to the sum of human happiness in their neighbourhood. Others, like myself, see the maintenance of harmless and even mildly fatuous beliefs as a bulwark against much grosser errors to which gullible people would otherwise be tempted.'

'I always suspected you were an idealist,' said Mr Boissaens. He was enjoying himself immensely. 'Wouldn't you like a glass of wine, and I think there may be some sandwiches?'

'You misunderstand me,' I said as I helped myself. 'I do not see my role as an impotrant one, or even as an active one. My reasons for becoming a clergyman were quite different. I was merely justifying my existence.'

'So I suspected. But you have not explained why you did become a clergyman.'

'Why should I explain? It is a free country. Anybody can become a clergyman who wants to.'

'But you do not believe half of what your religion teaches.'

'You are wrong in supposing that my religion has anything to teach. It is one of the great strengths of the Christian Church that it no longer teaches anything. Individual members can offer opinions and ask other people to agree with them. In theory, its purpose is to urge people to be good. In practice, it merely reassures them that they are good. As an occupation it is no more useless than any other. It helps pass the time until death.'

'Assure me that I am good.'

'Must I?'

'That's your job.'

'It is easier when people come to church. Their presence in the stalls is its own assurance. Well, you do nobody any harm.'

'Is that enough to be good?'

'Not really. That is why people come to church. You are obviously devoted to your daughter.'

'She is an extremely entertaining and likeable person. Also, she is affectionate. It involves no hardship.'

'Goodness need not involve hardship. That is a puritan notion, and totally unchristian. Existence itself is good.'

'You're not making a bad job of it, I must say,' said Mr Boissaens. 'Help yourself to whatever you need. Is the wine all right?'

'Excellent. And you have just given a large sum of money to charity.'

'But I don't believe in the charity.'

'That makes your action all the more disinterested.'

'And it didn't exactly hurt me.'

'The Church's purpose, nowadays, is to alleviate suffering, not promote it.'

Mr Boissaens changed his tack.

'The money I have given you comes in large part from some diamond mines in Africa. I have just read an interesting novel on the subject. It is based on one of my own mines, they say. Apparently when the negroes come up from underground, they have to have their bottoms searched before they leave the compound.'

'A necessary precaution, no doubt, against theft.'

'Would you like to have your bottom searched every time you left the pulpit?'

'Not at all. Nor would it serve any useful purpose.'

'Do you think it reasonable that your old age pensioners should expect to dance on the proceeds of my workmen's bottoms.'

'I think it unreasonable that they should expect to dance on the proceeds of anything except their own exertions. But they are the new *rentier* class. No doubt they will console themselves that but for the profits on which they are dancing there would be no investment in the diamond mines which employ negroes at a standard of affluence which is unparalleled throughout Africa. Moreover, they will probably suppose that you would not have given the money for the Hall if you could have derived more pleasure from spending it in some other way. So they have nothing to be grateful for.'

'I derive no pleasure whatever from giving it to them.'

'Of course you do. The sensation of generosity is entirely pleasurable, like compassion. Otherwise, how do you explain the success of women's magazines? If the exercise of goodness – making other people happy, for instance – was not a source of satisfaction to those who exercise it, nobody would be good.'

'You have quite persuaded me that I am good. But it is an academic point. The knowledge makes me no happier. I think I will have a statue put outside your Hall, showing a negro miner having his bottom searched.'

'They won't mind at all. Modern art is firmly identified with obscenity in their minds, and they are keenly in favour of anything modern.'

'You are a curiously bitter young man. I wish I could do something to make you happier, although you would probably be more boring. Hasn't Danae tried to make you happy?'

'What did she tell you?'

'She has been boasting about her conquest all day. At first, I was rather angry. It is impossible to be completely dispassionate about these things. But if you make her happy, that is all I care about. She must make up her own mind.'

I was surprised to hear such commonplace reactions voiced by a man whom I was beginning to admire. Perhaps he really was a student of *Woman's Dream*. More likely, his total ignorance of that magazine prevented him from recognising the pattern. Soon, he would start telling me that she was the only person in his life who mattered, and I would realise that underneath that tough, embittered exterior there beat a warm, compassionate heart. I helped myself self-consciously to some more champagne. Mr

Perrins was quite right. Although I have no claims to being a connoisseur, the Krug '52 appealed to me as exceptionally refreshing.

'Angela announced at lunch that you only had designs on my daughter's money. If so, I think you are behaving foolishly,' he continued.

I couldn't bear it. In another minute he was going to tell me that money was not the most important thing in life. He used to think so once, but experience and maturity had taught him that happiness was far more important.

'Angela feels that Danae should only look at suitors as rich as herself. She will have a hard search, and of course nobody is as avaricious as the rich. It is certainly true that money can add a powerful impetus to the sex drive. I have a cousin in Holland who is not only hunchbacked and very plain, but also possesses a most spiteful nature. Yet she has kept a devoted, intelligent and kindly husband for forty years. He fell in love with her money and it has never lost its fascination for him. He woos her assiduously night and day. She keeps him rather short, of course, and they are a most touching sight together, or so I am assured by those who have the good fortune to see them. I can only listen. They are like two turtle doves.'

'Ah yes,' I said. 'Somebody told me that your eyesight was rather poor.' I did not want to hear it again. He was as bad as the old age pensioners, only less subtle. They pretended to invite sympathy in order to embarrass you. Mr Boissaens unashamedly tried to make you feel uncomfortable.

'It gets around,' said Mr Boissaens, with modest pride. 'But if you are serious in your attentions to my daughter, I advise you to concentrate on her other qualities. She will be extremely rich, of course, and it would be silly to pretend otherwise. You will think I am being affected when I say that the sort of fortune she will be called upon to administer is more of' an embarrassment and a bore than a source of comfort.'

'Not affected, but inaccurate. You could give away all your money tomorrow, if you wanted, and so could she.'

'So could a tractor-driver give up his work and live on National Assistance. I have often thought of' setting up a charitable trust. But apart from the fact that there is no class of person to whom I feel so unreservedly well disposed that I wish to see its members prosper at my expense, I feel that the boredom of having nothing to do would be greater even than my present boredom.'

Poor fellow! It really did make one feel quite compassionate. 'What about Oxfam?' I said, with a nasty, satirical edge on my voice.

'It is already over-subscribed, both emotionally and financially. Where sudden famines are concerned, there is too much money chasing too little misfortune. A feature of modern life is that you have central governments with enormous resources controlling human beings with very little. Governments welcome famines and any sort of natural disaster as a means of justifying their existence.'

My mouth was full of sandwich. If I swallowed it too quickly, I would get hiccups.

'People are starving in Asia,' I cried passionately. It was something about which I felt extremely strongly, or sometimes imagined I did. Gillian's answer was invariably to give them contraceptives. But you can't eat washable sheaths and inter-uterine devices. 'Man does not live by the Pill alone,' I used to retort bitterly, hoping to annoy her by my irreverent misquoting of the great Ralph Waldo Emerson.

'Two thirds of the world's population are short of food. That is the only important statistic of our time.' Religion had no other significant message. All this talk of old age pensioners, free abortions for teenagers, a dynamic economy based on social justice was so much escapism. The most important thing in the world was to teach the Asians to grow more rice, or persuade the Americans to give them corn. 'The price of a rail ticket from Maidenhead to London would keep an entire Indian family in food for a month,' I cried, but it was no good. Remorselessly, inescapably, the hiccups were upon me.

Mr Boissaens listened to the first noises in silence.

'Never mind,' he said. 'I expect there is some wine left in the bottle. Try swizzling it with a fork and then drink it slowly. I never believe in the sudden shock technique. More suffering is caused by trying to cure hiccups in England than by all the witch-doctors in Africa. Hiccups is a state of mind, the symptom of an inner conflict. Do you hope to marry Danae?'

'Nobody has suggested it. Hic. I have only just met her. In any case – hic – I am already married.'

'I would have no objections to your marrying her, if that was what she wanted. I imagine that you feel the same. It is nearly two years since she took any interest in a man. She is a passionate girl, I think, and one does not like to enquire what she has been doing in the meanwhile. I imagine she masturbates. What will your superiors say?'

'The Church's new teaching on masturbation is that its dangers have been much exaggerated in the past. Hic.'

'You misunderstand me. Will you have to give up your vocation or whatever you call it?'

'If I decided to divorce my wife and remarry, I should almost certainly have to give up my living. But nobody has yet suggested anything of the sort.'

'A pity. I can't see you as anything except a clergyman. Is there no way around it?'

'None at all. Even if Gillian were to run away with a bus-conductor, or be pronounced incurably insane, I should be condemned to a life of celibacy. It's one of the conditions of employment, like abstaining from liquor if you are an airline pilot. Don't ask me why.'

'Perhaps they feel that too many wives would impair your efficiency. But few religions are not prepared to stretch a point where money is involved.'

'The Church of England has all the money it wants, and so can afford to preserve its integrity, at any rate so far as the clergymen are concerned. To find a congregation we bend over backwards in our efforts to accommodate. But the man at the altar is expected to behave exactly as the laity were expected to behave a hundred years ago.'

'Then you will have to give up preaching.'

His bland assumption that I was prepared to do so irritated me. It would entail far greater sacrifice than he could ever imagine. I happen to like composing sermons on the danger of inflammable nighties, and feel I have a vocation for it. Perhaps with Danae's fortune at my disposal I could build a church and hire myself a congregation of unemployed film extras, but it would not be the same thing.

'I might not want to leave my wife,' I said, with quiet dignity.

'In that case you would be mad, and I have no wish for a mad son-in-law. I see that my method has cured your hiccups. It is much better than holding your breath. Just a glass of flat champagne, sipped slowly. I can't think why everybody does not use it.'

I was not to be mollified. 'Not everybody has your advantages in life,' I said, and hiccupped loudly.

Danae was waiting for me in the drawing-room. In the hall, I heard her father being wheeled to the electric lift which carried him to his bedroom. She wrapped herself around me passionately.

'We can't go up to my bedroom. Angela is guarding the staircase like a dragon. She has been down twice already. Do you know it is nearly two o'clock ? I have read *Paris-Match* three times through and now I'm drunk. There are some rather good pictures of the Indonesian massacres.' We sat together on the sofa, turning over the pages. 'I like that one,' said Danae. A grief-stricken mother had a child of eight to her breast.

Danae's face was flushed and her eyes were bright. We were not touching, but I could feel her warmth and softness, and I thought of the terrible white Gillian waiting for me at home, like a pair of wet trousers on the grass.

'Look at this. Isn't it too terrible? The photographer must have been standing right in front of him.'

Mrs Boissaens came in, wearing a voluminous kimono. 'Are you still up? I was making sure all the lights were turned off.'

'Mr Trumpeter and I are discussing how to rescue the village's youth. I will turn the lights off.'

'I really think I ought to be going,' I said, standing up. 'It is terribly late.'

'Is your car at the front,' ? said Mrs Boissaens sweetly. 'I will turn the light on for you.'

'I didn't bring the car. It is no distance to walk.'

Danae jumped forward. 'I am going to run him home in my car. Don't wait up. Good night, Angela.'

Mrs Boissaens retired, beaten. I thought she gave me a curious, appraising glance as she left, but I was too embarrassed to return the stare.

'Angela is eaten up with jealousy,' said Danae. 'She's so desperate for a man she even got her claws into the Steward here. He was frightened out of his wits.'

'Poor Mr Perrins,' I said.

'You know him?'

'One meets these people around the place.'

As we climbed into the car, I gave a monumental hiccup.

'We'll soon cure that,' said Danae. 'Hold your breath.'

She punched me in the stomach and screamed into my ear. 'A good shock is the only cure.'

I was still hiccupping when she drove me to the car park of Middlewalk's disused railway station. I thought I was tired, but she soon persuaded me that I wasn't. When she dropped me at the front door of the Rectory, I had stopped hiccupping.

Gillian had fallen asleep pretending to read a novel. She was incapable of reading anything except *Woman's Dream* and medical magazines. She lay with the bedside light on, her mouth wide open, but she did not move. Suddenly, seeing her so vulnerable in that hopelessly unattractive posture, I felt a pang of tenderness for her. She might not have been much good, but at least I knew her. We had reached a stage in our relationship when she no longer had the power to irritate me. No suffering on her part, real or imagined, could affect me in the slightest way. I had already seen too much of it. But I wished her no particular harm. It seemed cruel to prefer Danae just because she was prettier, kinder, more amusing, wiser and more affectionate than Gillian. For a moment I must have approached the wisdom and compassion of God in my viewpoint, but then Gillian woke up as I was taking off my trousers and the moment passed.

'Where have you been? Do you know it is nearly three o'clock?'

'Mr Boissaens kept me talking about the new Hall. I think it is going to be all right. He gave me some letters to take to his lawyer.'

I turned my back on her to climb into my pyjama trousers. She stared mournfully at my bottom.

'I nearly telephoned the doctor. I was terrified. Suddenly, all the pains stopped and I felt a numbness creeping over my body. I tried fighting against it, but I could feel it fighting back.'

'Did you try taking an aspirin?'

'It was like the tentacles of a giant octopus. Invisible. I would not have minded if it had been a real octopus I could see.'

'Of course not.' None of us minded that sort of thing.

'I think it may be a sign that the last stages are not far off. I wish I had gone for that barium meal test at the clinic. It's all right if you can get at it in time. Now, it may have gone too far.'

'I should definitely take an aspirin in that case.'

'You wouldn't care in the least, I suppose.'

Normally my answer to this attack is to assure her in the most emphatic terms that I should care most outrageously, relying upon emphasis to impress her with my insincerity. After my conversation with Mr Boissaens, this was too near the knuckle. 'Of course I should mind. As a matter of fact, I should mind a lot,'

I said, trying to play the phlegmatic Englishman, mastering his emotion. It worked.

'Do you know, I really think you would mind.' said Gillian. 'You don't think you would. Who would get you your lunches?'

Those revolting meals! It was most imprudent of her to remind me at such a tender moment. I climbed into bed, thinking of Danae.

'You smell of scent,' she said. She sat up in bed and a hysterical note came into her voice. 'Nicholas, you've been going with that woman. It is true what they say in the village. You've been to bed with Mrs Boissaens. I wouldn't have believed it. And I thought Angela was my friend.'

How she deluded herself. 'You are quite mistaken. I scarcely saw Mrs Boissaens. It is too late for a long conversation. You are imagining things. Tomorrow, I am going to cancel your subscription to *Woman's Dream.*'

'Just you dare. I'll walk out of the house. So Mrs Swinger was right. She did take a fancy to you. I can't think why. I could have told her that you're about as passionate and original a lover as my hot-water bottle.'

An original lover! Once Gillian, from her study of some obscene manual, had suggested that we should try making love in what she described as the Italian manner. It was extremely difficult and self-conscious, and had not been a success. Gillian was now behaving in the manner prescribed for wives whose husbands are suspected of infidelity. First, anger, then self-pity. Finally, I knew from my scrutiny of the text-books, she would try and win me back by making herself more attractive and preparing my special, favourite dishes for dinner when I came back from the office in the evening. The first would undoubtedly involve heavy outlay on woollen clothes of grotesque hue. The second would mean Toad in the Hole. For some reason, Gillian had decided that I liked a dish she prepared from sausages and a sort of yellowy paste. Her mother decided it first. The dish was always produced with great flourishes when we visited her family home. In Gillian's magazine, the husband (called Andrew) was always subjected to this treatment by the wife (called Lynn) and it never failed to work. I began to see Andrew's point. Was even my darling, adorable Danae worth a whole week of Toad in the Hole?

CHAPTER FOUR

Chapter meetings usually start with a prayer, but Mr Tuck, whose evangelical leanings shied away from such things, had instituted a moment of silence instead. We stood self-consciously in front of our chairs, in the Rural Dean's study. Coffee, for which we paid Mrs Tuck fourpence a cup on the tacit understanding that any profits were given to charity, congealed in front of us. I wondered what was supposed to be the object of our meditation. The four last things, death, judgment, heaven and hell? Nobody could have looked less eschatological than Mr Heifer, who stood with a happy little smirk on his face. Mr Jackson could scarcely be expected to think about hell, since modern churchmanship tended to disbelieve in it. Possibly there was a somewhat less agreeable corner of Heaven where those people went who negligently brought into the world an unwanted child or expressed racialist sympathies. If there was no hell, there could be no useful purpose in holding a judgment day. Soon modern churchmanship would begin to disbelieve in death. Teenagers no longer believed in it, and that was the rub.

Perhaps we were meant to meditate on the dead of two world wars, those who had selflessly laid down their lives in the cause of freedom. A humbling thought, but nobody had suggested it. Mr Plimsoll looked bored and resentful, as if this silence were an unwarrantable intrusion on his valuable time. He resented it even more when he was asked to speak. Perhaps silence would emerge as the great blessing of religion. When liturgical and dogmatic squabbles had subsided into general apathy, the churches would remain as places of silence where people could take refuge from the noise of everyday life and sit with their mouths open and their minds blissfully vacant. Of course, the new religion would scarcely appeal to the working class. Workers demand a constant babble of noise around them or they develop melancholia which sometimes leads to madness. The worst punishment allowed by the English Government for any crime – the supreme penalty – was to shut up an offender alone. But then I have always doubted the religious potentiality of the working class. Religion is the opium of the bourgeoisie. After a time, I began to think about Danae.

So lost were we in our particular reveries that the whole period of forty-five minutes might have passed in silence had not Mr Heifer felt the need to urinate.

'Cyril can always be relied upon to bring us back to earth,' said the Rural Dean, and everybody tittered. I had often noticed the penchant for lavatory jokes among clergymen of my Faith, and thought it in extremely bad taste. Mr Heifer's affliction could easily have been the result of a war wound. When he returned, I gave him an especially warm smile. He winked back and sat beside me.

'In preparation for the Group Ministry, which we all hope will be instituted some time in the future, we are all going to produce progress reports on our departments,' said Mr Tuck in an officious voice. 'Who's going to start. Plimsoll?'

'I think the Rural Dean ought to start,' said Mr Plimsoll. 'Very well,' said Mr Tuck. 'My paper is entitled "Pets as an aid to religious life".'

'Religious what?' said Mr Jackson belligerently.

'Religious life,' said Mr Tuck.

'Religious life,' said Mr Jackson sarcastically.

'He's quite a character,' said Mr Heifer in an aside.

'In many modern homes today, pet animals are kept,' began Mr Tuck in a sing-song. 'They vary from large alsatians to lolloping spaniel puppies, small kittens, and of course I must not forget to mention the budgies. In wealthier homes, it is quite normal to keep a small pony for the children, but of course not all of us can run to that.'

'Not in the homes,' said Mr Jackson. 'They never keep ponies indoors. That would be cruel.'

'Textual criticisms can come later. I am concerned to impress you with the main argument. Nevertheless, it is generally admitted nowadays that pet animals have a large part to play. As a pleasant pastime for children, as a useful watchdog for the home, as a companion and solace in old age, they are an essential feature of the contemporary scene.'

His argument, when stripped of its horrible padding, went like this: Pets can be made the implements of a religious advance on two levels: on the highest level, people must be taught that the love and affection they lavish on their pet animals is in fact being lavished on Jesus, so that every time they clean the budgie's cage or empty the cat's tray of cinders they are performing a religious ceremony; on a slightly lower level, the Church must realise that the pet industry absorbs a large part of the national supply of affection, unselfishness and spare cash. Therefore the Church must identify itself more firmly with pet animals. Pets' services and prayers for sick or departed pets were not enough. Every clergyman should keep a pet, form a pets' club and know the names of every pet animal in his parish. Then he asked each of us what we thought, and how we proposed to conduct the campaign in our parish.

Mr Jackson informed us that his children kept white rats. Mr Heifer pointed out that he had got Roger, an enormous recumbent form under the table. I invented a cat called Tibbles.

'Good,' said Mr Tuck. 'I must come and pay a call on Tibbles soon.'

Only Mr Plimsoll objected: 'My wife does not like animals. They give her hay fever,' he said. I wished I could have thought of that.

'Then you must apply yourself especially hard to the pets under your charge,' said Mr Tuck.

'What am I expected to do?' said Mr Plimsoll. 'There is a perfectly good vet in the neighbourhood.'

'But not a spiritual vet,' said Mr Tuck. 'Do you suggest that the ministry no longer pays any attention to human beings because there are doctors who can look after their bodies?'

'I don't know,' said Mr Plimsoll, rather taken with the idea. 'Psychiatry has made some wonderful advances.'

'Mr Plimsoll is our efficiency expert,' explained Mr Tuck. 'He advises on labour-saving and keeps us in touch with the latest technological discoveries, so far as they apply to the ministry. You must tell me when I can visit your Tibbles. I really would like to get to know her.'

'Unfortunately, she spends much of the time out of the house. She visits a tom cat in one of the outlying farms, I believe.'

'Ah sex,' said Mr Heifer waggishly. 'I believe there is a great deal of that in your village.'

There was a slightly awkward pause. Could they suspect anything? 'I have been too preoccupied with plans for the new hall to notice,' I said.

'Isn't Mr Boissaens paying for that,' said Heifer, quite without malice. 'I believe Mrs Boissaens is the power behind the throne there. A most remarkable woman.'

The silence which followed was longer and even more awkward. Clearly, they had heard the rumours. With a tact which was depressingly obvious, Mr Tuck called on Cyril Heifer to read his paper on youth.

Heifer had prepared no notes. He had no use for young girls, who were mostly irredeemable. The important thing was to get the lads alone and give them a talking to. Sometimes showing them pictures helped to bring them out. They must be shown the sort of dangers to which they were liable to be exposed. It was the girls who led them up the garden path. He had a particular lad who came twice a week for pep-talks in the Rector's study. He

83

didn't ask the other clergymen to help, as he could see that it wasn't everybody's line of country. But if any of them saw a likely looking lad in his parish, Mr Heifer would be most grateful for the chance to have a talk with him.

'I like my lads to be between fifteen and sixteen,' said Mr Heifer wistfully. 'That is the best age, really.'

Another awkward silence followed. Then Mr Tuck cleared his throat. 'The important thing is to avoid any suggestion of scandal,' he said.

'You are wrong,' cried Mr Jackson. 'Avoidance of scandal is not the most important thing. The most important thing is Love.'

'Hear, hear,' said Mr Heifer.

'We are coming to that,' said Mr Tuck. 'Very well. You read your paper next, Jackson.'

'It is called "Towards an Aggiornamento",' said Mr Jackson.

'Towards what?'

'An aggiornamento.'

'You'll have to translate that if you're going to get through to the ordinary man in the street.'

'This paper is not intended for the man in the street. Can I proceed?'

'Please do.'

'As far as the man in the street is concerned, I should like to suggest three things as necessary before religion can have any relevance in his life. First, we must establish that belief in the existence of some hypothetical Deity is not essential to membership of the Church, and first class membership at that. We do not want any second class citizens, and, let's face it, very few people do actually believe in a Deity nowadays. Second, that the word God nowadays has a confused and misleading image. Many people still think of an old man in the sky. We must talk about Love, which everybody understands and which has a particular relevance to young people. Thirdly, we must strip down. All institutional forms and church services as we know them must be ended. They are time-wasting and often harmful to the image of true religion.'

'Hear, hear,' said Mr Plimsoll.

'Where do we come into all of this?' I asked. Nobody paid any attention. They obviously thought I had not yet entered into the spirit of Chapter meetings. Everything was being staged for my benefit.

'The Church, if it is to survive into the twentieth century, must come down on the side of the living. When confronted with a moral problem, we must ask what would be Love's answer? Would Love approve of unemployment? Would Love think £4 10s is an adequate return to an old age pensioner for her life of service to the community? Does Love think it suitable that men should spend their lives working themselves to death in mines and factories while others live in pampered luxury on the proceeds?'

'What about us?' I ventured timidly.

My remark was misunderstood. I merely wanted to enquire about the function of the priesthood in this new order. Nobody could suppose that we lived in pampered luxury, any more than that people were working themselves to death on our behalf. Jackson charitably decided to misunderstand me still further.

'The treatment of the priesthood is one of the crying scandals of the age. We are expected to work ourselves to death in a discredited cause for a miserable wage, and to live in conditions of mediaeval squalor. The first objective must be to modernise the priesthood. We must be streamlined.'

'Electronically tested,' said Mr Heifer approvingly.

'Re-housed in modern apartments and paid a salary commensurate with the importance of our work,' said Mr Jackson.

'Ah yes,' said Mr Tuck, profoundly bored. 'That is beginning to encroach on Plimsoll's territory. Before we hear Plimsoll, would anyone like some more coffee? Cyril still owes a penny from the last round, having given threepence, so that will be fivepence,

Cyril. There is change in the saucer. Now, Mr Plimsoll. He is our expert on efficiency, labour-saving techniques and technology.' Mr Tuck was a most remarkable man. According to Mr Heifer his life had been devoted to the imitation of Christ from an early age until one day he decided that his efforts had achieved total success. Having finally identified himself with the founder of the Christian religion, a new tranquillity settled on his life. Up to that moment he had been liable to collar passers-by and demand if he was truly Christ. Once that difficult question had been settled, he only referred to his divine status occasionally, usually in oblique asides and sly hints.

'Three main proposals this week,' said Mr Plimsoll. 'I have noticed that people still leave hymn books lying around the church after Matins on Sunday. 'This is extremely time-wasting. If they don't stack them neatly in the porch, I am not going to supply them. Ultimately, I hope to be able to dispense with an organist, too. Music and singing in the future must come from a tape, and the congregation can join in if it wishes in cases where there actually is a congregation.'

'I have noticed that fewer and fewer people come to early Communion on Sunday. It may be a coincidence, but I have observed that those who do are nearly always the troublemakers in the parish, and it is hard to avoid the conclusion that their only motive in fact is to make difficulties. I should prefer to abolish the Communion Service entirely. Eventually, I should hope to abolish the 11 o'clock Matins, too, and advance the 6.30 Evensong to about three o'clock in the afternoon, so that it does not compete with any of the religious television programmes.'

'A good idea,' someone said. 'People simply aren't prepared to leave the goggle box.'

'You must also think of the parson,' said Mr Plimsoll, argumentatively. 'He deserves a little relaxation. Sunday is supposed to be a day of rest, but for many of us it is the most arduous day in the week. We have successfully abolished all week-day services in my village. Now we must take a long, cool look at the Sunday arrangements. Many people, in my experience, prefer to get their religion in their own homes on the television set. It is more intimate, more of a family affair. It seems to me that the Church must either forbid all religious services on television, or use television exclusively as the only relevant medium of our time.'

The Dean and Chapter conferred. Were we going to forbid all religious services on television, or were we going to encourage them? I suppose that we had to pass the time of day somehow.

'The greatest problem confronting clergymen, as it confronts the whole of England nowadays, is the problem of leisure,' I said. 'How can we make our spare time more meaningful? None of us reads much, and the standard of television programmes is too appallingly banal even for our own tastes. Consequently we become lonely and bored. Our parishioners may all be God's creatures, but they are extremely limited in their conversation. Why can't we arrange special Chapter outings? One clergyman could always stay behind to conduct such religious services as are necessary, while the other four are on a fact-finding mission to the Continent, or even farther afield, to America and the Far East. I do not feel that in conscience we could take our wives with us. That would be too much like expense-account businessmen. But we must learn to look outwards nowadays, and see what is happening in the rest of the world.'

'I have never cared too much for foreign parts, myself,' said Mr Plimsoll.

'It wouldn't work,' said Mr Heifer. 'They wouldn't let you get away with it. Still, it might be worth trying. Some of those foreigners haven't got anything to learn, when it comes to sinning.'

'It would be oecumenical,' I said to Jackson.

'I agree that the Christian Church has tended to disregard sex in the past,' he said. 'But it is no good sweeping it under the carpet. Sex is probably the most potent force of our time.' He had plainly not had time to look up the word *oecumenical* in his dictionary. But it was an interesting point.

'I don't know what my daughter gets up to in London,' said Mr Plimsoll. 'I haven't asked, either.'

'I am sure you can trust Phyllis,' said Mr Tuck. 'It is those girls who haven't been brought up with a Christian background that I worry about.'

'What are your views on sex, Mr Trumpeter?'

I tried to remember the current doctrine. 'The most important thing we have discovered this century is that sex is enjoyable for women.'

'Is it really, now?' said Mr Heifer, greatly intrigued. 'I must say, I am glad that Nicholas has taken over from Mandarill.'

'Now that the fear of pregnancy has been removed, modern wives can enjoy lovemaking, and the Church should take a part in this, showing them how to enjoy it more and more. The first step, of course, is to teach them about contraception. Then they must be taught that sex is essential to a happy family life.'

'Many families in this neighbourhood already practise that,' said Mr Heifer doubtfully. 'There is a police court case next week.'

'We must take sex by the horns,' I said. My popularity was established. From that moment, I became the Chapter expert on sex, problems of leisure and oecumenicism.

'But I can't agree with the forcible feeding of contraceptive pills to animals,' said Mr Tuck. 'One has to draw the line somewhere. If the owners of a pet decide that in its best interests it should limit its family, that is all right. But there is no moral justification for putting out contraceptive food as they do in some large cities, so that pigeons eat it, without any knowledge of possible side-effects.'

'Perhaps not,' I said. 'But that is not the main point. There is no excuse nowadays for ignorance about the latest contraceptive devices. What does Love say?'

'Love quite agrees,' said Mr Jackson. 'Freedom from fear is essential. Sex without contraception is like…'

Invention deserted him.

'Soup without fish?' suggested Mr Heifer.

'Bread without butter?' I said.

'A dog without a tail? Port without lemon?' said Mr Tuck.

'Or too much port without any Alka Seltzer afterwards,' said Mr Heifer, becoming profound.

'Like a house without windows,' said Mr Jackson firmly. We all nodded our heads in agreement. What a happy collection of people we were! When I look back on my life, at occasional moments of joy snatched from the general run of boredom, it is to these Chapter meetings that I return with greatest pleasure. If ever Mr Good-Buller, the Archdeacon, turned up to one, we would abandon everything and pretend to be reading St Luke's Gospel in Greek. I don't know why he thought it a more useful occupation than any other. Neither Mr Plimsoll nor Mr Heifer had ever studied Greek. But it added a kind of conspiratorial glee to our discussions.

'You would be unable to see out of a house if it had no windows,' explained Mr Heifer sagely. It was much more apposite than his own analogy of soup and fish. You could always see out of them.

'It wouldn't be so cold, though, in winter, if there were no windows. I never see anything of interest,' said Mr Plimsoll.

'You need the sun. Electric light is no substitute.'

'You can buy ultra-violet lamps, which have all the health giving properties of the sun,' said Mr Plimsoll stubbornly. 'My daughter uses one for her eczema.'

We all looked sentimental about Mr Plimsoll's daughter's eczema.

'Are they any good for cancer?' I enquired.

'I don't think anything is much good for that.'

'No, I feared not.' But Gillian's trouble was plainly not cancer.

'What is your line on marriage?' I asked Mr Jackson. 'Would you remarry people who were divorced?'

'What does Love say?' said Mr Jackson. 'Of course I would. I see nothing abhorrent even in the idea of a marriage service for homosexuals who were planning a permanent relationship.'

'Now, now!' said Mr Tuck hastily. 'It would never do if Mr Good-Buller were to hear you. He would not even let me have pets on the altar for my annual pets' service. I sometimes think he is a most unintelligent man.'

'Evil,' said Mr Jackson.

'Unenlightened,' said Mr Heifer.

'Meddling,' said Mr Plimsoll.

'No doubt he means well,' said Mr Tuck.

'No he doesn't,' said everybody.

'He's a threat to the Church,' said Mr Plimsoll.

We all agreed that he was a threat to national survival.

When the meeting ended, we sent cordial messages to each other's wives. Mr Tuck drew me aside. For a terrible moment I thought he was going to press me with questions about my imaginary cat. Not at all.

'Please do not imagine that we are at all censorious about anything which might or might not be going on between you and Mrs Boissaens. I know perfectly well how men can be tempted. So few people today realise that I am a man of infinite compassion. People think I am a person of Dos and Don'ts. Yet my message is entirely one of love. You understand that, don't you? It is rather as Mr Jackson says, but more personalised. Why do young people today suppose that I came down to earth and suffered? Was it just to lay down rigid laws? Of course not.'

'I do assure you that there is nothing remotely improper in my relationship with Mrs Boissaens. I scarcely know her.'

'Hush, hush. I *understand*. All I require is that people should come to me when they are in difficulties. Do you remember the passage where I say: "Come unto me all ye that labour and are heavy laden and I will give you rest"?'

'Of course I do.'

'But I meant it. For my yoke is easy and my burden is light. I am meek and lowly in heart. Are you?' His intensity would have been embarrassing if it had not been so entirely unselfconscious.

'I don't know. I try to be.'

'That is all that matters. Whatever happens, we must prevent Father Good-Buller from hearing about it. If he comes anywhere near me, I am going to tell him that it will be more tolerable for the land of Sodom in the day of judgment than it will be for him. I nearly told him last Saturday. Do you know there are slightly more than 2,600 separate references to animals in the Bible? Why does he suppose that I put them there in the first place? But do you know,' his voice sank to a whisper, 'I don't believe Father Good-Buller believes in the Bible?'

Gillian was not in the drawing-room where she normally spent her afternoons, when I returned home. The Mothers' Union meeting was still in session. A dreadful hush fell as soon as I entered. All the women stared at me, their expressions varying from prurient fascination to prim disapproval. It was not hard to imagine what they had been discussing. People started to leave almost immediately.

'Next week I hope to have the man from Max Factor, and we can all try the lipsticks,' said Gillian brightly. 'We've had so much to discuss that we haven't done any of the routine things. What's showing in the cinema this week?'

'Mary Poppins,' said Mrs Allsopp. 'It's always Mary Poppins first week in the month.'

'Nothing we can complain about there, I'm afraid,' said Gillian.

'No. George has seen it fourteen times and he never saw anything,' said Mrs Swinger.

'I do feel they might give us something a little more adult occasionally.'

'There's not much good our going to Mary Poppins to see if it's all right,' agreed Mrs Hallowes. 'Waste of our time, really.'

'George always goes,' said Mrs Swinger proudly.

91

'Goodbye, Mrs Trumpeter. We'll be sending you some of our honey cakes, to see if they do any good,' said Mrs Allsopp.

'My man always used to like rabbit pie,' said Mrs Morelli. 'Only you can't get rabbits any more.'

'I will send you some tit-bits,' said Mrs Hallowes conspiratorially. She added in a whisper: 'Including the ointment.'

'My sister-in-law says curdled milk makes no end of difference to her husband's performance,' said Mrs Lackie. 'Only of course that's not what you're after, exactly.'

They imagined that I could hear nothing of what they said. Only Gillian was embarrassed.

'Remember what I said about rubbing yourself all over with Royal Jelly,' said Mrs Hallowes in a stage whisper.

'And I will pray for you both,' said the odious Miss Cornhouse, so loudly that I could not fail to hear.

They filed out of the door, avoiding me. Only Mrs Hallowes shook my hand.

'What on earth have you been telling them?' I asked Gillian, when we were alone.

'Only the truth. Oh, Nicholas, is it worth pretending?'

'What on earth are you talking about?'

'You know perfectly well what I'm talking about. But I'm not blaming you. Perhaps I have failed as a wife somewhere. There are always women like Mrs Boissaens waiting to step in. But for your sake, I'll try to like her. You can ask her round for supper if you like.'

'Oh, shut up.'

She followed me into my study. 'We're having a specially good supper tonight. Honestly, I don't mind if you ask her. When it's all over, perhaps we can go away somewhere. Then it will be like it was when we were first married.'

'Can't you see I have a lot of work to do?' Anything, rather than be reminded of those gruesome first weeks of marriage.

'I know, darling, but there are some things which are more important than work. Of course you are an ambitious, hard-working husband, and I am grateful to you, as well as proud. Somehow we never get time to say this sort of thing to each other. But I mean it. And I know that all your hard work is done for me. But just occasionally a woman requires other things. Do you like my new skirt?'

'No.'

'Well you should do. It cost three pounds and I bought it specially for you.'

'Then take it back to the shop.'

'Can't you have just this afternoon off from work, to be with your wife?'

'No, I'm sorry. It's quite impossible.' I had a new thriller by Ed McBain from the County Library. I think he may be even better than Erle Stanley Gardner.

CHAPTER FIVE

The first meeting of the Middlewalk Youth Club took place in the library of the Rectory. Sylvia Mullins brought her record player and we all listened despondently to her records for about ten minutes. Then Wendy Allsopp started dancing with Sharon Flitcroft, the farmer's daughter from East Hayes. Soon Sylvia and her brother Ted Mullins were wrapped in a sort of bear hug which passed for dancing, and Mrs Lackie's niece was dancing with Arthur Long, who had exposed himself to Minnie across the bar in the Bag of Corn and was at least fifty years old, but had turned up to give a helping hand.

'Come on,' said Danae, her eyes shining with excitement. I shook my head. Twenty minutes earlier, we had been making love on the narrow bed in Calvary. Dripping with sweat, finally she had yelled in triumph and pleasure. Even now she must have been reminded of our struggle, as she pranced about the floor encouraging the sluggish young people of Middlewalk. The Gutterling twins stood with their backs to the wall, infinitely aloof and contemptuous. Neither had left school. Kirk intended to become a steel erector, whatever that was, and Karen, who at thirteen was famous for having the worst legs in the village, was interested in micro-biology, hoping to work in the germ warfare station on Salisbury Plain. Their mother, who had lived alone since Gutterling emigrated to Canada, was thought to be so dirty in the village that nobody would talk to her except the odious Miss Cornhouse, who made it her business to know everybody.

I had no wish to dance with Danae. To my irritation, she found someone else who would dance with her. It was Lennie Hutton, the young journalist who had wanted to photograph me in bed with Gillian. They both danced extremely well, never touching each other, and communicating only by a cocky, wolfish look on the face of the young man which I found particularly offensive. If he had known our secret he would have wiped the smile off his face.

Afterwards, he approached me with a cheeky grin. 'Evening, Parson. How's tricks?'

'We have settled in very nicely, thank you.'

'What's all this I hear about you and a certain person up at the Hall.'

'It is a lot of malicious gossip. I scarcely know Mrs Boissaens.'

'Oh yeah? Never mind, I won't give you away. We never use stories like that anyway. Is she good news? Personally, I'm more interested in the daughter.'

Later, we sat drinking coffee prepared by Danae. Gillian had gone into London on some mysterious errand. She dropped plenty of hints, but I was too bored to pay any attention, imagining that it was a new outbreak of cancer. Hutton entertained us with stories of his sexual prowess. Later sensing disapproval in my manner, he became aggressive. He appointed himself the spokesman of modern youth, and affected an accent I had sometimes heard on television.

'Just explain to me in letters of one syllable what it is all about. OK, we've got the scene. This is youth. This is it. That's terrific. So where do we go from there? What are you trying to put over?'

'Nothing at all. The idea is to provide a place where young people can get together in the evenings and enjoy themselves.'

'Are you trying to make us all come to church or something?'

'Not if you don't want to.'

'Well, we don't want to.' He undoubtedly had the audience on his side. They had watched it all so many times before on television. 'You can't expect us to believe all the crap you spout in church, even if you believe it.'

'What do you believe in, then?'

There was a slight pause while he tried to remember the correct answer to this. I could have given it him, but he was prompted by Wendy Allsopp.

'Life,' she whispered.

'I believe in Life,' he answered bellicosely. 'Not in your sort of Life, Daddy. I believe in reality.'

'Reality?'

'There are Arabs living in the desert at this moment, man, near starvation, on a shilling a day.'

'Is that Life?' I had often wondered. Was their form of existence any more animated than Wendy Allsopp's? Probably it was. But in the eyes of God, Wendy Allsopp had equal claim. Inconceivable as it may sound, so did Mrs Morelli. Many aspects of Christian doctrine do not bear intensive scrutiny.

'You're beginning to bug me, man,' said my antagonist.

'Don't hurt him. He's frightfully intelligent,' said Danae. I was not sure to which of us she referred.

'Listen man. The desert is a sea of sand. No, I should say an ocean. I am in the middle of it. It pulsates and squirms around me just like the real ocean. Daddy, I am really part of that desert. No, I am wrong. It is part of me. It crawls through my veins like so many thousands of rats. I can't spit it out, I can't excrete it. It is part of me.'

It was no use trying to argue. I was beaten. Surprisingly, the rest of the company took everything in its stride. Perhaps this was the polite small talk of the new age.

'What about the locusts, Lennie? Are there any locusts?'

'Swarms of them. You can't see the noonday sun. They are eating my guts out. It's the only life, Daddy.'

'What about the cool of the evening, Lennie?'

'In the cool of the evening you feel too bitter to say much. You just sit around the fires, and try to spit some of the sand out of your hair. And you try not to think too much.'

Everybody present accepted this version of what life was about. I felt it could not go unchallenged.

'Do you spend much time in North Africa?' I asked.

'Who's talking about North Africa?'

'Weren't you?'

'Where is North Africa anyway? I was talking about here and now. The desert is your generation, you see,' he explained gently, as to a child. 'The locusts are all the people who listen to you and to the Church, like so many mindless sheep.'

'What are the camp fires, Lennie?'

'They're hope for the future. Not that there's much of that. But what the hell?' His voice now took on a note of phoney desperation. 'We're all here until the Bomb falls. What are we waiting for?' He picked up a bottle of Coca-Cola, part of a crate which Danae had brought down from the Hall, and drained it, throwing the bottle over his shoulder. I thought he might have been more careful with other people's property, but it landed harmlessly on a pile of old curtains. Danae, of course, was fascinated by him. After that gesture, he acted as if he was drunk.

So many recognisable influences shaped his behaviour – Western films which we had both seen, pretentious Left-Wing plays about students on television, Lawrence of Arabia, Osborne's *Luther*, Albert Finney in any part, James Dean, Vincent van Gogh as portrayed in a ghastly film of the last decade – that it was hard to believe he was a human being at all. He was a computer product. Feed all these things into a machine and out came Modern Youth in the form of Lennie Hutton. Had there ever been a human soul underneath it all? It was hard to imagine Lennie being delivered in a mess of after-birth, being suckled at his mother's breast, being taught his three times table, playing hopscotch and fishing for minnows. It was even harder to imagine him growing old in an awareness of death, watching his grandchildren set off to school as a fond and foolish old man, carrying his aching bones in carpet slippers to the grave. No, he was delivered wrapped in polythene as a ready-made modern youth. He would be re-wrapped or removed as soon as the model changed. He was nothing but a single, loathsome statistic in the post-war Bulge.

Some of these reflections I communicated to Danae by raising my eyebrows, but she only giggled nervously.

'Come on then, everybody, what are we waiting for?' said Hutton, still pretending to be drunk. 'Who's coming to Reading with me to burn the bright lights?'

'Me,' said Wendy Allsopp.

'Me,' said Sharon Flitcroft.

'I asked first,' said Sylvia Mullins.

Even the Gutterling twins looked less superior for a moment, but they were too timid to suggest anything.

'What about you, Miss Boissaens? Or are you too high-class for me? I wouldn't presume to call you Danae.'

'Call me anything you like,' said Danae. 'I wouldn't mind coming. Where are you going to?'

'Unfortunately, Miss Boissaens has to stay behind and clear up all the bottles you've been throwing around,' I said, giving her a secret glance.

'That's what you say,' said Lennie.

'Well, perhaps I'd better,' said Danae.

'That's OK by me, then,' said Lennie, with a great show of indifference. Even to secure his girl and to put himself in the way of an enormous fortune, it never occurred to him that he might offer to help. 'How about some other time then, Danae, eh?'

'Yes, of course,' said Danae with a giggle.

'I'll give you a phone call, then, OK?'

'OK.'

'Now which shall I pick of the remaining talent on offer?' he said. He inspected the remaining talent critically. 'You look the best of a bad bunch,' he said to Wendy Allsopp.

'Name?'

'Gwendoline Allsopp,' she answered breathlessly.

'Are you all right? I mean are you OK?'

'Yes.'

'Good. I don't want to waste my whole evening mucking around. Well, don't stand around gaping, girl. Get your coat, and we'll hit the bright lights. Good night, Danae. Good night, Mr Parson.'

'Goodnight, Lennie,' called Danae.

Afterwards, Danae suggested we should go up to Calvary again. She was insatiable. While I welcomed the attitude as being the opposite of Gillian's, I did not feel particularly inclined to acquiesce at that moment. It was about two hours since the last visit to our dank little love-nest, and on that occasion I had excelled myself by repeating three times a performance which needed at least a month's recuperation with Gillian. And a slightly priggish pernicketiness suggested that it might be more agreeable to wait until she had had a bath. In any case, Gillian might return at any moment.

'I wish I'd gone to Reading now,' said Danae. 'I wonder where they've gone.'

'Probably to a milk bar. Lennie didn't look as if he had his spending boots on.'

'That doesn't matter. I should have about eight pounds in my bag. Ah, no. I've got thirteen. And tons of change. Why can't we go somewhere?'

'Don't be silly. Gillian might be back at any moment. And I do think we should take more precautions.'

'Is George Swinger on to us?'

'It's not that. Everybody still thinks I'm having a passionate affair with your step-mother. Miss Cornhouse has been trying to convince them that it's really herself I'm keen on, but nobody believed it. Quite simply, I think it's wrong for us to go on like this without taking any precautions against having a baby.'

Perhaps I sounded pompous. One can never be sure. Danae, at any rate, was in no doubt. She laughed helplessly, only breaking off to groan and rub her sides. At that moment she looked most appealing, and I could probably have dealt with her there and then without bothering to take her upstairs, but we heard Gillian arrive at the front door. Briefly, she became serious.

'I'm not going to have anything to do with those things, and quite honestly I don't care if I do have a baby. Can you imagine asking for the Pill from Dr Plimsoll?'

Dr Plimsoll was a cousin of the Rector of Hatch Bottom. He was a splendid man, and once he had confided in me, while discussing Gillian's ailments: 'If they've got a temperature I give them a dose of penicillin, if they haven't I give them one of my bottles.' His bottles travelled around in the back of his car. All contained a pint of liquid, and each one was labelled 'The Mixture'. Some were green, some red, some brown, some colourless. In jovial moments, he would ask you which colour you fancied, before scrawling on the label: 'Take two teaspoonsfull three times a day, or more if needed.'

But still, I was worried. If the Church of England had any message at all for the youth of today – which I often doubted – it was that contraceptives should invariably be used on these occasions, and one did not like to be too hypocritical. Gillian, of course, would never divorce me. She would just cook me more Toads in the Hole. Danae was being irresponsible in laying me open to such treatment.

'We had better be carrying some crates out, or it will look suspicious,' I said.

'And I'm going to borrow this book, if I might,' said Danae.

It was called *A Manual of Sexual Practice*, compiled by a clergyman, a Methodist minister, two doctors (one female), a psychiatrist, a welfare officer and an industrialist. Gillian had bought it two months before our marriage, and it had somehow re-emerged during the last few days. On the front were two lurid strappers: 'Over two million copies sold', and 'Banned in South

Africa'. It was distributed for *New Christian Outlook* by Venus Books Limited, of Frith Street, Soho. I remembered what Danae's father had told me, and wondered if it was wise to allow unmarried girls access to such books. But she had slipped it inside her jersey before I had time to demur.

It was Gillian who looked guilty when we met her in the hall. She was carrying some curiously shaped bundles wrapped in paper and dropped several when she saw us.

'Hullo, Danae. I didn't expect to see you here. How's your mother?'

'Her mother is dead. No doubt you are enquiring after her step-mother,' I interposed.

'I don't know how Angela is. I have scarcely seen her all day,' said Danae.

'Not surprising, I suppose,' said Gillian, giving me a significant glance. 'It's no use asking Nicholas if he's seen her, of course. He would be bound to say "no".'

'As a matter of fact, I have not seen Mrs Boissaens for nearly a week.'

'No, of course not. Danae, I wonder if you'd like to stay for a late dinner? There are a few things I'd rather like to talk to you about.'

'I should have loved to stay. Thank you very much, Mrs Trumpeter. Unfortunately, I am expected back at home.'

'Couldn't you telephone them?'

'It wouldn't work. Daddy is very strict about that sort of thing.'

'Oh well, never mind. Another time, perhaps. It would probably have to wait, anyway, until my so-called better half is not hanging around listening to everything. When he's visiting the Hall on urgent business of his own, perhaps. I don't suppose you have much influence with your step-mother, in any case.' Gillian was talking in a very grown-up, matter of fact voice. Neither of us was deceived.

Danae gave me a wicked glance. Words cannot describe how much I loved her then.

'I think I may have quite a lot of influence with Angela,' she said.

Gillian waited until she had left, with a cheeky toot on the horn, before commenting: 'Such a nice girl, that. I can't believe that she comes out of that terrible family. What does she think about your carrying on with her step-mother?'

'We do not discuss it. Miss Boissaens is more interested in serious work for the children of people who are less fortunate than she is herself. She has very little time for idle gossip.'

'I don't believe in evading issues. I believe in bringing things out into the open.'

'But then you are an exceptionally fearless young woman.' Sarcasm was wasted on her. She preened and held her head sideways in a manner which she had always supposed to be alluring. 'Do you like my new stockings?'

'No.' They were white and made her skinny legs look like two sides of a goal post.

'I have made a big decision today.'

'Oh really?' No decision made by Gillian could be of the slightest importance, unless it was to divorce me, or die. Neither would ever occur to her.

'At least I made it yesterday, but have only implemented it today.' She was trying to be mysterious. A ghastly thought struck me. Perhaps she had decided to start a family. It was one of the ruses employed quite frequently in *Woman's Dream* by wives whose husbands were being unfaithful. I have nothing against children whatever, and I can see that for those who regard the continuation of the human race as an important matter, they have an essential role to play. But even if the physical role of assisting Gillian in her decision were not repugnant enough, nobody with the slightest benevolence towards his fellow creatures could wish to see any of them doomed to the role of being Gillian's children. I decided to make a stand.

'Then you can tell me about it tomorrow. I have so much work to do I don't know whether I'm standing on my head or my feet. I shall see you at dinner-time.'

I left her and returned to Ed McBain. There was nothing on television worth seeing, and I finished the book in twenty minutes. There was nothing to do. Whatever people say, the clergyman's life is not an easy one. For ten minutes I stared into space, thinking of nothing.

When the telephone rang in the Vicarage it made a long, plaintive trill. Although we were only thirty miles from London, the exchange had never been mechanised. No doubt the commuters in the area were happy, as it gave them an assurance, against all evidence to the contrary, that they lived in the country. Gillian came in looking extremely angry. 'It is your mistress,' she said bitterly.

'Who?'

'Angela. Your luvvy duck. I suppose you want me out of the room while you speak to her.'

'It is a matter of complete indifference to me.' I strode to the telephone. 'Hullo.'

'Hullo, Nicholas. May I speak to Danae, please.'

'I am afraid she is not here. She left about half an hour ago to return to you.'

'Yes, I know all about that, but I'm afraid I really must talk to her, if she's with you.'

'Well, she isn't. Do you think she could have had an accident?'

'Scarcely. It is only half a mile, and somebody would have told us by now. In any case, she apparently telephoned twenty minutes ago to say she was staying at the Rectory for dinner. She left the message with a servant, which is a typically thoughtless thing to do. I'm afraid it is really most important she comes up here immediately. It throws out the whole seating arrangement for dinner.'

'I am extremely sorry, Mrs Boissaens. She left here half an hour ago, as I told you.' How extraordinary that the most important thing in Mrs Boissaens' life at the moment should be that her seating arrangement was not upset.

'If I thought you weren't telling the truth, I should come down and fetch her myself', said Mrs Boissaens. A note of hysteria was creeping into her voice. 'Her father will be most annoyed.'

I doubted that very much. Nobody could be less concerned about seating arrangements. He very seldom sat at table when Mrs Boissaens received guests. 'All I can say, Mrs Boissaens, is that I am as mystified as you are.'

'But she said she was dining with you. I think I may have to come down and see just what is going on.'

She rang off in irritation. Gillian returned to the kitchen. 'May I come in now?'

'You have already come in.'

'What did your fancy lady want to say?'

'She said she may be coming down. She seems to think that Danae is still here.'

'She told me that. A very likely story, of course. I hope you asked her to stay for dinner? If you like I shall move into Bethlehem and she can share your bed for the night. She'll soon discover that there's not much fun to be had there.'

'You are torturing yourself unnecessarily. I don't even find her attractive.'

'Any more than you find your own wife attractive. Well, plenty of other people do.'

'Who?'

I should have tried to show interest in the answer. That was my mistake. But the suggestion that anyone could find Gillian attractive was so inherently ridiculous that I could not have managed to keep a straight face. As it was, my disbelief could have been forgiven, but not my boredom or my lack of interest. Gillian launched into a ten-minute harangue about how attractive she was, how this was wasted on me and how it was scarcely worth the trouble to remain attractive, as if attraction of the opposite sex was some onerous labour undertaken in a dull but worthy cause. Then she burst into tears and fetched my dinner from the oven, ending it all by saying: 'Toad in the Hole, although I don't know what you've done to deserve it.'

Neither did I. After a few minutes eating I said: 'You know, I really don't much care for Toad in the Hole.'

More tears, more abuse. The worst part of these scenes came when we had to make it up. Who can look wise, compassionate, loving and penitent with his mouth full of Toad in the Hole? Fortunately, Mrs Boissaens did not intrude on our domestic crisis. When the whole gruesome scene was played out, Gillian told me about her new decision.

'I have decided that it is no use our talking about what is wrong with the world any longer. We must do something.'

'Ah yes. I seem to remember making that the theme of my sermon quite recently. What have you got in mind?'

'First and foremost the problem of over-population. Everything else is subordinate to that, or springs from it: the crime wave, abortion, poverty, the underdeveloped nations. I have decided to set up an advice clinic.'

'Do you hope that many of the underdeveloped nations will come to be advised?'

'Please do not be facetious. I want to hear what you think of it.'

'It seems a very good idea indeed. As you know, I often say that married women need a hobby, and your earlier attempts to amuse yourself always seemed to me a trifle gloomy. I have often thought that a little positive action was needed, and less talk. But, of course, positive action can always go too far. Think of Stalin and Hitler. Your idea of an advice clinic seems the perfect compromise.'

'It will mainly be for married women, of course,' said Gillian timidly.

'Quite right. They are as much in need of advice as anyone else. All this talk of advice to teenagers...' I began, when a thought struck me. 'Oh my God, you don't mean a contraceptive clinic?'

'Family Planning advice will be included.'

'And to unmarried people?'

'If they come, you can scarcely refuse them advice.'

I paused. 'Let's get this straight, Gillian. Are you proposing to fit all the girls in the neighbourhood with contraceptives and to issue advice on birth control to teenagers?'

'Yes.'

'Here in the Rectory?'

'I thought I would use the old gunroom.'

'But you know nothing about it.'

'I went to the Clinic once myself, you know,' said Gillian demurely. 'Today I visited the Centre in Baker Street, and was taught how to measure. They gave me all the sizes and the literature. I can't prescribe the Pill, of course, but I have got the address of a doctor in Reading who does. All that remains is to order the stocks. Do you think it will be all right?'

Partly because I have a neurotic horror of saying the obvious, partly because I had never seen Gillian in such a humble mood, but mostly because at that moment I suddenly lost interest, I merely nodded my head.

'I expect so,' I said.

Gillian's eyes shone. For the first time I could remember, I read in them something akin to hero-worship, but all she could say was: 'I am so glad you have decided to be sensible about it all,' in a bored, grown-up sort of voice. 'You don't think the Church authorities will make trouble?' she asked.

'The exact teaching of the Church of England on the subject of contraception as worked out in the Lambeth Conference is that we are not prepared to say that under all circumstances it must be wrong. No pronouncement has even been made on the vexed question of birth control for the unmarrieds. No matter what they said, many people would disagree with it, so they have decided not to say anything. If too many people complain, I shall point out that it is simply my wife's hobby, and nothing to do with me.'

Once again, Gillian showed something which approximated to a spontaneous emotion. She choked on her food. 'I knew you would be sensible,' she said.

Naked adoration shone from her eyes. I decided to press home my advantage. 'Need I finish my Toad in the Hole?' I said.

'Of course not, darling, if you don't want. Aren't you well?'

'I am in excellent health, but it is possible I have been over-working myself recently. There is so much to do for just one man in a large parish.'

'Of course there is. In many ways, I think it is a good thing that you have got Mrs Boissaens to look after that side of life. It would be most unsuitable if I were to take a lover. People would point at you, and it would be bad for your position in the village.'

'I don't know,' I said recklessly. 'You might try. The only problem is that there are so few men of serviceable age in the neighbourhood. They are nearly all old age pensioners, and I imagine they feel that any unusual demonstration of virility would prejudice their chances with the Social Security interviewer.'

'Many of them are too proud to claim their just entitlement,' said Gillian argumentatively.

'Not in my experience. There is always Arthur Long, but I have reason to suppose that his sexual appetites fall short of actual intercourse. And George Swinger, we believe, finds adequate satisfaction in occasional acts of inhuman cruelty. Mrs Morelli's husband has the misfortune to be dead. Really, there is very little scope.'

'You don't understand,' said Gillian. 'Now that I have my advice clinic there is no problem. It was just that I could not have borne the knowledge that my life was entirely without purpose. Now I am happy. By the way, I forgot to mention that I will have to ask you for £70 to pay for stocks. The specimens I have now are only for measuring purposes. But in fact the margin between wholesale and retail in these goods is extremely generous, and before long we should be showing a profit.'

It was a small price to pay, but Gillian was wrong when she said that I did not understand. I understood only too well. An idea which had always been at the back of my mind since marriage had now retired into established fact: it was not sex which Gillian enjoyed and expected out of marriage; it was the practice of contraception.

CHAPTER SIX

'May the words of our mouths and the thoughts of our hearts be always acceptable in Thy sight. In the name of the Father, and of the Son, and of the Holy Spirit, Amen. Last week I mentioned the moral question raised for all parents by the inflammable nighties which are openly for sale in the market. These nightdresses are particularly dangerous to the young, because on the surface they seem such an attractive buy. They are in pretty colours, reasonably priced, and of an agreeable modern design. We cannot blame people, especially young people, for snapping them up. Yet you have only to stand briefly in front of the electric fire for them to catch alight instantly. In the heat, I am told, the artificial fabric tends to stick to the body, so that even if the unfortunate victim has sufficient presence of mind to tear the garment from her, she will be unable to do so. I have been in correspondence with the manufacturers in this matter. They say...' I read from a letter. 'These garments have been fully treated for fireproofing, but in the unlikely event of a mishap it is recommended that the affected area is plunged forthwith into cold water. An ordinary domestic housebath would be suitable for this purpose!

'Well, I have answered their letter, pointing out that many of my parishioners do not yet have bathrooms in their homes, and even those who do will find that it takes an unreasonable length of time to run a bath while their nightdresses are on fire. So far, I have received no response.

'It is easy to evade the issue, and say to parents something along these lines: "Do not let your children smoke in bed, and where there are electric fires, make sure they are properly guarded!" But we all know that this is impossible. You cannot keep your eyes on the children throughout the day, particularly in the holidays when many of them like to spend the morning in bed, after their hard work in the term. It is like saying to children that in order to avoid tooth decay, they should stop eating sweets, or clean their teeth every night. None of this is the parents' responsibility nowadays. It is for the Government to take action, if they think it necessary. I confess that I am often distressed to see children of fourteen and fifteen in this village with a complete set of false teeth, but at least the Government have done something about it in supplying the false teeth. But you can't supply children with a new false life.'

Couldn't you just, I wondered. Few of the children in my village responded to any of the stimuli which normally indicate animation. But a good sermon should not be controversial. Occasionally I could see one member of the congregation nod her empty, silly old head at some particularly fatuous commonplace. The applause of listening senates to command my lot forbade. This was the best I could hope for. With some difficulty I drew a pink nightdress from my trouser pocket.

'I bought this garment without any difficulty for twenty-five shillings. It came from Marlene's Boutique, in Twyford. One particularly horrifying thing about this purchase is that the nightdress is obviously not intended for children at all, so that no parent could vet it beforehand. I would like to ask you all to imagine for yourselves the fate of some bedridden old lady, trapped in one of these. Nobody can hear her cries for help! In all probability, she has no telephone. Do the manufacturers care?

'Of course they don't. Their concern is to sell as many of these garments as possible, and nobody can blame them. Nor can any of us be expected to do anything about it. We are bombarded constantly with advertisements telling us to buy things so that we don't know what we're doing. The garment, by the way, is called Gaylord and is made by Nu-wave Beautee Wear, but if I tell you that you will probably think it is an advertisement and go and buy some. It is not my job to preach at you, and I don't intend to do it. If you wish to go and buy yourself a Gaylord nightdress I can't stop you, and I wouldn't even try. The Christian message is not a list of "dos" and "don'ts".

'But what I am saying from this pulpit, and I don't care how much trouble it gets me into with the Government, is this: The Government must act. Immediately. Inflammable nighties are becoming a public scandal. And if the Government does not act, it cannot complain if the public takes the law into its own hands by refusing to buy any more inflammable nighties. In the name of the Father, and of the Son, and of the Holy Spirit. Amen.'

With great dignity, I folded up the nightdress and returned it to my pocket. It was a slight, fragile thing, its pinkness most striking against my white surplice. If I had been a Buddhist monk, I might have donned it and burnt myself to death at the altar rails as a protest. Unfortunately, as I remarked to Mr Jackson, we don't do things like that in the Church of England. But I really felt most indignant about these inflammable nighties. I gave a self-righteous sniff at Danae, who sat in the front pew and did not seem disposed to take me seriously.

Gillian was not in church. She spent all her time these days in the old gunroom, playing with horrible rubber objects. When I called, she would only look up to cry: 'It's not dirty. It's natural,' or some other breathless slogan as she turned them inside out or rinsed them in Dettol. So far as I knew she had only been able to experiment on the Mothers' Union up to now. As a Sunday treat I might try and send Danae to see her. For all I knew it would be a case of shutting the stable door after the horse has gone, but Gillian was very little trouble these days and deserved a bonus.

After service, I always stood outside the church door to meet my parishioners. They could meet me at any time, of course, but they seemed to attach more importance to the encounter after church, when I was still robed in my surplice.

'Good morning Mrs Lackie How are your nieces? Yes, I heard about that. Wasn't it a shame? Good morning Mrs Morelli. How are you Mrs Flitcroft? And your chilblains? And your daughter's cystitis? Isn't it a shame? Ah yes, Miss Cornhouse. Hello, Mildred, Isn't George feeling very well this morning, or is he just – ah – keeping a watch on the rectory? I should tell him to leave Mrs Trumpeter alone this morning. She's rather busy these days. Mrs Hallowes, you're looking very well today. Good morning, Miss Boissaens. Isn't it a lovely morning? How are your chilblains, Mrs Gutterling? It isn't chilblains? Let me guess. It's corns. No? Something to do with the feet, I'm sure. No, it's nettle rash. How silly of me. Isn't it a shame? We can't any of us live much longer. Isn't it a shame? Still, the thing is to be cheerful. I can see somebody wants to talk to me. Isn't it a shame?'

Both Danae and Mrs Morelli were trying to attract my attention.

'I was wondering about that nightie,' said Mrs Morelli with a self-pitying whimper, 'I don't suppose you'll have any use for it now, and I wondered if you would be thinking of giving it to the old age pensioners?'

'You mean to yourself.'

'There are some of us as can't afford new clothes every so often, and I was wondering if perhaps as you have finished with it you might let me have it for afterwards. One likes something gay to wear in bed sometimes, and the Government certainly don't give you nothing, as you was saying in church.'

'I am afraid you have misunderstood what my sermon was about.'

Mrs Morelli began to get nasty. 'I am sorry I asked in that case. It seemed only natural, seeing as how you was preaching about it, and how hard it was to be an old age pensioner. But there are some preachers, I believe, who don't stand by what they preach, not when you get them out of church afterwards. In church, there's nothing they wouldn't give. Outside, you can't even ask them for a nightie they've no use for. I heard you say the Government should do something about giving old age pensioners nice nightdresses – something they needn't be ashamed of to be looked at lying in when the doctor comes.'

'You don't understand. There's a danger of fire. I merely used this nightdress as a demonstration. Now I'm going to throw it away.'

'We'll all thank you a lot for that,' said Mrs Morelli. 'I'm not complaining, of course. I've got some nightdresses. But there are some as don't have a single nightdress to their name, poor dears. Lying in bed at night, they can't even hear the postman or the doctor at the door with their teeth chattering so loud. Some of them hasn't any teeth, either, or they've taken them out, so they can't even hear that. Seeing that most of the poor dears are deaf, anyway. I'm not worrying about myself. It's the other old age pensioners as might be worried, when they hear that the vicar's throwing away good nightdresses.'

'I'm sorry I can't help you Mrs Morelli, but you see it is a matter of principle. Yes, Miss Boissaens?'

'Daddy wondered if you'd like to come up to the Hall for a drink before lunch.'

'Drinks,' said Mrs Morelli.

'Tell him I should be delighted to. I will come up straight away.'

'Would you like me to drive you?' I sometimes wished that Danae's smile was slightly less conspiratorial.

'In my cassock? You must be mad. I will come up as soon as I have been home to change.'

'I don't think anyone would mind you in your cassock. I rather like it.' She would never really be happy until someone had made love to her in a bishop's chasuble with mitre and gaiters.

'Well, you must wait. I haven't finished my conversation with Mrs Morelli.'

'I hear Gillian has opened a birth control clinic in the village,' said Danae, as she drove me through the village. 'Very sensible indeed, if you ask me.'

'Aren't you being a little hypocritical? I think you ought to visit her yourself.'

'Perhaps I will,' said Danae, in the tone of voice which clearly revealed she had no intention of doing it.

'Don't you think we are being irresponsible? I have a good mind to insist that you go and see her. Babies aren't just an ogre invented by reactionary clergymen. They actually do arrive if you don't take precautions.'

'I don't care. Lennie agrees with me, anyway.'

'Lennie?'

'Lennie Hutton. He says that although he always uses them, because he doesn't think it fair to the girl, it is rather like playing a piano in gloves.'

'What does he know about playing the piano?'

'I expect he knows quite a lot about the other thing.'

'When have you been seeing him to exchange these confidences?'

'I saw him the other night, after I had left you. As a matter of fact, I bumped into him in Reading.'

A sharp pang of jealousy made me shut my eyes. 'I thought you said you were returning to dinner at the Hall.'

'Suddenly, I couldn't face it. By the way, I told them I had stayed to eat with you, so you'd better support me.'

'Why should I? If I had known you were running after that pathetic creature I would have told them.'

We were halfway up the drive to the Hall. Danae pulled into the side.

'Darling Nicholas, don't be so childish. We couldn't have got up to anything, because he had another girl with him. Wendy Allsopp. You are quite enough for me.'

We kissed. She was soft and warm and I loved her to distraction, but the position was most uncomfortable.

'I think we had better move on. They may be watching for us.'

'Daddy, as you may have noticed, has rather poor vision. If not, he will probably have pointed it out to you by now. And it really does not matter what Angela sees. She is so sex-starved that it would probably do her good.'

'Are you going to do *anything* about preventing an unwanted child?'

'Who said it would be unwanted?'

'But children need a father.'

Danae gave me one of her ravishing smiles. 'Now who's talking? There's nothing wrong with you, Nicholas. Why are you so diffident?'

'I hear you have been making inflammatory sermons against one of my products, Nu-Wave Beautee Wear,' said Mr Boissaens.

'Good Heavens, do you make them?' I asked.

'Not personally. My eyesight is too poor, and I fear that my other disabilities would make me rather clumsy on the factory bench. But I have a large holding of shares in Sanilan, the company which owns Beautee Wear and I have my own nominee on the Board, Mr Chaffinch. He is a hard working person, and honest, but totally lacking in imagination. His wife fritters away all his salary on Pekingeses. They breed them, allegedly for profit, but as she refuses to sell one unless the buyer can assure her that he will devote his entire life to care of the animal, few are ever sold. They keep a permanent staff of three Norwegian au pair girls whose only occupation is to brush the Pekingeses.'

'He must be mad,' I said.

'No madder than working class housewives who spend their savings on a tape-recorder. Money can only hope to secure pleasure, and who are we to criticise the pleasures of other people so long as they do not interfere with our own? Even if he were mad, that would be no excuse for trying to make him destitute, to drive his Pekingeses out into the cold world. Is that your purpose?'

'I am extremely sorry,' I said. 'If I had known that these nightdresses were made by one of your concerns, I should certainly not have attacked them from the pulpit.'

Mr Boissaens was enjoying himself. 'You wouldn't have done so?'

'Certainly not. It was extremely ungrateful and in bad taste. I can only say that I am sorry.'

'You mean you would have allowed all your old people to burn themselves to death rather than offend me?'

'Small children, mostly,' I murmured, as I tried to think of a way out of the trap.

'You would have made a bonfire of small children and old age pensioners rather than prejudice one of my minor investments? I am touched and flattered by your devotion. As a matter of fact I discussed the matter with Mr Chaffinch, my nominee in Doncaster. He told me that all these pretty pink frilly things that women like to wear are made exclusively of coal, so it is small wonder that they burn merrily. The choice confronting any purchaser is to pay a few extra shillings for something they can safely put into their electric fire whenever the urge overtakes them, or to save money and refrain from doing so, as far as they are able. I suggested we should put a label on these garments to say that they were highly inflammable, but Mr Chaffinch advised against it on the grounds that our customers would murder each other with them. There is no end to their deviousness, apparently. All a manufacturer can do is to point out the use for which his product is intended. If you wear my nightdress in bed, Mr Trumpeter, you will be kept warm, you will look fresh and youthful, and many people will find you sexually attractive. It will be no protection against bullets or knives or wild animals. If you set it alight, you will burn to death. If you try eating it, you will probably be poisoned. If you use it as a lawnmower, you will find it inadequate to the task.'

'I quite agree with everything you say. On the other hand, I feel the Government should prevent people from burning themselves to death in this way.'

'Why?'

I could think of no answer. Clearly, there must be one. Perhaps my repugnance derived not so much from the fact that people should, by the exercise of their free will, choose to risk immolation as from the fact that other people, like Mr Boissaens, should profit from their choice. But no doubt he manufactured non-inflammable nighties also. 'They might set fire to other people's houses at the same time.'

'Acceptance of that risk is part of the social contract. The Government can only supply a fire brigade.'

Loneliness had made him garrulous. Perhaps it was mixing with people of inferior intelligence which produced such an implausible argument, just as a first class chess player will make silly mistakes against a player whom he considers to be bad. At any rate, I could spot the flaw. 'Would you agree that it is part of a Government's function to discourage cruelty to children?'

'Certainly.'

'And to protect children whose parents were so negligent of them that they risked starving to death?'

'I suppose so. Yes.'

'Shouldn't this protection be extended to children whose parents were so negligent that they risked burning to death?'

'Possibly. I see what you are getting at. But why do you bother to tell all this to the villagers of Middlewalk?'

'Why do you bother to discuss it with me? One must pass the time of day, somehow.'

Mr Boissaens chuckled. 'You are quite right, Nicholas. I am sorry to be so aggravating; I enjoy your company a great deal, and would like to have you as my son-in-law. Unfortunately, you say this is impossible until you have disposed of Gillian. I hope you are plying her with Nu-Wave Beautee Wear nightdresses. As a matter of fact, I have no shares in the company, as far as I know.

Mr Chaffinch was an innocent fabrication. But I thought your arguments needed tightening up, as they were recounted to me by Perrins. You have convinced me. If I did possess a major shareholding, I should write to Mr Chaffinch and instruct him to stop manufacturing inflammable nighties in children's sizes. It would be hard on dwarfs who wished to equip themselves cheaply for the night, but hard cases make bad law. Why don't you marry Danae?'

'I am already married.'

'Don't be childish. She loves you, and as far as I can see you are fond of her. You do not like your wife, and she does not seem to feel much affection for you. You only succeed in making each other miserable. If you think she would be penniless without you, one could easily make ample provision for her. You are not suited to be a clergyman, as you believe in nothing.'

'I never said that.'

'But you know it to be true. Why can't you walk out on Mrs Trumpeter and come with us to Kenya when we move? Or you could go with Danae to Mexico and get a divorce, or anywhere you liked. My only purpose in life is to see Danae happily settled. Then I shall fold up and disappear, leaving Angela, you and everybody else to get along as best you can.'

It was impossible to tell him why I could not abandon Gillian. True, I disliked her as a person, found her boring, malicious and unintelligent; Danae was more attractive, nicer, cleverer, richer and more affectionate; but Gillian was my responsibility, the cross I had chosen to bear. While she was alive, I could never be happy. Somewhere a pathetic little mind would be torturing itself: 'Where did I go wrong? Perhaps I should have paid more attention to the physical side. Perhaps I should have tempted him to make love to me in new, more progressive ways. Or taken more trouble with my appearance. Or shown a greater interest in his work. Or cooked him his favourite dishes more often.'

'I can't do it,' I said.

Mr Boissaens became brusquer.

'Those who wilfully ignore the pleadings of reason are indulging in a form of insanity. It is a prevalent disease, nowadays, in England. One of the weaknesses in the arguments for a free market economy is that people seldom behave rationally or in response to economic pressures. They would sooner starve than leave their dingy little Northern towns. And starve they should, since the condition is self-inflicted. But we are too humane. We give them just enough money to keep them going and revel in their suffering. If there were no poverty, none of us could enjoy feeling compassionate or exercising our radical consciences to think of ways to abolish it. If I threatened to stop payment of my addition to your stipend would it make any difference?'

'No.'

'I didn't suppose it would. Idleness is every bit as much a dynamic force as avarice. It is time Danae found herself a husband. I am tired of waiting. But if you are just playing around with her, I should be grateful if you would allow her to return here for meals. On Friday I found myself sitting next to a terrible Belgian woman who spoke Flemish and with a Congolese accent. She had nothing whatever to say. Her first husband was murdered in the course of the independence celebrations. Why don't you take Danae into a corner and talk it over with her? The day she marries, I propose to give her the greater part of my fortune, which is the only way to prevent its being seized for the People when I die. Not that I think she needs it, or will derive much pleasure from its use. But I think it wrong that the money should be shared among an enormous number of people who have done nothing whatever to deserve it and whose capacity for enjoyment is even more limited than hers. Don't you feel a tiny bit honoured that she should have chosen you? It is no good pretending that you are the most handsome or even the wittiest person in the world. Or perhaps you find it natural that my daughter, a beautiful, clever and sweet-natured girl with an eventual fortune of some nine million pounds, should fall head over heels as soon as she set eyes on you.'

'Oddly enough, I think it was something to do with my clerical costume,' I said.

'Do you love her?'

'If I did, I should see no reason to confide in you.'

'I think you do. She is a lovely girl. But you are too idle to do anything about it.'

'Of course I love her, but I am already married. Our only hope is that Gillian will die.'

'Is she unwell?'

'She thinks she is.'

'We must hope she is right.'

All my prayers had centred round this one petition for six years. There was nothing uncharitable in this. If prayers are of any use, and there is such a thing as a Deity and an after-life, Gillian would have been much better off dead. If the whole apparatus is a delusion, my prayers could not possibly have done her the slightest harm; they were just one of those pious practices with which we clergymen while away the time of day.

Gillian was in a most disagreeable mood when I returned. She had burned my lunch and was drinking tea in an orgy of self-pity.

'How was Mrs Boissaens? How was your darling little Angela?'

'I did not see her.'

'Of course not. That is why you have lipstick on your collar. I think you might be a tiny bit more careful, when I am working myself to the bone in order to cover up your goings on.'

'How is the Clinic?'

'There has been a setback. Try as I will, I can't produce diaphragms at under three pounds. They are much more popular than the smaller pessaries. Nobody wants a pessary. But three pounds is too much for many people. When you are trying to live on four pounds ten a week and what little you can squeeze out of the Ministry of Social Security you can only just afford a few little luxuries in your life – an occasional packet of tea or some boiled sweets. There is absolutely nothing left for necessities. It is absurd that everyone can't order these things on the National Health. The Government is determined to make second class citizens of our old age pensioners.'

'Why do old age pensioners need contraceptives?'

'A typical question, if I may say so. The sort of insensitive, bullying remark one has grown accustomed to. I suppose elderly people have no right to self-respect? As a matter of fact, it is the older members of my Mothers' Union who are showing the way.'

'Aren't they long past the menopause?'

'You have one of the dirtiest minds I have ever met. All vicars are like that, I believe. What if the poor dears have passed the change of life? They still want to be part of everything that is happening in the world. They don't want to feel tucked away out of the mainstream, however convenient you may find it. In some ways it is more important for old people to be helped than the young. They have a right to be shown the modern methods and try them out for themselves. Teenagers are just indulging their own selfish appetites, and ought to be able to look after themselves, or take the consequences. Older people need help and understanding. I don't see how the Government can claim that it would be encouraging immorality among the old to fit them with free diaphragms.'

'So you don't want my youth club to come to you for advice?'

'They can do what they like. In my experience, they will be too timid. Their elders are putting them to shame.'

Suddenly, I felt tired. Gillian often had that effect on me. Just occasionally she suspected that there might be a weakness in her argument, but she invariably covered it up by doubling her normal aggressiveness. If I continued the discussion, she would start ridiculing my sexual efficiency.

My thriller was finished and I had nothing to do – sports results on television invariably produce a boredom which verges on nervous collapse – but I would sooner sit in the library and stare into space than continue this sort of discussion.

'I expect you are right,' I said. 'By the way, I brought you a little present. I thought of keeping it until Christmas, but I should probably lose it.'

'What is it? How most unlike you to think of other people,' said Gillian, but I could see that in her simple way she was pleased. I took the present out of my pocket. 'A nightdress. How perfectly sweet.' She suddenly became embarrassingly emotional. 'Nicholas, I'm sorry I was cross. This is one of the sweetest presents I've ever had. To think that you went off and bought it on your own without saying a word to anyone. Oh dear, it really makes me want to cry. I know I'm silly, but it's so unexpected. It will be my favourite nightdress from now on. it's such a pretty pink. Do you think it will suit me? It's almost too good to wear in bed. I should like to wear it as an evening gown.'

'Wear it whenever you like,' I said.

Mr Plimsoll was clearly agitated.

'I have no objection to any of the vicars' wives pursuing whatever hobby they like so long as it does not interfere with other people. But I was telephoned twice on Saturday evening and once again on Monday morning by someone who said he represented the Press. He wanted to know what I thought about Mrs Trumpeter holding sex lessons, whether I proposed to follow suit, whether I thought it was morally right that young people should know about those things or whether they should be kept in ignorance. I had no end of trouble – on Monday morning, too.'

'What did you say?' I asked.

'I said "no comment",' replied Mr Plimsoll proudly.

'Typical,' said Mr Jackson. 'Nicholas has taken the only meaningful step in this diocese for the last hundred years, and Mr Plimsoll has no comment to make. What do you think, Mr Tuck?'

'I have already made my position absolutely clear,' said the Rural Dean. 'Provided that Mrs Trumpeter does not try to force her own particular beliefs on those unable to dissent from them, I have no objection. But animals must be protected. Many people keep pets who lack any qualification to look after them properly. I know that we are divided in this Chapter on the subject of capital punishment, but I do feel that some sort of corporal punishment at least should be introduced for those people who go away on holiday and leave their pets unattended at home. Right throughout the New Testament I make it absolutely clear what my feelings are about animals. Are not five sparrows sold for two farthings, and not one of them is forgotten before God?'

'Could be, could be,' murmured Mr Heifer.

'But what do you think of the main issue? Here we have a brave woman who is prepared to go out into the world and protect unmarried women from a disaster which could ruin their entire lives. Are we going to denounce her publicly in the market place?' Mr Jackson was determined to embarrass us all somehow.

'Where?' said Mr Heifer.

'In public,' said Mr Jackson. He was a most humourless person.

'It depends on the circumstances,' said Mr Tuck. 'We don't want Father Good-Buller to interfere. We've been through all that before.'

'In the case of the Pets' Communion Services,' explained Mr Heifer.

'Sometimes I think you are all mad,' said Mr Plimsoll. 'Why do you want to create trouble for yourselves? Isn't there enough in the world today already? Look at South Korea.'

'Vietnam, you mean.'

'It doesn't matter where you look. Everywhere there are people trying to interfere and get you to do things. The whole idea of religion is that it should be restful. Yet you have to hold Pets' Communion Services and Sexual Welfare Services – they only cause a lot of trouble. My idea is to cut down on services, not to think of new ones. Nobody wants them any more.'

'True, but one has to pass the time of day somehow,' I said.

'Not making trouble,' said Mr Plimsoll. 'That is against the whole spirit of the Bible. The great, the only message which Jesus has for mankind nowadays is Peace.'

'I suppose so,' said Mr Tuck. 'I don't think I'd like Father Good-Buller to hear about it.'

'Cyril?'

'Include me out. This has nothing to do with me. If it makes her happy, I'd say "Go ahead", but you have to keep an eye open for Father Good-Buller.'

I could see that the meeting was going against me. 'What does Love say?' I asked in desperation.

'Love starts by asking itself "What right have we to interfere?" ' said Mr Jackson. 'But then it considers the context and decides we have a duty to help. There is a world population explosion. People are dying like flies from starvation in Asia. England is bursting at the seams. Young couples who wish to marry cannot find housing, and yet they wish to express their love for each other in its purest and highest form as the mystical conjunction of two bodies into one. How can they do this if they have the ever-present fear of an unwanted baby? How can they really give themselves with joy in the surrender? It is our duty to equip the world for Love.'

'Beautifully spoken,' said Mr Heifer, who was profoundly moved. 'But at what age do you think it's all right for them to start?'

'As soon as they can derive benefit from it,' said Mr Jackson. 'Love makes no distinction between age groups any more than it does between colour and class.'

'Ha, ha,' said Mr Tuck. 'Jackson always goes too far. But if we can keep it from Father Good-Buller, there can be no harm in it.'

The fiend himself visited us towards the end of the Chapter Meeting. Mr Heifer pretended to be reading from Bishop Caversham's commentary on the Sermon on the Mount, and we all nodded our heads sagely.

'Are we to deduce from Christ's reference to the lilies of the field and the birds of the air that we should abstain from servile labour? Nay, rather that our labour should be devoted to the glorification of His work. That the lilies toil not neither do they spin should be the object of our consideration, whereon we may ponder the Majesty of God's doings. But he who would aspire to emulate them must first attain the perfection of innocence that makes his existence wholly pleasing in God's sight, through diligent attention to Good Works and the Articles of Religion. For uncouth persons to live their days in idleness saying to all who would rebuke them: "Thus my Saviour bade me spend my days" would be in no way distinguishable from the habit of the Pharisees, described in the New Testament as a generation of vipers.'

'Don't pay any attention to me,' said Father Good-Buller. 'Of course Bishop Caversham was writing before the creation of the Welfare State. In those days people actually would have starved if they had not been prepared to do any work. Modern developments have made the Sermon on the Mount even more relevant than it then was. I am sure that Solomon in all his glory was never arrayed like some of my old people in their mini-skirts.'

Mr Tuck bristled. Although a man of infinite compassion, he could not abide flippant references to the Bible. At times he identified himself with it to an alarming degree; but even if lie occasionally believed that lie was Jesus Christ, it was a harmless enough eccentricity. We all had our little foibles.

'I don't see what mini-skirts have to do with it. There is not a single reference to them in the Bible. Clothes do not matter in any case. They are only the outward apparel. The Bible concerns itself with our inner clothing, Father. We shall be judged not by our outward display of garments but by the manner in which each of us has conducted himself towards the rest of my little creatures. Are not the sparrows sold for two farthings…?'

The Archdeacon and the Rural Dean sparred with each other like fighting cocks. Father Good-Buller was the more intelligent, but Mr Tuck had the greater passion. At length, Father Good-Buller became bored.

'It is not an open matter, my dear Mr Tuck. Animals do not have immortal souls but humans do. The distinction between vegetable matter and animal life is much smaller than the distinction between humans and animals, which is infinite.'

The atmosphere of the Chapter was strongly against him.

He may have sensed it, but the air of superiority with which he protected himself from the lesser clergy in the diocese was generally impenetrable. Perhaps it was to shatter his complacency that Mr Jackson spoke:

'How do you *know* that humans have immortal souls?'

There was an awkward silence. We all felt that something should be said, and spoke at once: 'Ah, that's the 64,000 dollar question' – flippantly (Mr Heifer); 'That's not what I said' – nervously (Mr Tuck). 'Mr Jackson was only speaking figuratively, of course' – tactfully (myself); 'This has got nothing to do with me. I don't know anything about it' – petulantly (Mr Plimsoll).

'I can see that Mr Jackson and I have a great deal to talk about,' said Father Good-Buller unpleasantly. 'But that is not why I came here. I would like to have a word with Mr Tuck and Mr Trumpeter after the meeting is over, about quite another matter.'

'It is time to end the meeting. We all have a great deal to do. Shall I say the Prayer, Father Thomas, or would you like to?'

'I shall say the prayer,' said Father Good-Buller.

When we had arranged Mr Tuck's writing desk to look like an altar, we reversed our chairs and knelt down in front of them. For some reason, Father Good-Buller's devotions always required this preparation. 'Our Father,' began the Archdeacon. We joined in with varying degrees of self-consciousness. Only Mr Heifer really entered into the spirit.

'Let us pray,' said the Archdeacon. 'Oh Lord, who hast revealed thyself to us in the Communion bread and wine which are of Thy substance, protect Thy Holy Catholic Church from internal falsehood as much as from foreign perversion and let not this Thy Rural Chapter in the diocese of Silchester be contaminated by foul scandal which delights the mind of heathen people but vouchsafe us all eternal Grace, through Our Lord Jesus Christ, who liveth and reigneth with Thee and the Holy Ghost, now and for evermore.'

'Amen,' we all said dutifully. Somebody was obviously in serious trouble, and it rather looked like me. What had I done? My conscience was never entirely clear. The other clergymnen avoided meeting my eye as they sidled out of the room. Mr Plimsoll would have climbed out of the window if he could have done so without drawing attention to himself. Mr Jackson clearly felt that Love had other matters to attend to, and even my beloved Cyril Heifer shuffled past with a preoccupied air.

'It is one of the less pleasant duties of a diocesan archdeacon to concern himself with the discipline of the clergy,' said Father Good-Buller, rubbing his hands together lugubriously. Clearly he found these duties far from unpleasant. 'Inevitably, a Bishop receives letters from cranks and misfits which I usually advise him to ignore. But it is most unusual to receive a letter from twelve respected citizens without looking into it. We have received such a letter from your parish, Mr Trumpeter. It makes some very serious allegations which both Dr Toplass and I feel require an answer.'

'Who has written to you?'

'It is not normal practice to divulge. On the other hand, so that you can know the full seriousness of the matter, I might as well show you the letter concerned.'

It was written in the sloping hand of the semi-literate, but the signatures at the end showed an impressive variety of style.

'My Lord Bishop,

'We the undersigned members of the Parish of Middlewalk would like you to know our feelings on the subject of our vicar's carryings on with a married woman by the name of Mrs Boissaens. We feel we can no longer overlook this matter in the light of what has been happening, as it is becoming a matter of public concern. Intimacy is known to have taken place on more than one occasion, and in the light of what Mrs Trumpeter must be feeling about this we feel we should bring it to your attention. All of us are churchgoers and none of us is a member of any political organisation whatsoever. We feel most strongly that something should be done on Mrs Trumpeter's behalf and for the good name of the Church in this parish. Furthermore, we feel that Mrs Boissaens herself should know better, coming from a more wealthy background.

Respectfully

Amelia Hallowes	Mildred Swinger (Mrs)
Joy Honeycomb	Mrs Lackie (OAP)
Mrs Morelli (OAP)	Mrs Gutterling
Mrs Allsopp (OAP) (widow)	Ursula Cornhouse (Miss)
Gwendoline Allsopp, 14	Kirk and Karen Gutterling (students)
	Leonard P Hutton.

It was the last signature which upset me. The ingratitude of old age pensioners is quintessential. Miss Allsopp and the Gutterling twins had no minds of their own in any case. The only surprising thing about their appearance in the list was the evidence it afforded of their ability to write. But Leonard P. Hutton was my friend, with whom I had spent many happy hours discussing the problems of youth in the modern age. Et tu, Lennie?

'What is your answer?' said Father Good-Buller, inspecting my face keenly for any signs of guilt.

'They are simply a lot of troublemakers. Half of them have never been to church in their lives.'

'But still the other half must represent a sizeable proportion of your weekly congregation.'

'Not at all. People are taking a much greater interest in religion nowadays.'

'Now come along. I have lived in the world far longer than you. I hope you are not trying to pretend that you normally have more than ten people at your services?'

'If you count the organ-player and the wardens and the bellringers who appear before Matins…'

'I don't count them.'

'Well, perhaps not quite ten.'

'So you must accept that the greater half of your congregation has decided to lodge a formal complaint about you. What would you do if you were in my shoes?'

'I should enquire whether there was any truth in the allegations.'

'Is there?'

'No.'

'You expect Dr Toplass to believe that?

'I don't see why not. It is my word against theirs.'

'Ah, but you are only a clergyman. Ordained ministers of religion are two a penny. Members of the congregation are a much rarer breed, and they are prized above their weight in gold. Rather than lose a single churchgoer we are prepared to assure our listeners that they are fulfilling God's purpose in whatever they do – divorcing, fornicating, lying, gambling, swindling their employers, but they expect higher standards from the clergy.'

'Oh really? I thought there was a shortage of priests.'

'Not nearly so great as the shortage of churchgoers. I think the only thing to do is to take a solemn oath on the matter. You have no objection in principle, I take it, to holding the Bible? You would not sooner affirm? One can never be sure with the younger priests.'

'I have no objection.' Behind his lonely sarcasm, I seemed to detect a tiny glint of sympathy in Father Good-Buller's stare. There could be no doubt that he thought me guilty of this revolting offence. As he prepared the altar for a solemn service of oathtaking, lie seemed to be reassuring me: 'You have only to come to confession with me afterwards – in private – and all will be forgiven.' I knew that he held these gruesome séances. Mr Tuck had been obliged to confess to him after the incident of the Pets' Communion Service, under threat of exposure to Dr Toplass, the Bishop. His penance had been to rise at five o'clock every morning for a week and recite a decade of the rosary. Needless to say, Mr Tuck had not felt obliged to do any such thing. In any case, he did not possess a rosary.

'Now, say this after me,' said the Archdeacon. 'I swear before Almighty God that I have never had unlawful intercourse with Angela Boissaens, never behaved improperly with her in any way nor looked lustfully upon her to bring scandal upon our Holy Mother the Church and to bring my Sacred Calling into disrepute, through Our Lord Jesus Christ, who liveth and reigneth with Thee and the Holy Ghost through all time, Amen.'

I repeated it.

'Now we had better have that in writing, to satisfy the Bishop and for my own files. Tuck and I will witness it.' As an afterthought, he sprinkled me with some water from a vase of chrysanthemums. Then the altar became a desk again, he sat down and began to type with one finger. At the bottom he left a space for General Comments: *Taken on the New English Bible.* Clearly that was my escape-clause. When we had signed it, Father Good-Buller said; 'When my clergy find there is something troubling their conscience, they often like to come and confess it to me in private.'

'Oh, really?' I said.

'Yes. They find it a great comfort. It has the additional advantage that anything told me under the seal of the confessional can go no further. Quite literally I would sooner die than tell the Bishop anything I had heard in these circumstances. And of course I could not allow it to influence me in my attitude to someone. Many people have found that there are solid advantages to be derived from making a good confession, quite apart from the sacramental grace. You need not even believe in it.'

'It is very kind of you, but I do not wish to make a confession at present,' I said.

'Very well. I cannot compel you. I shall show your statement to Dr Toplass, and he will decide on any future course of action. I am sorry you have decided not to avail yourself of the benefits of religion in this time of trouble. No doubt the Bishop will put his own interpretation on your refusal to do so.'

After he had gone, Mr Tuck said: 'You should have agreed to confess. Now he'll move Heaven and Earth to get you removed.'

'I had nothing to confess.'

'Dear me, you mustn't suppose that I mind. My heart is full of compassion for everyone, even the vilest sinner. It was typical of Good-Buller to make you hold the Bible. He enjoys seeing it profaned.' Mr Tuck seemed to be suffering from shock. His manner was more distracted than ever.

'I think he is a most tiresome man,' I said.

'Did you see the blood on his lips?'

'No. I think I must have missed that.'

'I did. And in his right hand he held seven candles. But I did not like the look of his horns this morning. Ten horns stand for the ten commandments and the seven crowns are the seven churches of Asia, representing the seven pillars of wisdom. But today I thought I saw an eleventh horn. What can that mean?'

'The end of the world, I should think.' It was better to humour him. Excessive attention to the Gospels often produced these symptoms. Personally, I have always thought that the Book of Revelation is manifestly the work of a raving lunatic, but we are supposed to take it seriously, and Mr Tuck was my only remaining friend.

'Perhaps you're right. Everywhere my prophecies are being fulfilled. Who would have thought that the Great Beast would have made his appearance inside the Church of England? Perhaps I should write to the Prime Minister.'

'I shouldn't do that, you know.'

'You are right, of course you are. All the kings of the earth and the chief captains will be hiding themselves in the dens and in the rocks of the mountains by now. By the way, how's Tibbles?'

'Tibbles?'

'Your dear little pussy. Perhaps you have forgotten that you offered to introduce me to her.'

As far as Mr Tuck was concerned my imaginary cat was much more important than that I had been unjustly accused of adultery and that my livelihood was in danger. But it was most important to retain his friendship.

'Of course. To tell you the truth, I am rather annoyed with Tibbles at the moment. She ate all my Sunday lunch and then made a huge mess on the kitchen floor.'

The Rural Dean clapped his hands in delight. 'How playful! Surely you can't seriously be annoyed? What I love about cats is their unpredictability. But is she *really* all right?'

'You mean spiritually?'

Mr Tuck nodded his head.

'I couldn't really say, I am afraid. I have been kept rather busy with my Youth Committee.'

'Of course. But if she is really in straits, you won't hesitate to send for me, will you? It might easily land me in trouble, but I don't think that even Father Good-Buller would dare deny them the Last Sacraments, do you?'

'He need never know.'

'I knew you would understand. There are so very few people around nowadays who are as intelligent as you. I think I'll call in early next week and see how Tibbles is getting on. We won't tell our little secret to anyone, will we?'

Gillian greeted me with a peck on the cheek when I returned home.

'The newspapers have been telephoning for you.'

'Do you think it is about the advice clinic?'

'I hope so. We need a little publicity. Trouble at the moment is that too few people know about us.'

When the telephone rang again, a voice said: 'Is that Mr Trumpeter? This is the Reading *Globe* here. We hear that there has been some trouble in your village over a married woman, and we would like to hear your side of it.'

The voice was easily recognisable as Lennie's. He was either holding his nose or talking through tissue paper in an effort to disguise it.

'There is no trouble in my village at all. I have explained to the diocesan authorities that it is all the work of a malicious newspaper reporter called Leonard P Hutton. Shall I spell it? LEONARD P HUTTON – who, in an effort to make a news story he could sell to his newspaper, persuaded some other villagers to write a slanderous letter to the Bishop. The mistake he made was in signing the letter himself. Now he can never use the story.'

'All right, Mr Parson, I see you've recognised me. You know, I can sue the Bishop for showing you the letter?' Lennie sounded extremely unpleasant now. I think he was imitating a television performance we had both seen.

'Go ahead.'

'You're wrong about my reasons. Since you're so holy, I'll tell you the real reason. There's a very decent young girl in the village whom you've perverted. I think you know who I'm talking about. The only reason she's keen on you is because you're a parson. Probably she thinks it makes you higher class, or maybe she just likes your sexy dog-collar. Whatever it is, I'm warning you now that if you don't take your dirty hypocritical hands off my girl friend, I'll have your name in every Sunday newspaper. You wouldn't look nearly as smart in civvies, you know.'

He rang off. I was due to meet Danae that evening, when we could have a good laugh over the matter.

'By the way, Gillian, I forgot to mention to you that I have decided to keep a pet cat.'

'You must be mad. There is far too much work to do in the house already.'

'I will look after it. I believe the Flitcrofts have three kittens on their hands at the moment. When it arrives, I hope you will remember to call it Tibbles.'

My visits to the Hall were becoming more frequent. Danae began to find them monotonous. It was true that I was never again quite so proficient as I had been that evening before the first meeting of the Middlewalk Youth Committee. One can't expect miracles every day.

'We need to be more adventurous,' said Danae. 'I have been reading that book of Gillian's and it mentions something called the Italian method of making love.'

'It is not nearly so amusing as it sounds,' I said. 'In any case, it is against the law. I am not even sure that the Church allows it.'

'The Church doesn't allow anything,' said Danae. 'Let's break the law.'

So we did, but our attempt was acutely self-conscious and unsuccessful.

'I could have told you it would be like that,' I said.

'The trouble with you is that you know everything and you have no idea of romance. At least Lennie would approach it in the right spirit.'

'He would probably say that it was like playing the violin with his feet,' I said, but my sarcasm was wasted.

CHAPTER SEVEN

It was only with the greatest difficulty that we discouraged Father Good-Buller from opening my Old People's Dance Hall. He had discovered an hour-long service which he thought would be appropriate. Instead, we decided to hold a fancy dress ball with prizes. Gillian dressed in a mini-skirt, which she bought for the occasion at great expense, and an old blouse of Mrs Mandarill's, explaining to all who enquired that she represented Art Nouveau. I thought it might be amusing to dress as a tramp, again using Mandarill clothing, but nobody laughed. Only Mrs Hallowes had made any effort among the older people. She wore a sheet, covered her cheeks with lipstick and described herself as the Scarlet Woman of the Bible. Danae looked almost unbearably attractive in black jeans with an orange cummerbund, as a pirate. None of the others had changed at all, regarding fancy dress as something laid on for their benefit, rather than as something in which they might be expected to participate.

'Our first number is the Gay Gordons,' I said over the Tannoy system which had been installed at a cost of £180. 'Take your partners everyone.'

Nobody moved as the music crashed through the Hall. 'It's too loud,' said the odious Miss Cornhouse. 'I can't hear myself talking. I think you might have some consideration for the older folk.'

I danced with Gillian. She was extremely energetic and accurate on the dance floor, her face set in a mask of concentration. 'Perhaps it is time you danced with someone else,' she said, when we were both exhausted.

'Who?'

'Ask Danae. You've got to get it started somehow.'

Danae and I danced the Dashing White Sergeant. The company sat around the floor watching us with total lack of interest. Clearly, they felt they would be more entertained at home in front of their television sets. If the vicar chose to give an exhibition of ballroom dancing they could only come along and watch, but nothing must be allowed to stand in the way of their right to complain.

'You look absolutely frightful,' said Danae as we took two steps backwards and stamped our feet. 'What on earth are you wearing?'

'I am dressed as a tramp.'

'I have never seen anyone look so silly. Half of the villagers look like that normally. I wish you'd get into your proper clothes.'

I was too much out of breath to reply. So far as I could see, I was going to spend the rest of the evening dancing to amuse my parishioners. Several of them had allowed their mouths to fall open and were staring into space. Others clicked their false teeth around resentfully.

'I'm tired of dancing now,' said Danae. 'You'll have to find someone else to dance with.'

Interest was re-awakened by the arrival of Leonard P. Hutton dressed as a clergyman. 'I have come as the Reverend Nicholas Trumpeter,' he announced. Everyone had a good laugh over that. Danae clapped her hands in delight. 'Lennie, you look marvellous,' she said. 'Don't you think he looks handsome?'

'No,' I said.

'You should become a clergyman,' said Danae. 'Really, it suits you.'

'I might at that,' said Lennie. 'Only I don't believe half the crap they teach.'

'Neither do any of us,' I retorted good-naturedly. 'That is no bar to ordination.' Lennie looked at me blankly. As he led Danae off into a St Bernard's Waltz, I heard him say: 'Is he pissed or something?'

Danae laughed. 'No, he's always like that.'

'Mrs Hallowes, will you dance with me?'

'I should be delighted to.' As we struggled round the floor, she eyed the other couple with interest. 'I don't hold with all this cheek to cheek dancing do you?'

'I have no strong feelings on the matter.'

'Oh, *Mr Trumpeter*! What would your wife say?'

'She would probably agree with you.'

'Have you ever tried callisthenic dancing, Mr Trumpeter?'

'No, I don't think so. Isn't it for girls to develop their figures?'

'It needn't be. As a matter of fact, I hold meetings occasionally. We just say a few words and then we go through these dances. We call ourselves the White Circle.'

'How amusing. I never knew you were interested in dancing.'

'It isn't dancing exactly. It's an ancient system, far older than Christianity.' Her butterfly-shaped plastic spectacles glinted. 'We meet down by the river. Would you like to come?'

'I don't really know that I would have time. As you can imagine, parish duties keep me rather busy. Religious life gives very few opportunities for outside interests.'

'But this is all very much tied up with religion. You see, we are expressing the love we feel for Nature in the hope, one day, of identifying ourselves with the Laife Force.'

Danae and Lennie had now left the dance floor and were deep in conversation. Lennie had her pressed against the wall, and they seemed oblivious of everything else. I had to keep talking to ridiculous Mrs Hallowes.

'That seems harmless enough. But, as I said, I am too busy.'

'You must come and see us, just once. There is no need to participate, if you do not want to. Miss Cornhouse calls us the

Witches of Middlewalk, but of course we are the Whaite witches.
We would never have anything to do with Dark Forces. We are
only interested in Laife. Some of our rituals derive from ancient
fertility rites, but nothing vulgar goes on. I should have thought
you would have been interested from the historical aspect.'

Lennie had his arm around her and Danae's hand was resting
on his hip.

'Ah yes, the historical aspect. That must be quite interesting.'

'Will you come, then? We have a meeting the day after
tomorrow, on All Souls Day. There is much evil around on the
night of All Souls Day, which we have to combat with everything
we've got.'

'Yes, yes, I'll come,' I said. Lennie had tried to kiss her and she
had turned away her head to look at me. That was the most
hopeful sign yet. 'I'm afraid I'm too exhausted to go on dancing,'
I said.

'You need practice,' said Mrs Hallowes. 'We sometimes dance
for two hours at a stretch. We don't seem to notice the passing of
time. Oh, and another small thing. At these meetings, we all call
each other by different names. I am called Sister Beatrice. The
dancing has been examined by scientists, and they agree that it
does actually succeed in harnessing the Laife Force, although, of
course, they can't begin to explain how or why. I think I had
better introduce you as Brother Peter. I'll send Sister Jane to fetch
you to the meeting.'

'Sister Jane?'

'Mrs Gutterling. We call ourselves by these names partly
because they *are* our names in the spirit and partly to avoid
embarrassment afterwards.'

'I must leave you for a moment, I'm afraid. There is so much
to attend to. Thank you so much for the dance.'

'You haven't seen anything yet,' said Mrs Hallowes with a
musical laugh. 'Wait until you see me under the influence of the
Laife Force. I am quite a different person.'

I caught Danae just before she left the Hall. 'Are you going?'

Lennie answered from the gloom of the car park. 'She has asked me to give her a lift back to the Hall.'

'Her car is already here.'

'But she has decided to travel in mine. Good night, Mr Parson.'

I ignored him. 'Good night, Danae,' I said. She refused to look at me.

'Goodnight Nicholas. I'm sorry we've got to go. It was a lovely party. I expect I'll be seeing you sometime.'

If she had chosen to punch me in the face, she could not have delivered a nastier shock. As she walked away towards Lennie's car in her absurd drain-pipe trousers I noticed how thin she was. What, in God's name, had I thrown away?

'You look as if you had seen a ghost. What on earth is the matter with you this evening, Nicholas?'

Gillian always regarded any misfortune as a signal for abuse. If she suspected me of feeling sad or depressed she went into the attack. 'What have you got to be miserable about, anyway? You never think of anyone but yourself.'

No doubt people were starving in China through lack of contraceptives; no doubt the lot of the lower paid workers in industry was most uncongenial; no doubt spastics presented a problem, and prisoners needed to be re-integrated into society, but as I removed my trousers and hung them on the rail at the end of the bed I could only think that my life had lost its purpose and I wanted to die. Through taking her for granted, I had allowed myself to forget how beautiful Danae was, how loving and how gay. Now there was only Gillian.

'I think you must have seen a ghost. Have you?'

'Yes,' I said, because I knew it was no good keeping silent.

'At least, I thought I did. It may have been my imagination.'

'What did it look like?' said Gillian breathlessly. Her women's magazine serials were peopled by ghosts which normally turned out to have a rational explanation. But suspense pre-supposed a belief in them, and occasionally a writer forgot to tie up all the ends of his plot, leaving the matter ambiguous.

'I didn't want to worry you.'

'But I want to know. I have a right to know. Even if this thing only has existence in your mind it might help me to understand better if you described it to me.'

'It was real, all right,' I said grimly. 'But I think it would be better not to discuss it. How's Tibbles?'

'She finished her tin of Top Cat. I think she's asleep now. Nicholas, I want to know. Do you think this house is haunted?'

'That nightdress looks most appealing against the white of the sheets. I think the pink becomes you.' So did the way she stood in front of the electric fire every morning, shivering uncontrollably.

'You are always frivolous about things which matter. It is true that I have often heard odd noises in the house. And sometimes, in an empty room, one suddenly feels unaccountably scared. I never told you because I thought you would laugh at me. But something has definitely worried you tonight. Oh Nicholas, do you think we should have the house exorcised? I hate to think of old Mr Mandarill creeping around the corridors. He was a very evil man, I feel sure. I never like going near his grave in the churchyard. I try to be sensible and think of rats and gutters expanding, but have you sometimes noticed an extraordinary smell in the house? I talked about it to George Swinger and he told me he couldn't smell anything. Perhaps he is not psychic. Do you ever smell anything, Nicholas? You're probably not psychic, either. It is only sensitive people who are affected by these things.'

As long as she continued talking I could mourn my loss. I remembered Danae laughing at my jokes, splashing in the bath with me one afternoon when Gillian had gone out, undressing shamelessly in front of the window, loving me, laughing at me, wrapping herself round me in a crowded room when nobody was looking. Gillian was still prattling away when I dropped into a dreamless sleep.

Mr Tuck seemed surprised when Gillian opened the door to him. No doubt he had forgotten all about her, as only people can who do not have to share her bed. I was standing immediately behind, and the Rural Dean's expression of relief on seeing me was highly comical. He ignored her thereafter.

'Nicholas, I hope I haven't come at an awkward moment? There are some things I want to talk about most urgently. Can we go into your study?'

When we were alone he dropped his bland air.

'How's Tibbles?'

'She's very well. Would you like to see the mess she made last night in the kitchen? Gillian refuses to clear it up, and I'm too busy. Perhaps you wouldn't mind doing it yourself. Otherwise we will have to wait until George Swinger comes to take out the dustbins.'

'Another mess? I think Tibbles must have a tremendous character. But I am chiefly concerned not with her corporal welfare so much as with what I like to call her essence.'

He was wrong, of course. If Tibbles could be said to have any essence, it lay on the kitchen floor, but theological argument is a total waste of time. The most important thing in the modern world is to show goodwill. So we searched for Tibbles up and down the house, occasionally making plaintive noises. We searched in the drawing room, in a hundred damp cupboards, even in Gillian's Planning Room, as it was now called. Not even the Planning Room contained a cat.

'Puss, puss, puss. Mew. Miaow. Tibbles. Puss,' we both cried in a high falsetto. We searched the bedrooms, finding another mess in Gethsemane. Eventually we ran her to earth in a small bedroom under one of the cupolas – Calvary. I had not been into it for nearly three weeks, and the multitude of memories and emotions it evoked nearly swamped me. An old china chamber pot in one corner had been improvised as a waste-paper basket, and in it Danae had chosen to leave a pair of laddered stockings. Others might have been disconcerted at this evidence of their guilt, but I felt nearer to weeping. Self-pity is something which is normally alien to my nature, and I am constantly irritated by people who suffer from it. But I had forgotten how enjoyable it could be. I sat on the bed of the only love affair I had ever known and great tears of sentimentality began to fill my eyes.

'Little Tibbles, there, pretty puss. Was she hiding from Daddy? You don't know me yet, but I want you to think of me as Uncle Billy. I am the Rural Dean, but you needn't be frightened of that because it only means I love you a little bit more than anyone else. Listen, she's purring. We are going to be the *greatest* of friends, you and I, and I want you to tell me if ever they think of performing any horrid operations on you. We wouldn't like that, would we, Tibbles? You just want to grow up in the love of Me, being pleased with feline things.'

'What do you want to do, baptise her?'

'I think it would be cruel. In any case, I have never been able to accept that baptism is necessary for salvation. Are not five sparrows sold for two farthings, and not one of them is forgotten before Me?'

'Before God,' I murmured without thinking. My mind was far away.

'Yes, yes, of course,' said Mr Tuck, suddenly embarrassed. 'In any case, baptism is unnecessary. So much of the Gospel is misunderstood. Besides the Archdeacon would be sure to hear about it.'

'In any case, I don't think that Tibbles is quite ready for baptism yet,' I said. To show that my heart was in the right place I stroked Tibbles behind the ear. When I tried to tickle her stomach, she bit me. Mr Tuck grew jealous.

'You must be careful of what you say in front of her. Cats are very sensitive. Of course there should be much more stringent control of those who are allowed to keep them. I personally would never allow anyone to keep a pet who did not regularly come to church. You might find an atheist whose heart was full of love, who had been driven away from church by someone like Father Good-Buller, but it seems an awful risk. Even among people who claim to be Christians, I am sorry to say, there is seldom a complete understanding of the responsibility involved. How long have you had Tibbles?'

'I can't remember.'

'She looks very young. Didn't you tell me about her three months ago?'

'Conceivably.'

'Yet I could swear she isn't more than six weeks old.'

'She has kept her youth in a most amazing way.'

'You aren't giving her drugs to stunt her growth? I have read that scientists can do it nowadays. They are called kitten-cats.'

'I saw them on television.'

'Do you approve? Do you think it is morally defensible?'

'I don't know.' He was profaning my love-nest with his lunatic ravings. I wished he would go. If I found Tibbles in there again I would throw her and all her spiritual problems out of the window.

'It would all hinge, I suppose, on whether you loved God or not,' said Mr Tuck, and there was an unpleasant edge to his voice. 'Other people exhaust all their love on worldly things like women. By the way, how is Mrs Boissaens?'

'I have no idea. I haven't seen her for weeks.'

'I'm so glad. The Archdeacon will be most relieved to hear it. He has started making enquiries again, you know. Have you been receiving many letters recently?'

Few Anglican clergymen receive less than two anonymous letters a month. Usually, they are written in capital letters with many underlinings and consist of personal abuse or vile accusations. Just occasionally they denounce another parishioner and are mildly entertaining. Gillian feels strongly about them, but I have always found them among the least onerous of my cares.

'No more than usual.'

'Well, he has. I have a good mind to send him a few myself.'

'I shouldn't, you know. These things only lead to trouble.'

'I think it is time somebody told him that there is nothing to choose between the Archdeacon of Silchester and Stalin, or Hitler. He is the great Beast of the Apocalypse.'

'He might guess who had written it.'

'Other people must have noticed. We could all sign it, from the Chapter. He gets on my nerves when I see him gloating in his chair, just waiting for the Last Trump to sound.'

'Aren't we all? Come downstairs for a cup of coffee. It's all right, there's no charge. You can bring Tibbles. What makes you think that Father Good-Buller is still trying to implicate me with Mrs Boissaens?'

'I saw it written on his forehead.'

'Oh, really?' So it was a false alarm. I need not have worried.

'And he asked me to sign a second affidavit to the effect that I had heard you take a solemn oath denying that you had any association with the lady.'

'You don't think he is trying to collect evidence for a consistory court?'

'He may well be, but the Bishop does not believe in them. In any case, nothing could be worse than going to confession with the Devil. What am I to say at the Last Judgment?'

'I should deny it hotly and hope for the best.'

In the kitchen, George Swinger was waiting for us in a state of high excitement. Clearly, he had seen something. 'I was in the churchyard this morning, tidying up around the graves, like,' he began.

'Oh yes?' I said. Far the best view of my bathroom could be seen from the graveyard. Could he still be interested in seeing Gillian naked? I should have thought that once was enough for anyone. 'The cat has made a mess in the corner. Mrs Trumpeter said she would be most grateful if you could clear it up.'

'Cats' messes I don't mind,' said Swinger. 'There's other things I draw the line at. There's been happenings going on in that churchyard, and I never see'd them. I didn't want to tell Mrs Trumpeter what I found, in case it upset her. I haven't even decided whether to tell Mrs Swinger yet, in case it has a bad influence.'

'What did you find, George?'

'I don't know how you religious gentlemen likes to call them, but I and my wife call them birth controls.'

'They are probably something to do with my wife's clinic. Perhaps they are faulty specimens which were thrown away.'

'Not at all. These were proper normal ones, not the religious ones your wife sells. Mildred showed us one she'd bought from Mrs Trumpeter, and neither of us could make it out. These were the proper ones you can buy at the barbers to stop having babies with. And they had been used.'

'How extraordinary,' said Mr Tuck.

'I knew you clerical gentlemen would be interested. Would you like to come and see them?'

'Not really,' I said.

'Where are they?' said Mr Tuck. So we followed him. Mr Swinger showed us his discovery, just behind Mr Mandarill's grave. There was something particularly sordid about the sight. And in November, too.

'How disgusting. I expect it must be the work of some of the teenagers in the village,' I said.

'You think it's teenagers, do you?' George Swinger gave me a long, hard stare. 'I never see'd what was going on here, so I can't say whether it was teenagers or not. But I know there are some as might think differently.'

It was intolerable that I should be accused of misbehaviour in my own churchyard. One had grown to accept the identification of religion with sex in the vulgar mind, even its corollary that the parson was the Man of Sex. But the next step, whereby a parson would automatically be accused of any sex crimes in his neighbourhood was false and objectionable. Our interest in sex derived partly from the fact that it was a very interesting subject, partly because modern thought had imbued it with all the mystique of a religion and partly because it was a way of drawing attention to ourselves. For no other reason. We were not, like musicians, exceptionally passionate by nature. In my experience, at least, there is nothing so exhausting as long hours of idleness. Few parsons' wives, I imagine, are satisfied with their sex lives, but that is part of their vocation. It would have been a waste of time to explain any of this to George Swinger.

'We must post a policeman to keep a watch on the place. They are desecrating holy ground, you know, and I think there may be a law against it. There is a law against sexual intercourse in any form if you read the law books long enough. And I daresay even contraception is illegal in public.'

'What shall I do with these things?' said George.

'I suppose you had better bury them.'

'Here in the churchyard? There's a fee for burying things in the churchyard.'

'The Parish Council will cover the bill. I daresay we can get it back from public funds. I am going to report this matter to the police.'

'PC Terence Winner, down at Twyford, is my brother-in-law. I'll have a word with him if you like.'

'Could you, George? That would be very kind. Now, Mr Tuck, we must go in for our coffee. They expect you to be in five places at once if you're a clergyman. And for the love of Christ, take that bloody cat away from here.'

Afternoons are always the most trying time for a clergyman. In the mornings we walk around smirking at children, cringing before the elderly or infirm, listening sympathetically to complicated and morbid case-histories of illness. In the evening, we have television to keep us acquainted with what is happening in the world, or a book from the library to serve as relaxation after our day's work. But there is always a long, baffling stretch between the time when our miserable luncheons are cleared away and the start of Children's Hour on television. Mr Plimsoll went to sleep, but he had a most unusual capacity for sleeping. Mr Tuck motored around in his Mini-Austin, looking for stray animals, or preaching to the fields and hedgerows. Mr Jackson sat in a trance in front of his typewriter. Mr Heifer visited the son of a workman who worked in a fish and chip shop in Twyford. They appeared to enjoy each other's company. For a long time I had been meeting Danae in the afternoons, so that we could discuss youth problems and other matters of general concern. Now I had no escape.

'Would you like to come to the cinema this afternoon?' I asked Gillian.

'How most unlike you to think of anything amusing,' said Gillian. 'What is on?'

At the Regal, there was *Mary Poppins*. Few people would describe me as an inflexible man, but I had made it a point of honour never to see this particular film. At the Odeon, in Maidenhead, there was *The Bridge on the River Kwai*. It had been showing off and on in the neighbourhood for eight years. Both the Gaumont and the ABC in Reading had nudist films. I am quite broadminded about them, but Gillian feels very strongly against the nature movement. Do not misunderstand me. I derive no sexual satisfaction, and only minimal excitement, from seeing parts of naked women on the screen. My claim is that a good nudist film may be slightly more interesting than television's Tingha and Tucker Club on an off-day. In any case, we were left with a three-hour film of the Bible in Slough, or a double programme of horror in the Twyford Essoldo: *Screaming Skull* and *Dracula's Teen-Age Daughter*. After some discussion, we decided that the second choice would probably be more adult.

'This makes me feel just as if we were newly married,' said Gillian, as we motored through the lanes. 'Will you buy me some bulls' eyes?'

'I wish I could, but I am afraid we can't afford it.' She made the most disgusting noises with them.

The Essoldo was nearly empty, as so many cinemas are in the afternoon. I have never been able to make out what people do with themselves at that time of day. A self-absorbed couple in the most expensive seats were indulging in a form of light petting. No doubt it would grow heavier as the film proceeded. A very old woman, obviously immobile and probably blind, sat in the back row eating potato crisps. Probably she had been left there by her relatives to get her out of the way. Or perhaps she was just another mute testimony to the problems of leisure.

The *Screaming Skull* was a disappointment on the whole, although I was amused to see Gillian wince every time it screamed. *Dracula's Teen-Age Daughter* was much more enjoyable. Cliff Redman, a writer, finds himself attracted to an extraordinary girl with teeth like a walrus whom he meets while he is writing a book on vampirism in Westphalia. He rejects her suggestion that they should have sexual intercourse together on grounds which are difficult to understand. Perhaps he felt that she was too sudden in her approach, allowing insufficient time for their relationship to develop and become meaningful. However, he is still fond of her, and when he discovers that she has the misfortune to be a vampire he decides that the only mature and compassionate thing to do under the circumstances is to hammer a wooden stake through her heart when she is asleep. As he is hammering, blood gushes out of her mouth and swarms of bats beat against his face, but he sensibly hammers on. Finally her teeth contract, her enormous bosoms subside and with the final words: 'Thank you, Cliff,' she changes into the corpse of a typical, decent teenager. Gillian was visibly affected by it all. Of course, I had seen too many typical, decent teenagers to be much impressed by the metamorphosis. Not so Cliff Redman. He announced as his intention at the end of the film that he would devote his life to good works, taking a menial job in Asia so that he could better understand the problems of underdevelopment.

It did not seem very important to me whether Cliff Redman understood the problems of underdevelopment or not, but then Gillian will point out that I am immature. Any conversation with her always comes back to that. It was to forestall such discussion that I recklessly bought her a Mars bar as we came out of the cinema. The loving couple ahead of us, faces flushed, had gorged themselves on a four-and-eight-penny double pack of Lyons Mint Chocs.

'Hullo, Daddy. I didn't know you went to the cinema. We're coming on.'

'Hullo Leonard. We sat behind you in the cinema, but failed to recognise you.'

'Snooping, were you? I suppose you didn't like the way we were carrying on. If you must know, Danae had a fly in her eye, which I was trying to get out for her, and then it kind of slipped under her jersey, so I had to get it out from there.' He made an indecent gesture with his hand. Danae had stopped being embarrassed and treated me to something like her old conspiratorial laugh. 'After that I'm not quite sure where it went, are you Danae? But any gentleman would have done it for her. It was a most *Christian* action, wasn't it Daddy?'

The situation was extremely awkward. I could think of no snub which would not make me look even more ridiculous. Finally, when his pawings took on a determined character, I said: 'Please, Lennie. Not in the foyer.' Even the woman behind the cash desk laughed at that. Danae threw back her head and shrieked, while Lennie gave a puzzled, stupid, sarcastic smile. There was no malice in Danae's laugh, just keen enjoyment. When she looked at me, standing in clerical dress with a Mars bar in my hand, there was warm affection in her eyes.

'Come on Danae. We're just hanging around.' The whining bossiness in his voice was familiar to me. I heard it every time I went into the village shop at Middlewalk, as children ordered their mothers to buy them an iced lolly or some barley sugar to rot their tender young teeth. It was the voice of power without responsibility, the prerogative of almost everyone in our democratic age.

Danae was not to be cajoled. She looked at me saucily, but I could only stare back with distaste, thinking of the clumsy hands which had been fondling her body and the odious, classless voice which had been whispering clichés into her ear.

'I feel I ought to come and see you about the youth club outing to Slough,' she said, not too sure of herself.

'I am afraid I am extremely busy these days,' I said. 'Perhaps I could give you a few minutes after Morning Service on Sunday.'

'That is too early. Couldn't you come to lunch at the Hall?'

'All his lunches are booked up for months in advance,' Gillian said unnecessarily. 'You must tell your step-mother I am very sorry.'

'All right,' said Danae bravely. 'I will get up for Communion and see you afterwards.'

'Come on Danae,' whined her paramour. 'Cor, do you think we have got all day?' It was hard to decide whether his use of 'Cor' was intended facetiously or not. In any case, nobody laughed. With one longing, lingering look behind, Danae followed him through the glass swing-doors past a brilliantly coloured studio-portrait of Gregory Peck and into the cold world outside.

'I must say,' said Gillian, 'I don't blame you for telling them off. If everybody behaved like that in the cinema they would all be closed down. I always considered Danae was such a sensible girl. You would have thought she could have waited until after marriage.'

After marriage! What gruesome memories those two words evoked.

'Will you get into the car?' I said. 'You are blocking all the traffic for many miles around,'

'Personally,' said Gillian, 'I think it is a very good idea to try things out a little while you are engaged.'

'So long as you take adequate precautions,' I said between my teeth. The car always made a hissing noise these days, as if to proclaim the seediness of its passengers.

'That goes without saying,' said Gillian, against whom sarcasm was not effective. 'I often wish we had been a little more adventurous in our courting, but of course it is not possible for clergymen to behave as ordinary people in these matters. Sensible experimentation has everything to recommend it. I daresay that when they are married, everything will go much smoother as a result. *You*, I seem to remember, Nicholas, were very slow. But I am not happy about young people doing these things unsupervised.'

'What makes you think they are going to marry?'

'Didn't you know? I thought everyone in the village knew about it. They are going to announce their engagement on Sunday.'

'It is not true.'

'Very well, it isn't true. Mrs Allsopp learned from Wendy, who had been shown the ring which Lennie bought. It cost eighty-five pounds. I think it is silly to spend so much money on a ring. Keep the money – you'll be needing it later on, that's what I say. If you remember, I insisted that you should not buy me a ring at all, then Mummy gave us one of her old ones. A perfect waste of money. But at least it shows a romantic heart. So few people have any spirit of romance nowadays. You know, Nicholas, I wouldn't really have minded at all if you had bought me an engagement ring. I would have been rather touched.'

I said nothing, having other things to think about. If I allowed Danae to marry the half-witted journalist it would be the wickedest thing I had ever done in my life. She was worth a million of him. I remembered the pleading look she had given me, and nearly died of self-pity and mortification. She was the loveliest, kindest, warmest creature in the world.

'Nicholas, why didn't you buy me an engagement ring?'

'Shut up. Can't you see I'm driving?'

'Nicholas, why didn't you buy me an engagement ring?' Her voice now had the authoritative, slightly hysterical tone of a schoolmistress.

'Because you said you didn't want one.' It had been a holy crusade of hers at the time. Enlightened womanhood did not require such baubles to bolster its self-esteem. Far better spend the money on something sensible and modern like a washing machine. So in fact, I had bought neither, pointing out that it was against my principles to invest in a washing machine. One might as well give one's money straight to the Communist Party.

'Just because I said I didn't want one, it doesn't mean to say that it might not have been rather a sweet thought to have given me one. Women need occasional tokens of affection.'

'If you shut up I'll bring you some flowers next time I come back from the office, and say how attractive you're looking.'

'That would be something. If only I could feel it came from the heart.' Gillian had never understood my *Woman's Dream* jokes.

'Look, I gave you a Mars bar, didn't I?'

'Yes. It was very sweet of you. It is just that sometimes one longs for a little more – something with imagination behind it.'

'What about your pink nightdress?'

'Yes, that was rather sweet. You may not have noticed that I wear it every night. I don't think you notice much.'

Of course I had noticed. Every time she walked towards the electric fire I held my breath, and the strain was beginning to tell.

'You still haven't told me about the ghost you claim to have seen,' she added.

'I have no intention of telling you. It would only alarm you unnecessarily.' That last word was a master touch. Gillian was determined to be alarmed. She had a right to be alarmed, wasn't she a mature, adult woman?

'Perhaps we ought to get the house exorcised. They say it can only be done properly by a Roman Catholic priest. Or perhaps we ought to get to the heart of the matter and make sure that Mr Mandarill troubles us no more.'

I had visions of Gillian hammering a wooden stake through Mr Mandrill's coffin. Would blood gush from his mouth and his face change from one of demoniac evil into that of an ordinary, decent, half-witted old clergyman? Of course we would never know, as his coffin was ten feet underground. While Gillian burbled on a new resolution began to form in my mind. The only way to restore sanity to the world was for Gillian to leave it. Basically, there was nothing wrong with the underdeveloped nations, or even with old age pensioners. It was Gillian who caused every perplexity and misery existing on the face of God's earth. I could never kill her because that would be immoral, and in any case I lacked the courage. Gillian must somehow be expunged. At last my life had a purpose.

'Do drive carefully. You nearly bumped into that cyclist,' said Gillian.

'I'm sorry, dear. I failed to see him in the dark,' I said wearily.

'Well, just keep your eyes open, then,' said Gillian.

CHAPTER EIGHT

Danae sat in the front pew, looking very meek and devout. Beside her knelt Mrs Boissaens, with an 'I'm praying for patience' expression on her silly superior face. Why do you come to church in gloves, you fat white woman whom nobody loves? Otherwise there was only Miss Cornhouse, who sat sniffing miserably at the back of the church. These early morning services were a waste of time. Nobody wanted them. The Church of England would never move into the second half of the twentieth century. I decided to deliver an impromptu sermon, just to annoy them. They think that by coming to early morning service they will get away in half an hour. I was going to show them differently.

'May the words of our mouths and the thoughts of our hearts be always acceptable in Thy sight, in the name of the Father, and of the Son and of the Holy Ghost,' I said.

'Amen,' whispered Danae humbly, sweetly, piously. She was the most damnable hypocrite. I was not going to have any of it. My sermon at Matins was to have been on the problems of old age, pointing out that whereas Christians may derive comfort as well as grace from helping placid and agreeable old people, it was a much better test of Christian resolve to help old people who were downright unpleasant. In other words, they mustn't leave everything to the vicar. For the Communion Service I chose a sterner text:

'Moreover the Lord saith, Because the daughters of Zion are haughty, and walk with stretched-forth necks and wanton eyes, walking and mincing *as* they go, and making a tinkling with their feet:

17 Therefore the Lord will smite with a scab the crown of the head of the daughters of Zion, and the Lord will discover their secret parts.

18 In that day the Lord will take away the bravery of *their* tinkling ornaments *about their feet*, and *their* cauls and their round tires like the moon,

19 The chains and the bracelets amid the mufflers,

20 The bonnets and the ornaments of the legs, and the headbands and the tablets and the earrings,

21 The rings and the nose jewels,

22 The changeable suits of apparel, and the mantles, and the wimples, and the crisping pins,

23 The glasses and the fine linen, and the hoods and the vails,

24 And it shall come to pass *that* instead of sweet smell there shall be a stink; and instead of a girdle a rent; and instead of well set hair, baldness; and instead of a stomacher, a girding of sackcloth; *and* burning instead of beauty.'

Throughout the reading, I gave a bitter emphasis to certain words: *wanton*, *tinkling*, *scab*, *secret parts*, the *crisping pins*, STINK. On each occasion, I paused and gave Danae a long, merciless stare. Her eyes met mine in demure, dog-like adoration. Perhaps it was all a lie that she was going to marry Lennie.

'The words of this passage from Isaiah have a curiously old-fashioned ring about them nowadays,' I began. 'But like so much of the Bible, one finds the deeper one goes into it, the more its relevance to our everyday lives becomes apparent. Women today are not like their Victorian grandmothers, and nobody would like to see a return to the Victorian Age. If the Church stands for anything, it stands for progress. One hears a great deal about the problems of' young people – how all too often they are prevented from marrying by inadequate Government grants or for some other reason, and we all know that it would be unrealistic to deny them the fullest and purest expression of their love for each other merely by economic arguments. On the other hand, there are risks. We all know about venereal disease' – I gave Miss Cornhouse a malignant stare – 'but how many of us really know about the dangers of unwanted babies? And how many of us are prepared to be frank about it? I have just heard of a youth – I can scarcely call him a young man – in this parish who has boasted that he always refuses to use family planning because it reminds him of playing the piano in gloves. The selfishness and hypocrisy of that sort of statement takes one's breath away. What sort of preparation is that for marriage? There are circumstances which justify even playing the piano in gloves. After all, people come to church in gloves, why shouldn't they play the piano in them, too? But I am coming round to the view that there are no circumstances which justify the ultimate expression of human love, when two bodies are as it were united in one, without taking proper precautions. There can be no love without true charity, and there can be no charity where there is selfishness or irresponsibility. If a girl in my parish came to me and said she was thinking of marrying a man who was in that state of mind, it would be my duty to warn her against it. And if she persisted, I would refuse to celebrate the wedding.

'The trouble with people nowadays – and this especially applies to young people – is that they tend to think of Church as something that happens on Sundays – if then. Here we are told, of the daughters of Zion, that the Lord will discover their secret parts. Of course he will. Nothing is secret from the Lord, even the innermost private happenings of the marriage bed. Selfishness and irresponsibility are as much sins inside marriage as out of it. Marriage is a terrible and awe-inspiring responsibility. Nowadays people rush into it without a second thought. Obligations to parents, friends and voluntary organisations like the local youth club are completely forgotten in one mad rush, like the Gadarene swine, to the altar rails. When I think of how much unwanted misery is brought into the world by this sort of callous indifference to other people's feelings, I honestly begin to think it would be better if no woman ever began to think of marriage before she had reached full maturity, say at about fifty. Marriage before thirty should be forbidden by law. But it is no good formulating a set of rules for life inside a Christian community, when all too many of our fellow-citizens are not Christian at all. I would like to see the mother who produced an unwanted child – and who can say, with their hands on their hearts, that any children are wanted nowadays? – punished by a large fine. Instead, we see the Government actually giving them money. All we can do is to create a little Christian community inside ourselves – we, the four people in this church – and regulate our own lives in the way which we would like to see everyone else regulate theirs, to the best of our ability. In the name of the Father and of the Son and of the Holy Spirit, Amen.'

After church, Miss Cornhouse came to congratulate me on my sermon. She, of course, had not allowed herself to be rushed into marriage. As for bringing unwanted children into the world, she was equally blameless.

'If everyone was as sensible as you, Miss Cornhouse, there would be no housing problem, no unemployment, no problem of lower paid workers...' No old age pensioners, no teenagers, no life on the planet of any description, except the occasional stray budgerigar which has escaped from captivity, performing its pretty tricks to itself alone in the wilderness. Miss Cornhouse would have to be forbidden under some other clause.

'Have you heard Danae's good news?' asked Mrs Boissaens.

'No, what good news?' I said.

'After what he said in the sermon, I feel we shouldn't tell him,' said Danae.

'What sermon?' said Mrs Boissaens. 'I didn't hear any sermon. Danae is going to get engaged to Mr Hutton. I think it's such a good idea. Girls of her age should always have an outside interest.

We're trying to win Eugene round, but of course it has been a terrible blow. Anybody would think he didn't like Leonard by the way he's carrying on.'

'I don't suppose he does.'

'Of course he does. Eugene is just a little bit old-fashioned, isn't he, Danae? We're having Lennie to dinner tonight. Perhaps you would like to come, too, and we can discuss plans for the wedding.'

'I am afraid that I am too busy.'

'Well, come after dinner, then,' It was a command rather than an invitation. 'Now, we must go.'

'First I want to see Nicholas alone for a minute,' said Danae.

'You can say anything you want to him this evening.'

'Haven't you ever heard of pre-marital advice, Angela? I don't suppose you needed it, anyway.'

'There isn't much Mr Trumpeter can teach you.' The atmosphere was distinctly nasty.

'It is quite normal for girls to come to the vicar for advice before marriage,' I said. 'For instance, I believe that your fiancé doesn't come to church much. Normally, I advise girls not to think of marrying before they have persuaded their would-be husbands to become regular church-goers. In your case, Danae, I think I would persuade you to forget about marriage in any case, at least for a while. Marriage isn't all it's cracked up to be, I can assure you. Lennie might not be the sort of person to make a good husband. We all know he is most amusing, and very good company. But is he mature enough? Will he be able to take on the responsibility?'

'There's nothing wrong with Lennie,' said Mrs Boissaens decidedly. 'Or at any rate he's better than any of Danae's other young men. Do you remember Roger Cushkind, Danae? He spent a whole evening trying to persuade us that he was a drug addict. Of course, he was nothing of the sort. Or the Venables boy, who did take drugs and told Eugene that for twenty thousand pounds down he would never see Danae again, but otherwise they were off to Gretna Green. And at least Lennie isn't married. I must admit, I never thought Eugene was a snob before. Of course, I'm only her step-mother, but I'd much sooner see Danae marry a decent lad from a working class background than some awful middle class little man.'

Like myself, no doubt.

'You are quite wrong in supposing that the working class are in any way superior,' I said. 'They are almost as varied as any other class, and their only common attribute is a comparative lack of intelligence.'

'They are more natural,' said Mrs Boissaens.

'No they are not,' I said. 'It is just that their behaviour patterns are less familiar to you than those of the other classes and so create a false impression of spontaneity. They have few original impulses, and frequently lack the means of expressing them if they had.'

'That is one point of view,' said Mrs Boissaens. 'But I am surprised to hear it from you. I thought you were supposed to be a parson. Aren't we all equal in the eyes of God?'

'Indeed we are, but none of us can quite claim to share His sublime vision. In any case, you have just said that the working classes are superior.'

'I wish you would both stop talking about me as if I were a piece of meat,' said Danae.

I seemed to have heard it before. Perhaps it was *Woman's Dream*, but more likely it was in a film about getting through to teenagers, whatever that might mean.

'We were not discussing you at all,' I said. 'And in any case I have never heard meat discussed in that way.' What she meant, I fancy, is that we should return to the subject of her affairs and curtail our discussion of more general matters. It was a complete fallacy to suppose that the working classes were more honest – let alone more articulate – than the middle classes. Nor, as a class, did they have warmer hearts. Nor, I am convinced, do they make better lovers. It is a myth assiduously promoted by men in the communications industries. Artists have always been social parasites, and they have often felt bound to flatter their patrons, but there is no reason for those who are neither artists nor patrons to be taken in by it all. Ministers of religion had a greater duty to the cause of truth. The existence of the working class may be an unfortunate necessity, but certainly nothing to rejoice about.

'I beg your pardon,' I said.

'Are we going to have our pre-marital talks or not?' said Danae.

'Oh, all right. I hope we can resume our conversation some time, Angela. The mistake of so many people nowadays is to make a virtue of a necessity. Necessity is never virtuous, nor virtue necessary. The two are logically irreconcilable. Where there is necessity, or any other form of compulsion, there can be no virtue.'

'I see,' said Mrs Boissaens. She looked mystified, but was plainly not anxious to continue the conversation. Few people have either the stamina or the honesty to follow their thought to its logical conclusion.

'Have you gone stark, staring mad?' Danae asked as we walked towards the Rectory. I allowed myself a little half-smile as I followed her. She walked with a stretched-forth neck and wanton eyes, mincing as she went. When I looked at her feet, in smart white Italian shoes over brown patterned stockings, I could swear I heard a faint tinkling.

Gillian greeted us coolly at the Rectory door. Plainly she had still not quite forgiven Danae for indulging in unsupervised sexual experiments with Lennie.

'Miss Boissaens is engaged to be married,' I said. 'We are going to have a little talk together. I always try to give people some pre-marital advice before they take the plunge.'

'I'm very glad to hear it,' said Gillian. 'So many people get married nowadays without even knowing the facts of life. Somewhere I've got quite a sensible little book on the subject.'

'I know,' said Danae. 'I have already seen it.'

'After Nicholas has spoken to you about the spiritual side of marriage, or whatever he likes to call it, perhaps you would like to come to me for some solid help. Actions speak plainer than words. I expect Lennie will grow into quite a sensible young man eventually. But it is no good listening to my husband. A child of six could tell you more than he knows about marriage.'

We ignored her hysterical, gesticulating figure. At times, I began to think that her new hobby was more trouble than the old. If only I could persuade her that excessive contraception has been proved to be a contributory factor in the rise of certain types of cancer – that would really put the cat among the pigeons. She was beginning to be sceptical about the unnamed Californian institute of cancer research I used to produce from time to time, but it had served me well. Many forms of sausage meat had been discovered to contain carcinoferous materials, I said. For a brief and wonderful period there had been no more Toad in the Hole. Then it reappeared, but I noticed she always left the pieces of sausage on her plate. It had come as a great relief to know that she was trying to murder me. Any action I took thereafter could be construed as self-defence, but she seemed twice as healthy, and soon she would have to change her nightdress. Clearly the next step was to identify family planning in all its forms with cancer. If the Californian institute was out, I would have to rely on experimental research behind the Iron Curtain. Nobody could contradict me on that.

'Have you gone mad?' said Danae. 'What on earth were you talking to Angela about?'

'She raised a point about the differing intellectual ability of the various social classes. It is an interesting subject, and one which receives insufficient attention nowadays – probably because it is incompatible with the glib egalitarianism to which we must all subscribe.'

'Well, so long as you're happy,' she said, giving me an odd, sideways glance. Just like a daughter of Zion. I was torn between the urge to smite her and the urge to know her secret parts. She might have been right. My mind was a little confused these days, or perhaps it would be more accurate to say that it worked with brilliant clarity on a series of unrelated and incongruous subjects. Only continuity was lacking. I did not feel up to the concentration needed on this occasion. Other people were a bore and an infringement. It would be grossly impertinent to expect them to interest me, but they should have been interested in what I had to say.

'Why did you want to see me?'

'Just to explain why I was getting married and to see if we could remain friends. I'm still extremely fond of you, and wouldn't mind at all seeing you from time to time, but you see I have to get married some time, and you don't seem to be in the market.'

'I agree that I am not in a position to marry you, but your argument is faulty. There is no need for you to get married. Gillian can't live forever, in any case. And why on earth choose Lennie?'

'He's not as bad as all that.'

'He is quite literally sub-human. He has no character and I very much doubt whether he has any free will. He is an advertiser's brand-figure. He was never born, he was collated. He is a sociological abstraction.'

'I'm sorry you feel like that about him.'

'Worse than a brute, he is a machine.'

'He is not brutal at all. He is very kind.'

'If you had listened, you would have observed that I never said he was a brute. I would prefer the company of Miss Cornhouse's budgerigar, or even Mrs Tartfoot's Scottie. You say he is kind. What has he ever done which is kind? He may be able to mouth the approved sentiments, but his selfishness is total and absolute. When you can't say that a fellow is witty, or handsome, or well-born, or rich you have to say that he's kind. He's nothing of the sort. He's a drain on our productive effort, a threat to national survival. It's people like him who are responsible for the decline of England. He is responsible for the juvenile delinquency, the illegal abortions, the upsurge of crime, above all, the general lack of any sense of purpose.'

'As a matter of fact, he told me that he voted Liberal.'

'It is the sort of cretinous, conceited thing he would do. His whole life is spent trying to draw attention to himself, just like Mrs Swinger having a hysterectomy or that ridiculous Wendy Allsop having a complete set of false teeth at thirteen. Of course, there is nothing in Lennie to which attention can be drawn. He is not a person, he is the voice of Youth trying to assert itself.'

'If that's how you feel, then there's no more to be said. I wouldn't have minded seeing you. Lennie can't expect to have me with him the whole time. He's supposed to be modern, after all. But I think you're going funny in the head. Nothing you say seems to make much sense. I've got to get married, you see, or I would spend the rest of my life cooped up with Daddy and Angela.'

'But you can't get married to a sociological abstraction. He will insist on your having 2.05 children and will divorce you in seven years.'

'Then we can get to know each other again. Can't you see, Nicholas, we couldn't go on the way we were.'

'You are talking in clichés. Lennie has been getting at you.'

'There is some truth, I am afraid, even in clichés. I'm sorry, Nicholas, to see you the way you are. At least I've been able to insist with Lennie that you should marry us both. He wanted a civil ceremony in Reading, but I knew you wouldn't like it. If he divorces me in a few years I shall come back to you, if you still want me. But I think you are too much tied to Gillian.'

This was preposterous. My feelings for Gillian simply did not enter into the matter. In any case, I had none. The only reason why I had not agreed to run away with Danae was that it seemed rather a drastic and unnecessary step to take. But it was too late to explain.

'Don't be silly. I could never marry a divorced woman. Father Good-Buller would be certain to hear of it. You are making a terrible mistake in getting married to Lennie, and I would not be doing my duty if I failed to warn you. Now I am beginning to regret that I ever got involved with you. At least, I hope you will have the sense to go and see Gillian, who would like to give you some advice about family planning.'

'It is kind of her, but I am not really interested. You were wrong when you said in the pulpit that Lennie did not take precautions. Of course he does. And he's got much more imagination than you have.'

The Italian manner again? Was it going to haunt me all my life? Nobody else seems to realise that even if it is physically possible, it is a much less satisfactory way of setting about things than the method which nature designed. But I am obviously out of touch with the times. Perhaps I am wrong.

'What do you mean? Lennie has no imagination whatever.'

'Yes he has. He has bought a little book, written by an Indian. It has all the different things we can do – when we're married of course. We were reading it together in the churchyard.'

At least I was glad that they were not anticipating the delights of marriage. Opinion about pre-marital intercourse is much divided in the Church of England, but I have always felt that the traditional doctrine has much to be said for it. Only after she had gone did I realise what had been happening in the churchyard and it made me sad. One should never expect anything but hypocrisy from the young.

'Well, goodbye, Nicholas,' she said.

I kissed her passionately. Perhaps it would be the last time I tasted her warmth. A lifetime of Gillian's frigid pecks stretched before me, and I clung to her desperately. Eventually she disentangled herself with her mad, irresponsible laugh and started tidying her jersey.

'I really must go. I am going to call on Lennie's mother.' It was inconceivable that Lennie had a mother.

'Don't go,' I said. 'I need you.' We both recognised something from a film or a television play and Danae laughed shyly. But she liked to think she was needed. 'You're all I've got in the world,' I said, with a half-embarrassed smirk. The tragedy of this was that it was true, which made it all the funnier in a way. We both laughed and Danae kissed me on the cheek.

'You've still got Gillian,' she said.

The mention of Gillian's name conjured an image of her waiting outside.

'There's one more thing, Danae. Could you please go and see her about family planning?'

Danae shook her head. 'Why should I? If that's the way she gets her kicks, I have no objection, but she can't practise on me.'

The vision of Gillian's hurt feelings and gloomy disapproval froze my soul. It was more than I could endure. 'Please Danae. If you've ever loved me, just do this one thing for me. It will make Gillian so happy.' She would make my life unbearable for a month if she had been forbidden her treat. Any mention of the wedding would revive her disappointment and I would have to listen to interminable harangues on the irresponsibility of modern youth.

'Why should I wish to make Gillian happy?' For the first time I saw a flash of affronted womanhood in her eyes. 'But if you ask me like that, I can't refuse.'

Meekly, she allowed me to lead her to Gillian's planning room. 'Do come in,' said Gillian. 'I'm so glad you have decided to be sensible.'

I left them with a lighter step. I had saved myself an enormous amount of trouble, as well as taking a positive step towards relieving congestion on what is, after all, an uncomfortably crowded island.

In the afternoon I had promised to join Mrs Hallowes' White Circle for one of their devotional periods. These meetings were a great embarrassment to me. Mrs Hallowes always greeted me in a white frilly nightdress, and her eyes glinted with pleasure behind enormous diamanté butterfly spectacles:

'Good afternoon, Brother Peter. Ai'm so glad to welcome you to our little meeting. Today we are going to practise the harvest rites performed to the great god Osiris on the banks of the River Naile. Here we have a little statue. The idea is that we pretend to worship it while the sun beats down on us and decides which is worthy to be the receptacle for the Laife Force in the coming year. Unfortunately, there is no sun, as you can see, but the River Thames should supply enough current for the Laife Force. It is much more turbulent than the Naile.'

Four or five women from the village then shuffled round a teak statuette of the sort that travellers bring back from Port Said, or Mozambique, or Lourdes, or wherever there is a flourishing tourist trade. Sister Jane (Mrs Gutterling) fell to the ground in a paroxysm of ecstasy, but the others suspected that she was showing off and ignored her. Afterwards, as we all sat in a damp wooden hut heating some Oxo cubes in a billy-can, Mrs Hallowes said: 'Ai hope you like our little meetings. The Church people have been rather against us in the past, but all that is changing now. I believe that we are actually more *scientific* than some of the things you practise in church. But you don't disapprove, do you?'

I thought about it. 'The only thing that worries me about your meetings, Mrs Hallowes…'

'Sister Beatrice, please.'

'Sister Beatrice, then. The only thing that worries me, as a clergyman, is the clothing you wear. Has it been fireproofed? A good many of these nylon nightdresses are highly inflammable and I couldn't condone the wearing of them in a religious ceremony if they didn't carry the guarantee of the British Standards Institute.'

'Ai thought you maight have some tainy religious scruples. But I think you're being a little old-fashioned. You must try and shake off all the centuries of ancient dogma. In the past, I know, the Church of England has always been resolutely opposed to inflammable nighties, but that teaching dates from before the population explosion and all the other exciting and wonderful things which are happening in the world. Your Church must move with the times, like the rest of us.'

'There may be something in what you say.'

'In any case, we only wear our robes in the winter. In summer, we meet unwrapped. You feel so much freer and somehow more receptive to the Laife Force which is pulsating all around us. Can you feel it now? Can you feel the presence of something very strange and wonderful?'

I didn't think so, but a denial would sound very churlish.

'What would that be, then?'

'Love,' said Mrs Hallowes. 'Love is the only protection we poor mortals have against the Dark Forces. Ours is the force of life, and creation, theirs is the force of death and destruction. Surely you can't disapprove of what we're doing?'

'No, indeed not. In summer, of course, it is different. So long as you keep your nighties discreetly in the background, I don't see that I can have any objection. Of course, creation is all very well, but you've got to have a sense of responsibility to the community. There is nothing in your creed which forbids sensible family planning?'

'We have nothing to do with sex at all. Indeed, if our bodies were not immaculately pure, they could never be conductors for the Laife Force. Our main occupation is preparing ourselves to engage in combat against the Dark Forces.'

'Are there many of them around?'

'We are not sure; but we are watching Miss Cornhouse. She spends a lot of time alone. However, we are ready for her when she strikes. Have you had any experience of the Dark Forces?'

'I don't think so, but my wife complains of strange noises in the house. She thinks they may be caused by the unquiet spirit of Mr Mandarill.'

'Mandarill,' breathed Mrs Hallowes. 'That is very interesting, and would explain a lot of things. Did you hear what Brother

Peter said, sisters? I think our moment may be at hand. I am very glad you came to me about this. We may be able to help you.'

'You know, Danae, I think, but have you met Leonard, who is going to be my son-in-law?' Mrs Boissaens was full of glee.

'Stepson-in-law,' I said. 'Yes, Lennie and I are old friends. We don't always agree, of course. He even took exception. with me on some point of behavioural judgement, and wrote in complaint to the Archdeacon.' I gave a full, fruity clergyman's laugh.

Lennie was not prepared to enter into the spirit of my little joke. He was looking resentful and truculent with a huge brandy glass which he kept swilling around ostentatiously, as if to emphasise the difference between our stations in life. He was also a little drunk.

'That's nothing to what I've got on you now, Mr Parson, if I decided to use it. Those riverside parties of yours must be quite interesting.'

'I haven't the faintest idea what you're talking about.'

'It's all right,' said Mrs Boissaens. 'We have had a little discussion and Leonard has agreed not to write the story. As you are going to officiate at the wedding, we thought it would only result in complications if there was a big scandal beforehand. Leonard is giving up his job at the end of the week in any case.'

'Oh really,' I said. 'What is he going to do?' I tried to sound sympathetic and interested in a grown-up sort of way, as if I was discussing a child's career with one of my parishioners. Danae gave me a glass of brandy. She was my only friend in the room and I loved her passionately, but I could not help noticing that it was a smaller glass than Lennie's.

'We haven't decided yet,' said Mrs Boissaens. She, too, was playing grown-ups. I was mysteriously included among those who would decide. 'We think he might like a stint running a coffee farm in Kenya, but my husband seems to think he should start in business.'

'From the bottom,' I said. 'It is the only way.'

'Vicar at witches' coven,' said Lennie dreamily. 'I can just see the headlines. Riverside orgies. Prehistoric cults. Strange happenings shatter the calm of peaceful country hamlet. It would certainly make the national dailies, and I shouldn't be at all surprised if some of the foreign papers picked it up. Just what do you get up to with the Magic Circle, Mr Parson?'

'It sounds fascinating,' said Danae. 'Do you think Mrs Hallowes would let me join?'

'I'm sure she would, but it is not really half as exciting as it sounds.

'Is it true that you have sexual intercourse and then sacrifice a sacrificial animal?' asked Lennie.

'No, of course not. They are White Witches.'

' "We are White Witches," explained the go-ahead Vicar of Middlewalk when confronted with reports of growing disquiet among his parishioners. His Archdeacon, Father Thomas Good-Buller, however, takes a different view.'

'Good Heavens, you haven't informed Mr Good-Buller?'

'Of course he hasn't. He's only joking,' said Danae.

'I'm not so sure,' said Lennie. 'It seems to me we may have a duty to bring this to the light of the authorities. Here you are posing as a man of religion, taking everybody in with your glib, pious talk about making love to each other and how we can only have abortions in certain circumstances when all the time you're practising witchcraft on the quiet.'

'You don't understand anything. If you ever came to church you might not sound quite so ignorant when you talk about religion. Have you ever heard of the oecumenical movement? So few people are interested in religion nowadays that the clergy have decided to pass the time of day together in a spirit of friendship. Also, it is very confusing to the average layman or man in the street who might be thinking of taking up religion as his hobby, when he finds so much freedom of choice and so much disagreement. It is this disagreement which is turning people away from religion in large numbers, or so they say, and the market won't support as much consumer choice as in the past. We are meeting people of other religions all over the world – not only Christians but also Jews, Buddhists, Mahommedans, in order to show them that we are all much the same, and it doesn't really matter what you believe in so long as it is religion. It is one of the great things which is happening in our time. I was not present at this meeting as a participant, merely as the official representative, locally, of my Church in the role of an observer. If I did not think it was vital work, I could scarcely spare the time.'

'Exactly. One can so easily get the wrong idea about things through reading the papers. I never read the papers for that reason,' said Mrs Boissaens. 'In any case, you can be quite sure that Leonard was only pulling your leg. He wouldn't want to pick a quarrel with his in-laws at this stage, would you Leonard?'

'That's all very well, but we journalists have our professional code,' said Lennie. 'We wouldn't mind stretching a point for a pal of ours, but if anyone tries coming over on us, he's for the chopper.'

'You're not a journalist any longer, Leonard. You must try and conduct yourself like the manager of a coffee farm, or a management trainee in the copper mines, or whatever we decide you should be.'

'I often think that our relationship with the Press is the field in which most development is needed,' I said in my blandest clerical way. 'So many people have the wrong image of the Church nowadays. They think of us as something old-fashioned and out-dated whose image is somehow only for the old and disappointed.'

'You're bloody right we do,' said Lennie.

I was about to give him the second half – how our message was one of love, compassion, modernism and keen enjoyment of the good things – when a bell rang.

'Good Heavens, that's Eugene. I had quite forgotten him,' said Mrs Boissaens. 'He particularly wanted to see you, Nicholas. Come along now.'

As we were leaving the great drawing room, with its red and gold decorations, I saw Lennie shifting uneasily on his carved Empire chair.

'Do you remember why it was you wrote to Father Good-Buller last time, Lennie? It has completely passed out of my mind, but I am sure Mrs Boissaens would like to hear about it.' I did not pause to watch the effect of my remark. Even to someone as drunk and naturally unintelligent as himself, the threat must have been unmistakable.

'Angela, please,' said Mrs Boissaens as she hobbled across the white marble hall.

'I beg your pardon.'

'I said you must really try calling me by my Christian name. There is not all that difference in our ages, after all.'

'I am sorry. I was not thinking.'

In the passage leading to Mr Boissaens' study, she turned to confront me. 'I just hope it will all turn out for the best. We can only keep our fingers crossed. Eugene can't stand him. My husband refused to have dinner with us this evening, and has shut himself up in his study all week, moping. You must try to cheer him up.' She was attempting to create a grown-up alliance between the two of us against the pathetically immature rest of the world. She may even have been trying to establish something else, but I was too much preoccupied to pay attention to it.

'Such a nice young man, Lennie,' I said, in the tone of voice which suggested that the conversation was over.

'I always say that sort of person is the salt of the earth. So unaffected and natural,' murmured Mrs Boissaens automatically. 'I only wish they were both a little older. Marriage seems such a drastic step to take at that age. Perhaps you disagree, being a clergyman. You must come up and we'll have a little talk about it some time. I am free most afternoons.'

'Yes, indeed. If Mr Boissaens has sent for me, perhaps we ought not to keep him waiting any longer.'

'What about Tuesday afternoon, then?'

'Alas, I have my Mothers' Union.'

'Wednesday?'

'There is a Chapter Meeting.'

'Thursday?'

'Confirmation class.'

'Friday?'

'Young Wives.'

'Saturday?'

'I must visit Mrs Tartfoot's father-in-law, who is dying. Perhaps it would be better if I got in touch with you.'

'Now I come to think about it tomorrow afternoon, Monday, might be all right.'

'I've got to visit Mr Heifer's Boy Scout troop at Silvercombe. I'm afraid they keep you rather busy as a clergyman.' With the exception of Wednesday, all my engagements were lies. But I did not want to be involved in any cosy chats with Mrs Boissaens. They might prove to be the occasions for sin. In any case, untruths whose sole purpose was to avoid hurting other people's feelings were white lies. I have no doubt that Jesus forgave me.

'Come in, Mr Trumpeter. I imagined that you had forgotten your appointment. You will find some sandwiches on the table. Angela will no doubt show you where the wine has been put before she goes away. I wish I could show you myself. What do you think of my new son-in-law?' My patron spoke more loudly than usual, with a nervous jocularity which I had never heard before.

'He seems a most remarkable young man.' I heard the door shut behind Angela, and felt able to speak more freely. 'So original of Danae to choose a husband from the working class. Whatever one says about the strides they have taken since the war, one still seldom thinks of them as marriage partners.'

'I do not share your English obsession with class,' said Mr Boissaens dryly. 'To hear Angela talk, you would think that Danae had chosen her mate exclusively on sociological grounds. But if you disregard the virtues which are proverbially associated with his class, do you think that he has anything to recommend him?'

'Perhaps not, but it is nevertheless a splendid gesture. Simple people are so much franker, more honest and despite their rough surface they often have a pretty shrewd brain under their warm hearts.'

'Sometimes I doubt whether you are being entirely honest with me, Nicholas. Do you really like him?'

'Of course not, but one has to be careful as a vicar. Nothing that one says must ever be construed as a criticism of the man in the street. In the case of Lennie it would be truer to say that underneath a mean and stupid exterior he hides such deep reserves of imbecility as make one doubt that he can be a human being at all, let alone a member of our English working class. Perhaps he is a changeling, the natural son of some property speculator in Slough.'

'Why a property speculator?'

'Religion teaches us that they are the lowest form of life nowadays, like the Pharisees of olden times.'

'I merely ask, because by coincidence one of the development companies in which I have an interest is undertaking a large project in Slough at the moment.'

'So, no doubt, are the Church Commissioners. Parables are not supposed to be taken literally. Why did you send for me?'

'To ask whether there was the smallest chance that you could prevent this frightful marriage from taking place.'

'None at all. Danae has made up her own mind, and she is quite old enough to do so.'

'Couldn't you have married her yourself? There was a time when she seemed fond of you, and you must know that I would put nothing in the way.'

We had been through all this before. I answered him wearily: 'I have the great misfortune to possess a wife already. Not much of one, it is true, but a wife nevertheless. It seemed unreasonable to expect Danae to wait until she dies. There is no question of vicars being allowed to divorce, at least until ten years' time when the shortage becomes acute. And I am simply not prepared to give up my job. Once you have been a vicar, anything else would be undignified and dull. I am wedded to it.'

'You are wedded to nothing but idleness.'

'Not at all. Here in Middlewalk I am an integral part of the community. I have an essential role to play. By my presence, I reassure the meanest and least reflective citizen that *somebody* believes they have an immortal soul and a greater importance than their useless existence seems to indicate, even if they lack the intellectual curiosity to enquire about it themselves. By my cheerful obsequiousness to all and sundry I establish a bridge between the social classes, removing much of the bitterness and envy with which they might compare your lot, for instance, to their own. By listening to a series of complicated medical complaints every morning I relieve pressure on the over-taxed Health Service. I also provide a focus for gossip, which is essential in any community of people who have little to do and who are constantly thrown upon each other's resources. And when the older ones die, poor dears, I am there to attach my stamp of importance on an event which might otherwise pass unnoticed. Ours is not a large community, Mr Boissaens, but there is something to be said for the plight of a big fish in a small pond.'

'Very well, then, I must reconcile myself. It is all I can do at this stage. One does not like to name figures, but do you know that Danae and her husband, as they wake up after their wedding night, will be in virtually sole control of a fortune of some eight million pounds?'

It seemed much too much at their age. 'Is this really wise?' I said.

'It is the only way in which we can be sure of avoiding death duties.'

'Do you think it right to avoid taxes? Many people would equate it with stealing. Think of the welfare centres the Government could build, the kidney machines it could buy, the assistance to those in need, the teachers, the exciting social experiments, the aid to the underdeveloped...'

'...the gallons of free milk, the boundless horizons of prosperity and progress. I like having a clergyman around, Nicholas. You are well worth the pitiful allowance I make you. Your ideas are so novel, so exciting, so passionately felt.'

We both had a good laugh over that. It was seldom in life that one could laugh because one was amused. People in the village were liable to laugh if one complained about the weather, and it was always one's duty, as spiritual leader, to laugh back. Gillian never laughed, except bitterly, as a debating gambit. Cyril Heifer and I occasionally laughed at Chapter Meetings, but it was not encouraged.

'Are you trying to convert me to your Church's way of thinking?' asked Mr Boissaens.

'I don't think that we have any particular way of thinking.' I said.

'Probably not,' said Mr Boissaens. 'In any case, I think it is too late to convert me to anything. I am beginning to lose interest. What does your Church teach about Communism?'

'My Church feels most strongly that while it cannot accept at this stage the regrettable anti-religious bias apparent in some Communist countries, nevertheless when Communism reaches maturity it will understand that such institutions as the Church of England can be a positive help in the foundation of a more equitable society, in which we all believe. Many of the things in which Communists place their faith – like more comprehensive social security schemes and cheaper housing – are directly in line with Anglican thought, and there is certainly room for a dialogue. So long as Communists do nothing to interfere with freedom of choice in matters of religion, or with the traditional rights of the Church, there is no reason to suppose that we would do worse under Communism than we do under the present system.'

I had drunk nearly a bottle of champagne and was feeling loquacious. It was so seldom that one met people who were interested in what one had to say. Nearly all conversation was either a pathetic effort to bolster one's own and other people's self-esteem or an unheeded succession of monologues.

'In other words, your Church teaches nothing whatever about Communism, and has no feelings on the subject. Neither have I. It is a monument to human stupidity, but the stupidity is already there without such an obvious monument to it. It is not a thing you can fight against or regret.'

'Well said. I have always thought that you are basically an Anglican, Mr Boissaens, however much you may resent the suggestion.'

'You may say so, but I shall never come into your ridiculous Church nor give any money to your ridiculous causes.'

'Nor do most Anglicans. Fortunately, we are self-supporting.'

'But I have decided to make a further gift to the Old People's Hall. You may remember that we discussed it. A statue. I commissioned it from a very highly thought of young sculptor in London, Ian Sturgeon. Do you know his work? He is a brother of John Sturgeon, the painter. I think we might inspect it together. Perhaps you would be kind enough to push me to the lift. The work of art is stored in the cellar at the moment, but I thought we might erect it in front of the village hall after the wedding. You must understand that I commissioned it not so much as a gesture of goodwill towards the villagers, but because I thought it might amuse you. Having lived with a joke for so long, I find it has palled. The theme of the composition, I am told by the artist, is man's exploitation of man, but what I asked for was a simple scene at one of my diamond mines, from the proceeds of which your Old People's Dance Hall was built.'

In the lift, he continued to talk in a nervous and distracted way. I pushed him through the corridors by which I had once entered the Hall.

'Typical, really, of the conceit and pretentiousness of our young artists to give it an abstract title, although the subject is clear as daylight. Do not suppose that I wished to encourage modern art, or make a name for myself as patron of the arts. Patronage is nowadays a municipal affair, and what alderman has ever been able to tell a human breast from a cabbage? Private patrons are either looking for a commercial investment or anxious to ingratiate themselves with art critics. You will understand that I have not been able to inspect the statue, but I have got the feel of it with my hands. It is one of the few disadvantages of blindness that one cannot enjoy the arts. My father, you know, had the most beautiful collection of paintings in Brussels – Breughels, mostly – and another collection of the early French Romantics in Amsterdam. We never took any of our pictures to South Africa, because he thought the climate would damage them. I suppose I must have seen most of the world's great paintings in my youth, and I have no reason to suppose that anything worth looking at has been painted since. You go down to the end of the corridor and it is the door on your left. The light switch is behind you.'

Ian Sturgeon's masterpiece was one of the most revolting things I had ever seen in my life. It would have been funny if it had been more pretentious. A bronze group, about twelve feet long and life size, showed a huge man in Nazi uniform, with jackboots, brandishing a whip over a naked bending negro. His foot was firmly planted on the neck of another negro, whose emaciated body merged into the ground. A second jackbooted figure was peering into the negro's behind.

'Is that what it really looks like?'

'How can I possibly know,' said Mr Boissaens in irritation.

Gillian listened to my story with pursed lips.

'How very childish,' she said automatically. 'I think Sturgeon may have a point, though. What he is trying to get at, unless I am very much mistaken, is the new theory of psychologists that the roots of human motivation are not sexual, as Freud thought, but anal.'

'Is that what they think nowadays?' I asked as I turned my back on her and prepared for sleep. 'How very interesting. I wonder why they never thought of that before.'

In my dreams, Mrs Boissaens came to me. She spoke with her head turned aside, as if to indicate that she would forget the words as soon as they were out of her mouth:

'If you would like to be sensible and come to bed with me we can go upstairs now. We shall both forget about it afterwards. It will be the greatest fun. There is something new I would like us to try, called the Italian Method.'

I woke in a panic, sweating horribly.

'You look awful,' said Gillian, who was still reading her magazine beside me. 'Are you unwell?'

CHAPTER NINE

'I publish the Banns of Marriage between Leonard P Hutton, resident at the Bag of Corn, Middlewalk, and Danae Immaculata Gwendolen Boissaens, of the Hall at Middlewalk. If any of you know cause or just impediment why these two should not be joined together in holy matrimony, ye are to declare it. This is the third time of asking.'

Each occasion had wrung my heart, but even as I desperately searched the congregation for a response I knew that there would be no cause or just impediment. Three old women and Mrs Boissaens were the only people who had responded to Christ's message this morning.

After Morning Service, Mrs Boissaens approached me coyly from behind a tombstone. Mrs Hallowes, Miss Cornhouse, George Swinger and Mrs Gutterling stared at us, standing in a speechless group outside the porch.

'I am still waiting for you to say when you can come up and see me. We must talk about the ceremony.'

'Everything is already arranged for the wedding. Danae came to me for pre-marriage instruction and we held a brief rehearsal yesterday with Mr Swinger standing in for Lennie. Nothing can go wrong.'

'I was not referring to the marriage. That will soon be over and then we can settle down to serious life again. You know that they are honeymooning in Kenya? As a result Eugene and I are staying in England until March. It is extremely generous of him, I suppose, but really most inconvenient. Why can't they go to Barbados like everyone else? There is nothing for them to do in Kenya except entertain the neighbours, and I don't think Lennie plays Bridge. He can always learn, of course. The other day he tried teaching us a little game of his own, called Jack Snap or something. So amusing. Unfortunately it ended rather unpleasantly as I hadn't understood about the money part. But I certainly can't see the Hampsteads mastering it, or the Butch-Etheringtons, or even the Bullocks. Sam Bullock is such an unusual man – he looks just like a farmer, with a very violent temper. They say he murdered his first wife. One year, I hope you'll be able to come out to Kenya with us if everything goes well. As you know, there are a lot of coloured people there which should be interesting to someone in your job. Most of them are absolutely charming, although you have to be careful nowadays not to offend them. Will you come to Kenya one year?'

'I should be delighted.'

'Good. I'm so glad. One really only gets to know people abroad. What I want to discuss with you is the ceremony for Eugene's statue. We both think it a very good idea that there should be something modern in the village. It will liven them up and stop them becoming too stick-in-the-mud. Of course, I can't understand it, but then nobody could understand Michelangelo in his lifetime, could they? One just has to be humble in the face of genius like Ian Sturgeon's. Eugene says it's all about South Africa. I used to like visiting the Cape, but it has become much more difficult now. You have to pay all sorts of social security contributions for your staff and guarantee them a day's holiday every week. How can you possibly guarantee them a day's holiday when, for all you know, they might be needed? Soon it will be as bad as England. You have to pay much higher wages than in Kenya, and they're only interested in money. Honestly, I can quite understand why South Africa is so unpopular with other countries nowadays. Too much prosperity always spoils people. They lose touch with the spiritual side. That's what the statue is trying to say, I think. But we must discuss it all together. When are you free? I am so excited by the whole thing.'

As I suspected, she was anally orientated. If the statue had the same effect on everyone in the village, the place would become uninhabitable. Perhaps it was a clever piece of humanist propaganda designed to pervert our village life. In any case, it must be resisted with all the power and majesty of the Church.

'I am much too busy. I have not a moment to spare. Not this week, next week, or ever. My work is too important,' I blurted.

I stared straight into her stupid, puzzled eyes and walked past, giving a wide berth to the soft, sybaritic bottom exposed enticingly to the world under its tweed skirt, and elastic panties. Then, still in my surplice and stole, I picked up the skirts of my cassock and ran back to the Rectory.

Wednesday morning dawned as one of those freak December mornings when the sun shines, birds sing and there is a sweet, timeless smell in the air which reminds us of the beauty of God's creation. I had passed a troubled night and rose early to walk around the garden. It was still nearly dark, and I saw a light in Mrs Tartfoot's window. Why do old people always get up early? They have nothing to do, and every waking minute seems a torment to them. Then I remembered that old Mr Tartfoot was dying upstairs. I had called on him twice to see how he was getting on, but he seemed no worse. It was intolerable the way they could find no room for such people in hospital. He might lie there for three weeks putting everyone to endless inconvenience. I often wished the Church of England was more militant. We should march and demonstrate and shout our convictions, insisting on our right to be heard and demanding an immediate improvement in the Health Service. If only I could mobilise my troops — Miss Cornhouse, George Swinger, the White Witches, the Youth Club, the Mothers' Union, the Young Wives — into a fighting force ready for combat and sparing no punches, we might be in a position to influence events and it would no longer be necessary for me to face the damp, reproachful stare of Mrs Tartfoot every other morning. The vicar's job was to speed the dying on their way, and I had let her down.

'Well, Mrs Tartfoot,' I would say with a brave smile. 'We must try again. You hold the book and give the responses in a loud, clear voice and I'm sure it won't be long.'

Mr Tartfoot looked out of his bed, half understanding what was going on – neither pleased nor annoyed nor even much interested. It was difficult to know why one bothered:

Self: 'Oh Lord, save Thy servant.'

Mrs Tartfoot: 'Who putteth his trust in Thee.'

Self: 'Send him help from Thy holy place.'

Mrs Tartfoot: 'And evermore mightily defend him.'

Self: 'Let the enemy have no advantage of him.'

And so it went on. Then I would fix him with an embarrassed little smile, as if to assure him that there was no need to take it too seriously, and read the prayer:

'Take therefore in good part time chastisement of the Lord. For whom the Lord loveth he chastiseth, and scourgeth every son whom he receiveth. But if ye be without chastisement, whereof all are partakers, then are ye bastards, and not sons. Furthermore, we have had fathers of our flesh, which corrected us, and we gave them reverence: shall we not much rather be in subjection to the Father of spirits, and live? For they verily, for a few days chastened us after their own pleasure; but He for our profit, that we might be partakers of His holiness.'

A curious picture of family life, I sometimes reflected. Was it normal, in Biblical times, to whip your children for fun? The idea that modern parents corrected their children, or that children reverenced their parents, was hopelessly out-dated. It was all a gigantic waste of time. What possible reason could there be to perpetuate the existence of Mr Tartfoot? Or my own? The Church of England had a vital role to play – in urging the improvement of the Health Service, in combating the new anal orientation of modern society, and in providing a reasonably civilised existence for its priests. Mr Tartfoot was an irrelevance.

The wedding was arranged for the unfashionable hour of eleven-thirty, because the young couple had to catch a four o'clock aeroplane to Nairobi. Long before eleven the first motor cars began to arrive – huge Bentleys and Rolls-Royces, carrying directors of Mr Boissaens' English interests, Jaguars and Mercedes-Benzes carrying the English representatives of foreign companies, Austin Princesses and Rovers carrying bank managers, accountants, solicitors and their wives. Once a great Cadillac arrived carrying a Dutch cousin, but when the occupant – a tiny, wizened dwarf of a woman in her late fifties – discovered she was early, it drove away again. A brother of Danae's mother appeared, a handsome, proud Belgian of Portuguese extraction with more than a touch of the tar-brush – possibly he was from Goa or Mozambique. A message the previous evening had told me that Danae was to be given away by Mr Orison, the Canadian adviser, as Mr Boissaens could not reconcile it with his conscience to attend church. Lennie arrived five minutes early, looking more than usually fatuous in a grey morning suit, but strangely confident.

Finally my darling Danae – serene, radiant, devastatingly sexual in a long heavy silk gown of the purest white.

'Dearly beloved, we are gathered together in the sight of God, and in the face of this congregation, to join together this man and this woman in holy matrimony...'

Danae stood still, polite attentiveness written all over her wicked, beautiful face. Lennie fidgeted with his waistcoat pocket and cocked a satirical eye at me. Members of the congregation began to relax and look around.

'And therefore is not by any to be enterprised, nor taken in hand, unadvisedly, lightly, or wantonly, to satisfy men's carnal lusts and appetites, like brute beasts that have no understanding; but reverently, discreetly, advisedly, soberly and in the fear of

God; duly considering the causes for which Matrimony was ordained…'

Mrs Boissaens was fluttering her gloves to me in a chirpy way. The whole scene was a torment. As I glanced round the elegant company I did not see a single person who was not impeccably dressed, or whose countenance was not correct in every particular. Was it for this that Christ came to earth and was crucified, that men had fought and died, built great monuments and shut themselves up in cells for all their natural lives? Even if it was all a ghastly mistake, it deserved better than this.

'Wilt thou, Leonard, have this woman to thy wedded wife…?' Of course he would.

'Wilt thou, Danae… *So long as ye both shall live?*' Something of the desperate appeal in my voice must have communicated itself to her, because she fixed her great brown eyes with a tender and compassionate regard on my face before replying that she fully intended to love, honour and keep her sub-human mate in sickness and in health, for as long as she lived. And I, the witness to this grisly deal, had only Gillian. While the angels wept, I pronounced my Blessing.

As I climbed to the pulpit, I heard the congregation shifting around to more comfortable positions. Soon, I hoped, they would be sitting up. What I had to say was going to electrify the whole neighbourhood, not to say the whole country.

'In the name of the Father, and of the Son and of the Holy Spirit,' I said. All around the church, people began pretending to read their prayer books, or staring into space, or cupping their faces in their hands and dozing off.

'Marriage is the ceremony by which the Church witnesses a sacrament bestowed directly by God upon two people. It is not, as unreligious people might suppose, merely a licence provided by Church authority for the connubial embrace known to us all as sexual intercourse. Sexual attraction is undoubtedly the motivating force behind the decision to marry, just as Freud has taught us that sexual drive is the motivating force behind many of our actions. The Church fully accepts Freud's thesis, and welcomes it, adding only that we must accept it as a holy, as well as a natural, thing that two young people should feel attracted to each other and, to put it crudely, want to hop into bed. It is an example of God's working in our everyday lives when this happens. The consummation of this urge, which we understand and Freud does not, lies in the conception and rearing of children, but all along the line it is a holy and God-given thing.'

Five years ago, any mention of sex from the pulpit would have had all sitting bolt upright and writing letters of complaint to the Bishop. Nowadays, it was expected. Sonorous words like abortion, promiscuity and divorce rolled over their heads unheeded, just as words like damnation, retribution and hell had lulled earlier generations to sleep. Few appeared to pay any attention at all. So long as they occasionally made out familiar phrases – young people today, underdeveloped nations, concern for the elderly, hopeful future, venereal diseases, church unity, preoccupation with sex, modern age, welcome the challenge – they were reassured that, at any rate for the duration of the service, God was in His Heaven and all was right with the world. But they had heard nothing yet. I was going to attack their complacency at its very roots:

'But there is a murkier side to the coin. As we all know, the Church welcomes sex and blesses it – indeed we are gathered together to give it our blessing today, as a life-creating and wholesome thing designed by God to satisfy our lives, to increase our knowledge and love of each other and, where necessary or prudent, to perpetuate the species. Sex is the life force through which we become aware in one part of our bodies and through the whole of our consciousness of God's undiminished activity on earth. Now we all know that there are powerful, almost as ancient forces at work to frustrate God's purpose. Just as God works through the reproductive organs of the human body, these forces of evil are centring their activities around the human anus.'

Nobody seemed much concerned by my revelation. Rows upon rows of faces exhibited only the polite blankness which every clergyman recognises as the countenance with which Englishmen receive Christ's message. Danae seemed to be listening, and looked worried. Of course, she had something to worry about. Few of the people present, I should guess, were totally untouched by the modern evil I was castigating, but so great was their complacency and hypocrisy that they pretended not to hear.

'If our sexual organs are the instruments of life and hope, the anus is our symbol of death and rejection. Why, then, do people seek to elevate it, pretending to see there a mainspring of our human activities, and aspirations and concerns? Is it conscious perversity, or a misguided quest for truth, or merely a symptom of some illness in our society? Whatever it is, the new anal fixation is something we must fight against whenever we see it – on advertisement hoardings, on television, in the more sensational brand of newspaper – and be on our guard never to let it influence our own behaviour patterns, regardless of anything that may be fashionable or smart or expected of one, in the disturbing complexity of modern life.

'Above all, we must see it as a challenge. As Christians and human beings we must keep sight of the fact that the engine in which it has pleased God to house our immortal spirits is carefully and intelligently constructed. We use our eyes to see, our teeth to chew, our fingers and hands in the countless occupations for which they were designed – cleaning our teeth, lighting our cigarettes, fondling our lovers, adjusting our television sets, opening a tin of food. Is there any good reason why we should not keep the anus in a similar perspective? I am not one to argue that a sense of shame should attach to what is, after all, an entirely necessary and natural function. That would be to return to the Middle Ages, with its poor living standards and inadequate social security arrangements. Indeed much misery has been caused, we are told, by the guilt which was traditionally

associated with going to the lavatory in Victorian times. But now
the pendulum has swung too far. Our society has lost its purpose,
and seeks to rediscover it in an anal explanation for all the things
which have puzzled us in the past. This is a false orientation. It is
time we returned to our traditional standards. We must not be
afraid to stand up and be counted among those who, against
prevailing fashion, believe that the basis of human compassion,
wisdom and motivation is sexual and not anal. We must not be
afraid of being denigrated as traditionalists. That is what religion
is about. Our fathers, for several generations, recognised the
sexual urge as nature's great force on which all human patterns
were shaped. Religion, after a time, accepted this. If sex is the
highest expression of love known to mortal intelligence, and God
is love, as we are taught by St John, then it must follow that
human understanding of God can best be reached through sex.
There are those who will maintain that the present anal obsession
is a development from this. It is not. It is a perversion and a
denial.'

Nobody was interested. Nobody wanted to know about the
most important discovery I had made. But then, nobody was
listening. There is something about a sermon in church which
causes people to transfer their attention, just as certain television
sets have been trained to switch off during commercials. I might
have been advocating a nuclear crusade against China or
euthanasia for the mentally sick or a thousand other novel and
exciting ideas. They simply did not want to know about it.

'Man has been around for millions of years and it is time he
raised his eyes above his anus,' I shouted. 'Do you suppose that
our resurrected bodies will have anuses? Of course they won't.
There isn't a single anus in the whole Kingdom of Heaven. Those
who seek happiness on earth through their anuses are wasting
their time and my own, standing in this pulpit talking to a lot of
sleepy hypocrites. Life began in the womb and will return to the
womb. The anus is an irrelevance, and those who talk of it in the

same breath as they talk of the womb are committing a blasphemy before God and before man's intelligence.'

I had allowed my voice to rise to a scream, and I thumped the pulpit with my prayer book. A few members of the congregation nodded sagely, their minds far away. A few others squirmed uncomfortably. They had not been warned that there was a violent, Left-Wing sort of clergyman in Middlewalk. The only well-bred thing to do was to ignore the whole thing. I had to admit defeat. Mrs Boissaens looked brightly alert, her head cocked on one side like a parrot trying to endear itself. Clearly she had not listened to a word.

'In the name of the Father and of the Son and of the Holy Spirit,' I said.

A huge marquee had been built on the lawn for the reception. In it congregated those of humble station, to be given shallow glasses of Moët and Chandon's non-vintage champagne.

I left Gillian there and walked into the great painted saloon, where more important guests were served with goblets of Dom Perignon. The large dining-room, which I had only seen used once, after my induction, was laid for forty people. There was no place for Gillian. Danae stood at the end of a long line, with a kind word for everyone.

'Nicholas, darling. What a lovely sermon. Do you know, I think you have converted me to the Church. No honestly, I'm serious. It's so seldom you find sincerity nowadays. Can I come and talk to you about it when we get back? No, really, I was most impressed.'

I kissed her just under the place where the jaw-bone joins the neck. It was always a favourite place of mine.

'Ha-ha. Rector's privilege,' I said, and kissed her there again.

'Come on, break it up,' said Lennie, whom marriage had mellowed. 'Couldn't make out the sermon myself, I'm afraid. Miles above my head. But if you want some hard liquor, ask Manuelo for the whisky. He's keeping some under the table.

Never try to fob clergymen off with the soft stuff. Ha ha.' He indicated the butler.

'Ha-ha.' I gave my fruity clerical laugh, and kissed Danae again.

'Come along,' said Mr Perrins, who was Master of Ceremonies. 'You're keeping the queue waiting.'

I was hustled away with just time to squeeze Danae's hand.

At lunch I sat between a blue-haired American lady who told me she kept Java sparrows and the atrocious Mrs Boissaens. There was still no sign of Mr Boissaens. I was not feeling well, and did not enjoy the food. Afterwards, Mr Perrins drew me aside and said that my presence was required in the library.

After the inane chatter of the drawing-room I found the atmosphere in the library strangely exhilarating. Four desks were drawn together on which a profusion of documents was neatly arranged. About eight men stood around with other documents waiting to be signed. In the quiet efficiency of it all, nobody spoke above a murmur.

'Parson's here, sir,' said Mr Perrins.

'I wonder if you would kindly consent to witness some share transfers and other transactions which must be attended to. It shouldn't take more than a couple of hours,' said Mr Boissaens. 'You and Perrins are the only witnesses required. Hutton and his wife signed everything necessary this morning. If you would like anything explained to you, perhaps you will ask Mr Orison. Mr Forsythe will explain any legal matters. You already know Mr Kitchen, of Lillibet and Sprigman. Señor Perreira will explain any matter of Brazilian law. Mr Rubinstein is an expert on international monetary regulations, and this is his counsel, Mr...'

'Keating,' said a pert, precise young voice. 'How do you do.'

'Mr Orison you know. Do you know Lucius van Witte, from London, an old friend? Captain Kerby can fill in anything about Katanga or Rhodesia or Zambia, and Delano Kaptain you probably know about.'

'Thank you very much, but it will not really be necessary,' I said.

'I never sign anything until I know what I'm signing,' said Mr Perrins.

'Quite right,' said Mr Boissaens. 'You are a man after Forsythe's heart.'

'Here we have 250,000 Ordinary shares in California Railroad and Steel investments, held in Mr Boissaens' name. They do not constitute a majority holding, of course, but in conjunction with this block of 75,000 held in the name of Witwatersrand Securities and a further block of 102,000 held by our two Dutch companies it will give Miss Danae and her husband effective control.' Mr Orison spoke in a discreet sing-song.

'Junk,' said Mr Kaptain. 'You're doing a smart thing to get shot of them, Eugene.'

'Not at all,' said Mr Boissaens. 'California Railroad owns some of the potentially most valuable property in San Francisco. As soon as we can close down the train services, shares will be worth three or four times their present value.'

'The holding in Société Mutuelle of Brussels is complete, except for a one-third holding administered in her lifetime for the benefit of Mr Boissaens' cousin, Madame Schaverno. Seven different holdings in Dutch KLM, Shell and English Shell add up to no more than a satisfactory investment. In Canada we have a fairly satisfactory picture…'

His voice droned on and on. I signed everything put in front of me. At the end Mr Kaptain said: 'Phew, what does that leave you then, Eugene?'

'You see me now as I arrived into the world, in the state of unaccommodated man. Perhaps there is just enough money left to pay the Stamp Duty.'

A few of the more knowledgeable people laughed. 'We needn't worry too much about that, Mr Kaptain. He still has enough to keep the wolf from the door. Few of the English investments have been touched.'

'Who wants anything to do with English investments?' said Mr Boissaens. 'I would not burden a cat with them. It is thought immoral to own them, and this is only permitted until the Government can think of some way to remove them which will not plunge the country into economic ruin. There is no fun to be had from subsidising the living standards of the English working class. When I die, they will nearly all be confiscated anyway. It will leave Angela enough to live in some comfortable hotel at Bournemouth, and go on cruises twice a year. What more can an unimaginative person possibly want?'

'I heard your marriage had run into difficulties,' said Mr Kaptain, with the delicacy of a wounded elephant. 'Nobody was sorrier to hear about it than Myrtle and I.'

'Myrtle?'

'Mrs Kaptain,' murmured Mr Orison.

'My fourth,' said Delano Kaptain proudly. 'You probably knew Mary.'

Mr Boissaens was bored. 'That will do. I won't keep you all any longer. Thank you very much. Goodbye. Thank you very much. Goodbye. I won't keep you any longer.'

His rudeness was always unbelievable. As I left, he said: 'Would you like to come up for dinner this evening, Nicholas? We won't have any of the women. I feel rather like a game of chess. There are too many people around today.'

When I returned to the Rectory, it was plain that Gillian was tipsy. She had drunk far too much champagne at the wedding and had now finished my bottle of Cyprus sherry, bought for Danae nearly three months before.

'I have been working while you were trying to pass yourself off as a member of the upper classes at the Hall.'

'Oh really? What have you been doing?'

'I have decided to strip all the paint off the panelling in the planning room. It is too gloomy for words. Did you have fun?'

'You must be mad. It would take four men a week's work.'

'One has to make a start sometime. I know I can expect no help from you. I'm not sure I would be prepared to trust you with the paint remover, in any case. It is deadly poison – even if it gets on your skin it can affect you. I think I will keep it locked up, away from naughty little boys. Do you know, I had a caller?'

'Oh really?' Who could conceivably wish to see Gillian?

'I had a long talk with somebody. We discussed so many things. I think he is quite interested in me. Of course, you would not be able to understand that anyone should see me as a woman. A few people, you know, might find me attractive. It was quite like civilisation, discussing personal problems over a glass of sherry.'

She was correct in supposing that I would be intrigued, but I was not going to ask her for the name of her demon lover. It would be bad for her character if I showed too much interest.

'I suppose you finished the sherry.'

'No, there is plenty left.' I could see the empty bottle from where I sat. 'Aren't you even going to ask me who it was?'

'If you wish to tell me.'

'I think it right that you should know. I do not believe in underhand dealings, like you and that absurd Mrs Boissaens. If I decide to have an affair, that is my business. You certainly have no cause to complain after the way you have treated me. Cyril was most sympathetic.'

'Cyril?'

'Heifer.'

I threw back my head and laughed helplessly. There was no malice in it. Perhaps I had had too much to drink, too.

'I am glad you think it's funny,' said Gillian. 'Cyril was far more sympathetic than you have ever been. Also, I think, he is more mature. Certainly, he is much more of a man.'

It would have been unkind to point out what most of the world already knew, that my great friend Cyril was only interested in boys. Just because he did not wiggle his behind and talk in an affected voice about modern art nobody would ever have described him as a homosexual. He was a plain, old-fashioned bugger. Poor Gillian.

'What did he want?'

'I imagine he came to see me.'

'Apart from establishing a clandestine liaison with my wife, did he have anything to tell me?'

'There is absolutely nothing clandestine in our relationship. Of course, small boys always think of sex as something wicked and dirty. That's half the fun of it for people like yourself. As a matter of fact he did mention something about Mr Tuck having a nervous breakdown.'

'Has he, now? That's interesting. I can't pretend I'm surprised. If they will over-work us the way they do, it is all they can expect.'

'Cyril didn't think it was genuine. Father Good-Buller has had him removed to a special institution in Wiltshire for clergy who have had nervous breakdowns. Cyril thinks that it is a stratagem of Father Good-Buller's to remove progressives and other people who don't toe the party line.'

'He may be right. I wonder who will be next to go?'

'Typical of you to be more interested in selfish affairs than in your wife's personal relationships. I waste my time talking. If it's all the same to you, I am going to the toilet.' She rose with icy dignity and left the room.

In years of marriage, I thought I had trained myself to exclude her from my thoughts. Now that something interesting had happened, she would never stop intruding her own fatuous concerns. Gillian was an irrelevance. One day, I would have to dispose of her. Like everyone else, she was anally orientated. Indeed, she had started the rot which it was my mission in life to stamp out. Without any clear idea of what I intended to do, I picked up the empty sherry bottle and carried it to Gillian's planning room. Contraceptives lay in neat rows upon the shelves. The white coat which Gillian affected when she was planning hung on the door. In a corner, I saw where she had started work on stripping the paint. A tiny patch of panelling was paler than the rest. She would never finish it, of course. The tin of paint remover was open on the floor. I picked it up and carefully poured about half into the sherry bottle, which I returned to the sitting room.

After that, I felt the effects of shock and decided to leave the house for a time. Mrs Hallowes sometimes served parsnip wine when I called on her in the afternoons. It was very nasty, but nobody could pretend that a priest's vocation is all roses. I had been quite right to put some of the paint remover safely in a bottle. It was extremely dangerous to leave it open and unattended. Besides, if one was completely honest with oneself, one never knew one's luck. But somehow I preferred to be out of the house.

'Brother Peter, Ai'm so delighted to see you. Will you tray a little of my parsnip waine?' Mrs Hallowes' diamanté butterfly spectacles glittered like the Crown Jewels in the last rays of the afternoon sun. She was a most fascinating woman.

'I had rather hoped to find you in,' I said.

'And here I am. But Ai had been rather hoping to see you, my dear. We have arranged a little meeting for tomorrow evening.'

'I'm afraid I'm rather busy these days.'

'But you *must* attend. It concerns you. We are going to order the spirit of Mr Mandarill to remain at peace.'

'As a matter of fact, he has not been causing much trouble recently. In any case, after today it may not be necessary.'

'In that case, we shall hold a service of reconciliation and thanksgiving. But Ai must beg you to attend. We may need some of the facilities of the Church.'

'Oh, all right. But you must never let anyone know about it.'

'Of course we shouldn't. It is inconceivable that any of us, even under pain of death, would impart information to anyone who was not an adept of the Mysteries. If anything comes out, deny it and we will support you. Of course, when summer comes our meetings are more enjoyable. Then, I hope, you will become a fully-fledged member.'

I stayed with Mrs Hallowes until half past seven. Hers was a warm, hospitable hearth, and I did not look forward to my return. Back at the Rectory, I could see no sign of Gillian. The bottle of sherry had been taken from the sitting-room. My heart missed a beat when I saw it. Suppose there had been an accident? Accidents in the home accounted for more deaths annually than either road casualties or cancer. It was high time the Government did something about them. But I lacked the courage to investigate.

The house was eerily quiet as I drove away in our little Morris Minor to keep my dinner date at the Hall.

Mr Boissaens was despondent.

'If you insist on moving your Bishop into a fatuous position threatening my pawn, which is guarded, I shall take your Queen.'

'I am sorry. I did not notice. Can I take it back?'

'Certainly not,' said Mr Boissaens. 'It is no reason why you should be protected from the consequences of your actions to say that you are unobservant. But it will remove much of the enjoyment I can expect to derive from the game. I suggest that you should admit yourself beaten. We shall not play another. Your game lacks both intelligence and originality, although normally you can avoid simple mistakes like this one. Shall we play piquet?'

'If you wish.' His cards were special ones, with Braille marks at both ends and, most unintelligently, on both sides, so that I could often see half the cards in his hand as he did not know which way they faced. It was very little help in a game of piquet, but distracting nevertheless.

'How many people at the wedding, do you suppose, believed in the existence of God?'

'Very few,' I said. 'But belief in the existence of God is not necessary for membership of my Church, merely a willingness to believe. If you would like to believe in God, you are more than half of the way there.'

'I have no particular desire to believe in anything so plainly absurd. You are the elder hand. Are you ready?'

'Or even a feeling of goodwill towards your fellow men.'

'I have very little of that. How many cards have you taken?'

'Five. But you do not enjoy the thought of human suffering?'

'Not particularly. I will take three.'

'In fact you think, on the whole, that it is something to be avoided. I have a point of six, a minor quart – is that good? – a tierce, three aces and three knaves. Twenty-nine points.'

'Not at all. I have four queens and three kings. Seventeen points to me, twenty-three to you. Your lead. Just because I do not happen to relish the thought of human suffering, there is no need to visit church every Sunday and celebrate the fact.'

'That is rather the new idea inside the Church. I should definitely say you were a South Banker. Ace of Hearts led. The new idea is that you should exercise your compassion for lower paid workers, etc. at home. Now the King of Hearts. Twenty-five.'

'I have no compassion for the lower paid worker. If he is unhappy, he should move to another part of the country and get a better paid job. If he's not unhappy, he should shut up about it. What have you led?'

'The knave. I don't think you have any Hearts left. But of course people enjoy feeling compassionate, and our job is to promote this type of enjoyment. You can't wish to deny a little honest enjoyment to simple people, of lower intelligence than yourself – ordinary working people, who have few sources of pleasure. Twenty-nine. That's my last Heart.'

'I cannot understand this cult of the working class. Many working people may be delightful – a great many, of course, are not – but if one has to describe those qualities which are peculiar to the working class one would have to say that they are by and large less intelligent, less adventurous, less ambitious, less amusing and altogether less interesting than members of any other class. Does that exclude me from the Church of England?'

'Certainly not. It adds up to no more than an interesting contribution to the general dialogue. There is no point of belief or disbelief so extreme that it cannot be accommodated inside the Established Church. That is what we are here for. Ace of Clubs led. That's thirty. Now my knave to your king. That's thirty-one.'

'Eighteen,' said Mr Boissaens. 'Damn. You haven't left me anything to lead. Is there nothing I can do to put myself outside the pale of your Church?'

'Nothing that won't be forgiven immediately you've done it. You see, our God is all-merciful. Formerly we used to say that pride was the ultimate sin, and that anybody who died in that state, having consistently held it over a long period would be in trouble hereafter. But few people nowadays are prepared to accept the idea of eternal punishment for what is, after all, only an extension of self-respect. I think despair is the only really dangerous thing. We used to talk about Faith, Hope and Charity. In modern terms, they mean occasional attendance at church, optimism and compassion for those less well situated than ourselves. The first is not really necessary, and the third is highly enjoyable in any case. Optimism is the most difficult for rational people, and therefore the most important. Eight of Clubs led. You haven't any left. That's thirty-six, forty-six for the cards and you have nineteen. Are you optimistic? It's purely a discipline, and comes naturally to those who try hard enough. Your elder hand. I'll deal. Would you like to cut?'

At the end of the game he was Rubicon, and I had won £5 6s. at 6d. a point. I have never thought it cheating to glance at the bottom card when dealing a minor hand. It is merely a sensible precaution.

'I have been waiting for Danae to marry these last six years,' said Mr Boissaens. 'If only she could have chosen a reasonable human being, I should be so happy now.'

'Nonsense,' I said. 'Leonard is a capital fellow. So natural. So much straightforwardness, and so much zest for life. You'll get to like him tremendously, before long.'

Perhaps he realised that I was merely trying to inculcate the spirit of optimism.

'Do you think so? Well, I won't keep you any longer. You must be wanting to go to bed. Goodnight, Nicholas.'

'Righty-ho. Goodnight, Mr Boissaens. Thanks for the dinner.'

No lights were on in the Rectory. I rather dreaded what I might find when I went in, but of course my fears were ungrounded. Gillian switched on the light as soon as I came in.

'And why,' she said in the sweet, menacing tone of voice one hears sometimes in the cinema, 'did you try to poison me?'

'Who, me?' I said guiltily. 'You must be mad. I don't know what you are talking about.'

Gillian told the story of how she had found paint remover in the sherry bottle – 'I thought it funny at the time because I knew the bottle was empty' – and knew I had been trying to poison her.

'Don't be silly. I put the paint remover there because it was unsafe to leave it lying around open. It was merely a sensible precaution.'

Gillian continued her harangue, half venomous, half self-pitying.'…I knew something was odd as soon as I came out of the toilet. It isn't even safe to go to the toilet nowadays.'

I was already bored and embarrassed by her behaviour, but at the repetition of that dreadful and insulting word, something inside me snapped. 'Toilet, toilet, toilet,' I screamed. 'You can think of nothing but toilets. Your miserable world is centred around toilets. I know all about it. You think life began in the anus, don't you? Admit it.' I might have strangled her on the spot if she had not fled from the room to spend the night in Bethlehem. When the nuisance of her and her abominable anus was removed, I prepared for sleep. Clearly the problem was worse than I realised. It was not a question of anal orientation so much as anal obsession. Was I alone in the world able to see the dangers of this? If so, what should I do?

A loud knocking awoke me. It was morning. Gillian and George Swinger stood at the end of my bed in a state of high excitement. It appeared that Mr Boissaens had died in the night. He was suspected of having taken an overdose of sleeping tablets. I groaned. More work. As I confronted my uncouth early morning face in the mirror, cleaning my teeth, I reflected that it was a great pity: I had been beginning to make a convert.

CHAPTER TEN

As Rector of the parish and curator of all the benighted souls in the neighbourhood it fell to my lot to unveil the Boissaens memorial statue. So soon after our benefactor's death, and while his mortal remains were still under the scrutiny of pathologists and supercilious medical students in Reading, it seemed to me rather tasteless. But Mrs Boissaens was adamant, and nobody likes to gainsay a widow in these matters.

A murmur of appreciation greeted the statue when it was unveiled in its full horror, outside the Old People's Dance Hall, on a biting December day.

'It is a very humbling moment for us all. Here we are in the presence of what will undoubtedly be hailed one day as a great work of art. At present, perhaps, we can only see its meaning, as St Paul says in his First Epistle to the Corinthians, through a glass darkly. We can only conjecture what was in the artist's mind when he conceived the first idea for this masterpiece, and rejoice that our friend who has departed, Eugene Boissaens, left us this fitting memorial. Is it perhaps a searing indictment of *apartheid*, the system practised in South Africa and other countries to deny our fellow beings their equal rights? Is it a modern representation in symbolic terms of Christ driving the money-lenders from his temple? Does it illustrate the Christian virtues of patience and humility? We may never know in our life-times. All we can say for sure is that it is modern, and that is a good thing. The modern age presents a challenge to us all, in one way and another a challenge which Eugene Boissaens was never frightened to face. He was essentially a modern man, and would have loved to be present today to hear your reactions to his last gift.

'My own interpretation of this sculpture, is one which has immense relevance to the present day. I will not go into details, but if you look closely you will see that all the action of this tremendously vital work centres round a certain part of the anatomy of one of the participants. One would need to be a psychologist, as well as an art expert and moral theologian to understand completely what the artist is getting at. But what I think the artist saw, in a flash of inspiration which must be rare among those so young, was the horrifying, overpowering vision of our own society's anal preoccupation.'

Father Good-Buller, for some reason, had turned up at the ceremony and I had to be very careful what I said. The Archdeacon was listening intently to every word, seeing if he could spot anything at variance with the Thirty Nine Articles of Religion or the Nicene Creed. But not even the Anti-Christ himself was going to prevent me from delivering some part of my message. I wondered about Father Good-Buller's relations with that part of his anatomy.

'There is no need for me to preach a sermon today when you have this eloquent sermon in bronze to remind you of the disease which is creeping over our civilisation. Perhaps this anal obsession which we see in every quarter is not a disease in itself but merely the symptom of a much more profound sickness. Whatever it is, we must fight it with every ounce of energy we have left, and every drop of blood, until we have expunged it from our national psyche.

'I now declare this statue well and truly laid.'

After the Blessing, I was approached by Mrs Boissaens and Father Good-Buller simultaneously. It could not have been a less fortunate combination. Mrs Boissaens was shrouded in black like a nun, which was clever of her, as her husband had only been found dead that morning. But the heavy black veil – I wondered if it was made of inflammable nylon – created the impression of a disguise.

'I don't think you know Father Good-Buller, the Archdeacon,' I said.

'I must apologise, but I failed to catch the name of this lady,' said Father Good-Buller, acting as if he were a Bishop.

'Angela Boissaens,' she said with bell-like clarity.

'Ah yes. We have met, when your husband very kindly gave me lunch after Mr Trumpeter's induction. I can't tell you, dear lady, how we all feel for you in the diocese, but words are so seldom adequate on these occasions. So brave of you, if I may say so, to appear in public so soon.' His tiny pig-like eyes fixed on us both in undisguised suspicion.

'I merely wanted to ask you, Nicholas, if you would care to come up for dinner this evening. The house is rather empty, as you might imagine, now they've taken Eugene away.'

Pigs' eyes settled on me in horror. The invitation was a tempting one. Since her ridiculous scene of the night before, Gillian had not addressed a single word to me and had avoided my company. The atmosphere at the Rectory was not restful; on the other hand, one had to balance the repulsive nature and lecherous inclinations of Mrs Boissaens. Under the boiled gaze of Father Good-Buller, I chose the path of duty.

'Unfortunately that will not be possible. I have far too much work to do.'

'Very well. But I hope you will come up and see me soon. It is at moments such as this that one most needs spiritual comfort, and I have so many arrangements to make about selling the Hall.'

After she had gone, Father Good-Buller said: 'I could not quite follow your sermon, I am afraid. Some of the points seemed a trifle obscure.'

'I should have thought they were simple enough,' I answered. One did not, after all, need a Doctorate of Divinity to understand plain English.

'But that was not really what I wanted to talk about,' said Father Good-Buller. 'You may have heard that poor Mr Tuck has had a nervous breakdown. Until we can find a replacement, it will mean that your Chapter will have no Rural Dean. Since the Bishop did not consider that any of the remaining incumbents were – how shall I put it? – suited to the responsibilities of the post, I have decided to act as your Rural Dean until Mr Tuck is out of hospital, or until we find a replacement. This will be in addition to my usual office as diocesan administrator.'

I suppose he expected me to congratulate him.

'What was wrong with Mr Tuck?' I asked.

'A simple nervous breakdown. I shall not trouble you with the details, just to say that I would not have been excessively troubled when he applied to my office for a faculty to marry two animals – many of us suffer from overwork – but on enquiry I discovered that the service had already been held. Even that would not have been too alarming – the Church's history is replete with eccentrics – but he had chosen to marry a spaniel bitch of some fourteen years with a neutered female cat, in the presence of the entire village. It was going too far.'

So my poor friend had gone too far.

'Surely it would not matter if they were – at any rate originally – of the same sex? There is no question here of condoning the unnatural.'

'One could argue the doctrinal implications endlessly,' said Father Good-Buller in a surprisingly pleasant tone. It was the sort of thing he enjoyed doing, of course. 'But the fact remains that poor Mr Tuck is ill. When I arrived he was ranting about the Devil, and calling down terrible curses on my head. If he cooperates with his treatment and takes his medicine he should be back with us inside twelve months. So many of them refuse to take their medicine, thinking that one is trying to poison them, of course, poor dears.'

I realised now what was the matter with Gillian. She was mad. 'My wife has the same sort of trouble,' I said. 'Would you like to come and see her?'

'Scarcely,' said Father Good-Buller. 'One such experience is quite enough for a week. Has your wife tried to implicate animals in her activities?'

'Not yet, although there is a small cat called Tibbles I am rather worried about. Why don't you come back for a glass of sherry? I can get a bottle in the pub on the way.'

No Anglican clergyman, be he never so High, can resist a glass of sherry.

'Very well, perhaps I will.'

The pub was closed, but I went to the back door to buy a bottle of the same Cyprus sherry which Gillian had finished with Mr Heifer. On the lawn in front of the Rectory I removed the cork and pretended to slip, not getting up until half the bottle had poured away.

'Bother,' I said. I thought the Archdeacon gave me rather an odd glance, but he could not conceivably have guessed my plan. It was going to be most interesting to see Gillian's reaction when I offered her and Father Good-Buller a glass of sherry from a bottle which she thought to be poisoned.

However, fate intervened in the form of a remarkable coincidence. Personally, I believe it was destiny, and yet another example of God's working in our everyday lives. Those who do not enjoy the benefits of a belief are free to think that it was coincidence. As we were going into the house I heard a plaintive noise from above. Looking up, I saw that Tibbles had somehow got herself stuck on the roof, and was adorning a peak above one of the smaller Byzantine domes, crying raucously. I pointed this out to Father Good-Buller as an amusing diversion.

'Should we not do something about it?' he asked.

'I don't think that will be necessary. Cats have the surest way of looking after themselves.'

'What's this?' demanded Gillian, who had come out when she heard our voices.

'Your cat is stuck on the roof. We were wondering if we should do anything about it.'

'Of course you should,' said Gillian, flying into a rage at another example of ecclesiastical complacency. It was not enough that we tried to poison our wives while they were in the toilet; now we even allowed helpless animals to suffer. 'If you aren't going to lift a finger, I certainly shall.' She stormed up the winding staircase to Calvary.

I turned to the Archdeacon. 'You see what I mean?'

He clearly didn't. Being unmarried, he had no experience of the normal give-and-take of married life. Perhaps he thought we were both a little eccentric. 'It's this animal thing coming out,' I explained. 'Like poor Mr Tuck. I thought it would.'

Father Good-Buller recovered his poise. 'We ought to be helping. You go upstairs, and find where the creature is located, and I shall direct operations from the ground, out of doors.'

I reluctantly climbed the stairs to my desecrated shrine. Gillian was looking out of the window in a state of high excitement. 'She's immediately above us. What can we do?'

'We could tempt her down. Have you any cheese on you? Or an apple?'

'Don't be so stupid. If she could come down she would have done so already. As I suspected, you are quite callous. You preach about kindness to animals every Sunday, but when it comes to doing something practical, you refuse to lift a finger. Well, I am going out for her.' Gillian started tucking her dress into her knickers.

'Is that really necessary? You can be seen by the entire village.'

Gillian snorted and started to climb out of the window. 'You might at least help me, or are you too frightened to do that?'

She balanced on the sill. For a moment, the wicked idea entered my head that it would be very easy to give her a little push. To this day, I thank God that I resisted the temptation. It may have been cowardice and prevarication rather than stern moral fibre which prevented me from taking the step which both self-respect and logic suggested, but there is something entirely repugnant about destroying a human life. Christian morality is not so wildly out of tune with man's natural inclinations as its opponents maintain. Far below us, I saw the small black figure of Father Good-Buller, and even from that distance I sensed the brooding suspicion behind his gold-rimmed spectacles.

Gillian was standing on a rounded, three-inch rim which ran around the dome, making endearing gestures towards the cat, which I was unable to see. Only a cast iron gutter stood between her and the ground.

'Is this prudent?' I enquired. Something about my manner must have irritated her, because she turned sharply towards me and in so doing lost her balance.

It was with an extraordinary feeling of *déjà-vu* that I watched her slip down the dome. One was familiar with the scene from television perhaps, and I watched it with all the detachment of a television viewer. Now the gutter was going to break, and Gillian would fall with a terrible, bloodcurdling cry. Her death would be as much a cliché as her life, which was entirely suitable.

Sure enough, the gutter broke under her feet and she resumed her downward slide. But at the last minute her fingers found a tenuous hold on the metal rim. Her angry, frightened face stared into mine for a moment. 'Help me, you bloody fool,' she said.

It was all very well to request help in that peremptory way, but the distance from my window to her wrists was a very long stretch, and there was a small metal spike belonging to the window latch which threatened to impale my stomach. I had also noticed that the window-sill was covered with dust and what looked like mice droppings. Gillian was always most displeased with me when I dirtied my black suits. I was still debating the matter, and had reached out my hand in a half-hearted sort of way, when she lost her hold and fell, taking a large part of the gutter with her. Contrary to accepted tradition, she made no sound whatever. Perhaps she had no time to reflect on which platitude the occasion demanded, but I, with great presence of mind, leant out of the window and cried: 'Watch out, Father Good-Buller. She is falling.'

I think I may have saved his life. Both the gutter and Gillian missed him by inches. I saw him walk away from the paving which surrounded the house and sit on the grass, looking shocked and distraught.

'Hold on, I'll be right down,' I called in my best Bulldog-Drummond-takes-command voice. Gillian lay on her back, her dress still tucked into her knickers. Would it be accurate, I wondered, to describe her as having the appearance of a broken doll? Probably not. Even in that absurdly undignified position and seen from a great height she looked strangely formidable.

As I ran down the stairs, I found that my knees were weak with excitement and shock. I sat down at the bottom of the stairs to collect myself.

'Father Good-Buller, are you all right?'

He stared at me dully, still sitting on the grass. 'Your wife,' he said, pointing. 'Is she?...is she?'

It was almost inconceivable that she wasn't. I walked over to where she lay.

'I'm afraid that she may be,' I said.

The Archdeacon looked even more distraught. Reluctantly, he walked over to where I stood. My shout from the top window had brought George Swinger to the scene, and soon there was a small crowd of villagers gathered at a respectful distance.

'Isn't there something we should do? Oh dear, oh dear, I wish I had returned to Silchester. Surely there's something we should do?' According to the text-books, he ought to have produced his prayer book and embarked on any amount of the mumbo-jumbo which was so dear to his heart. Gillian would have pointed out this inconsistency. But the Archdeacon was plainly upset.

'Isn't there something called the Kiss of Life?' he asked eventually.

Both of us had been reading the newspapers. There was a passing craze for mouth-to-mouth respiration as a means of reviving corpses. Scarcely a day passed without some exhibitionist or other arriving at the scene of an accident and administering the Kiss of Life. It never seemed to work, but I could remember no occasion on which a priest of the Church of England had attempted it. Whatever one might say against the Archdeacon, he had a good nose for publicity. In my mind's eye I could already see the headlines:

'PRIEST ADMINISTERS KISS OF LIFE.'
TRAGIC FALL AT RECTORY.'

I tried to demur. 'Surely, it is too late for that to be of any use.'

'Nonsense,' said Father Good-Buller, who had taken command again. 'Give her the Kiss of Life.'

I sighed. Nobody could call the life of a clergyman easy. Even in moments of acute personal anguish one was expected to play the part. I knelt beside my wife's body and applied my lips to her own, which were as cold and lifeless as they had always been.

'Blow,' said Father Good-Buller.

I blew. The air concentrated in the space between her lips and teeth to escape with an irreverent sound.

'Open her mouth and blow harder.'

It was like blowing up an exceedingly strong balloon, or a car tyre. If I did not remove my mouth in time, the air was blown back into my own lungs.

'It seems to be achieving nothing,' I said.

'Then you must persevere.' He beckoned to George Swinger. 'My good man, do you think you could be so kind as to telephone for an ambulance? There has been an accident.'

Even as I bent over my undignified and useless task, I admired the nerve of someone who could refer to George Swinger as 'my good man'. It required all the self-confidence of an earlier generation. Perhaps I would try it out one day, but I doubted whether I could ever sound casual enough.

After ten minutes blowing I felt faint. There is a medical explanation for this, I believe. 'It is no good. You will have to take over,' I said.

'Nonsense. The ambulance will arrive before long.'

I could not be bothered to explain to him about the occupational hazards of glassblowing in Northern Italy, or the dangers of excessive oxygen intake. He was an imponderably ignorant man.

'I feel faint,' I said.

'Very well, take a few minutes' rest. There is no hurry.' The ambulance took half an hour to arrive. Goodness knows what it had been doing – perhaps shuttling a party of old people around on a shopping expedition; or to collect their free medicine and pensions in the nearest town. Sometimes one despaired of the National Health Service.

The ambulance driver took one look at Gillian: 'I'm afraid there isn't much we can do for her.'

It seemed to me that the situation called for some expression of regret on my part. 'Oh dear, oh dear,' I said. They all looked at me. 'She's my wife, you know.' I would have had no difficulty in disguising my true feelings, if I had had any. As it was, I had no feelings at all, and have never been able to dissimulate from a void.

'Sorry about that,' said the driver. 'We'll pretend there's still some life in her, otherwise we're not allowed to take her away. Easy there, Bob. Head in first. He's new on this job. Can you tell me the exact time and I'll send a report in.'

Tibbles chose this moment to give a wild cry from the roof. We had all forgotten about her in the excitement. The crowd's sympathy shifted at once.

'If you can't do anything for my wife, you might at least do something for that poor cat,' I said.

'Sorry, sir,' said the ambulance driver, with the callous indifference of a High Priest or a Levite. 'That's not our concern. I should try the Fire Service.' It was typical of the bureaucratic attitude to welfare.

'I suppose the Good Samaritan asked the man who had fallen among thieves for his National Insurance Card first,' I said bitterly.

'I beg your pardon, sir?'

'Nothing. Forget it. Just a little lesson in practical Christianity. Can't you hear that poor cat suffering?' Tibbles under-wrote my censure with a truly blood-curdling howl.

'I think she's on heat,' said George Swinger.

'Nonsense,' I said. 'Go and summon the Fire Brigade.'

'We must all remember that Mr Trumpeter has just suffered a most terrible shock,' said Father Good-Buller. 'Let's go inside and sit down, Nicholas.'

'I shan't move until that cat is safe,' I said.

A fire engine arrived with blue lights flashing and horn blaring eight minutes later. The crowd had now grown. Most of the village was there. In six minutes a ladder was sent up, two intrepid firemen tied Tibbles into a cradle and she was lowered to safety amid general applause.

'My wife was trying to rescue that cat when she fell to her death,' I said to the Chief Fire Officer.

'She shouldn't have tried that,' he said sternly. 'That is what the Fire Service is for. Half our troubles come from people trying to do things for themselves. You wouldn't believe some of the stories I could tell you. I must say, you've got a very nice cat there.'

Eventually the fire engine drove away, the crowd dispersed and life returned to normal.

'And now, Father, we might go inside for that glass of sherry,' I said.

'Do you know,' said the Archdeacon. 'I really think that it would be most welcome.'

When we were ensconced in my study, he became quite maudlin. 'You have been through a great strain, Nicholas. At least you have the comforts of religion. Many people find that at times of stress there is nothing so settles the soul as the sacrament of Penance. Would you like me to hear your Confession?'

'Not at present. My mind is too confused. Perhaps later.'

'You can be sure that anything you tell me under the seal of the Confessional would never be repeated. Perhaps your conscience is troubled. If the matter concerns anything which happened this afternoon, I would have to deny any knowledge of it after you had come to me for absolution, even if it concerned something which I had seen with my own eyes.'

He was inviting me to nobble the only witness in the supposition that I had pushed Gillian off the roof. But my conscience was clear – I had resisted the temptation. Clearly his eyes were not so good as he thought.

'No, no. You misunderstand me. Gillian was not pushed, she fell. If it does you any good I will tell you I pushed her for Confessional purposes, but in fact she fell.'

'In that case it would be a waste of the sacrament of Penance,' said Father Good-Buller, much disappointed. 'But we might have a sacred oath.'

'All right, but later. What I want to ask you is not to reveal to anyone what you know about my wife's mental condition prior to the accident.'

'Her mental condition?' Clearly, he had forgotten.

'Yes, yes. I was telling you about it. How she constantly thought people were trying to poison her, how she began taking an exaggerated interest in animals. But there were more cogent reasons than that for supposing she was mad.' His eyes widened as I told him about Gillian's anal obsession, how it started as an erotic perversion and reached the stage when she was never happy unless she was either in the lavatory or talking about it. I was beginning to describe the way in which this obsession had spread, like a hideous canker, throughout the village and beyond until it threatened the entire fabric of our contemporary society, when the front-door bell rang.

'How most unfortunate,' said the Archdeacon. 'Of course, you have just suffered a terrible shock. I will not breathe a word, and I now earnestly suggest that you do not confide in too many people. Perhaps we can arrange a holiday for you somewhere.'

My visitor was Police Constable Terence Winner, the brother-in-law of George Swinger. 'I am extremely sorry to intrude at such a moment,' he said, 'but we must make a brief report on all accidents in the home involving a fatality for presentation to the coroner's court in the event of an inquest. I wonder if you two gentlemen could assist me in describing briefly what happened.'

After we had done so, PC Winner measured the distance from the wall to the place where we estimated Gillian's body had lain, and asked me to take his measure up to Calvary so that he could write down the length of drop. He also found a button which had been torn from her dress when the ambulance men were putting her on the stretcher. He picked it up ostentatiously – and I thought offensively – in a pair of tweezers and put it in an envelope, which he licked down.

'You understand that I am both the diocesan Archdeacon and temporarily Mr Trumpeter's Rural Dean. In each case I am his immediate superior, and would be most interested to hear of any developments in this case before they become too widely known. Mr Trumpeter has just had the most terrible shock, and we would not like him to be too much exposed at present, if you see what I mean. If we can avoid any necessity for him to attend the inquest, I am sure it would save him much mental stress.'

I could not make out what the Archdeacon was talking about, but PC Winner seemed to understand.

'We always try to be considerate, where there has been a bereavement,' he said.

'Wouldn't you like to come in for a drink?' I asked.

'The police constable is far too busy,' said Father Good-Buller. 'In any case, he is not allowed to drink on duty.'

Ten minutes later, after the policeman had gone, Father Good-Buller prepared to leave.

'I know that I am only getting in your way. At such moments of acute distress, the soul's only refuge is in prayer and private devotions. I should advise you to go to bed, and say a votive Mass tomorrow morning. Of course, I shall remember you both in my prayers. Tomorrow you may be over the first shock, and we can discuss the idea of a holiday for you. If there is any difficulty in finding a locum, I might be able to take over your parish duties myself for a short time.'

'That is very kind, but I should not like my work to be interrupted. My place is here, in the parish. Please don't go – there's still some sherry left.'

'Then we shall finish it tomorrow morning. I must return to the Close, as I have a deputation of ladies arriving from Silvercombe. They wanted to see the Bishop, but Dr Toplass suspects that they may wish to complain about their Rector, and he has no interest in hearing complaints. He only wishes to hear messages of love from now onwards. It is a new idea which has occurred to him – we are composing a pastoral letter about it at the moment. If we all loved each other a little more how much more agreeable life would be.'

I enjoyed hearing him talk in this subversive way. It was like living under a totalitarian regime, where the tiniest twitch of an eyebrow could reveal a cynical detachment from platitudes which one was obliged to mouth.

'Try to put in a mention of this anal thing. It is far the greatest perversion of love with which we have to contend. Until one has come face to face with it, one can have no conception of its ramifications. At a guess, I should say it is more widespread and certainly more pernicious than drug addiction.'

'Of course I shall.'

'What do the women of Silvercombe wish to complain about? I should not have thought that my good friend Cyril Heifer would harm them.'

'I can scarcely be in a position to tell you that until I have seen them. Perhaps your remark contains the seed of their complaint. But your Chapter has been causing a lot of trouble recently. Only Mr Plimsoll and Mr Jackson seem to be able to survive without it. In the first case, this may be because nobody knows that he is there at all. Do you know how many Easter communicants Mr Plimsoll counted this year? None at all. Mr Jackson sent in a figure of 2,200, but on enquiry he revealed it as the estimated number of people who had eaten luncheon in his parish. The two operations were essentially the same, he said, provided one ate one's luncheon with love. He is very advanced in his views, of course. Still, his generous estimate helped to swell the diocesan figures for Easter communicants, and that is the main thing. We would not like to think that we were losing ground.'

His cynicism revolted me. Perhaps Mr Tuck was right. If not even the Archdeacon pretended to believe in God any more, how could we hope to deceive the laity? Mr Jackson might be entitled to his opinions, but Father Good-Buller certainly was not.

'If you are hinting that Mr Heifer has unnatural inclinations, I can assure you that you are wrong. As a matter of fact, he was slightly in love with Gillian. Only yesterday, she told me, he came and sat in this room and revealed his love.'

'And did anything follow from this revelation?'

'No. He was too good a man for Gillian. Possibly something about her manner put him off. You see, she had this fixation...'

'I know all about that. Now I must go, and I do most earnestly entreat you to rest. You have been under a great strain. I should not talk to many people until you have seen a doctor. Shall I ask Dr Plimsoll to call?'

'There is no need – in any case, I believe he specialises in cancer. If you have a temperature he gives you penicillin, otherwise it is a bottle of the Mixture. Gillian must have drunk twenty bottles of different coloured mixtures, and they never did her any good. If you can't stay, I must say goodbye. Don't believe a word those fiendish women from Silvercombe tell you. They are all liars.'

'You forget, Mr Trumpeter, that I ran parishes for twenty years. Hell hath no fury like a woman scorned.'

It was no good his quoting the Bible at me. I wasn't going to agree with him whatever he said.

'One should feel pity and compassion for them,' I said. 'It is probably not their fault that they are wrongly orientated. They are no more than products of their environment, and society nowadays not only condones but actively encourages the present confusion.'

'No doubt, no doubt. Well, I must go. Get some rest, Nicholas. You look very tired, and I am worried about you.'

When I was left alone in the house, some of my earlier exhilaration returned. I emptied out Gillian's planning room in a frenzy of excitement, which only abated when £70 worth of electronically tested modern appliances were spilling out of the dustbins. Then I began to realise that it was dark, and switched on all the lights in the house. The television was playing a programme called: 'Research for Tomorrow – the fast-changing technological, scientific and medical scene' which normally would have been enough to prompt the deepest gloom, but tonight it had the freshness of a spring daisy. I also turned the wireless up to maximum volume in the kitchen, although this was more a gesture of defiance than anything else, as there was no one except Tibbles to hear it.

After a time, I became aware of the silence which lay like a surface of snow around the two islands of noise and warmth. If I turned the television off, I could hear the beating of my own heart. If I moved around the room, I was frightened by the noise of my own footsteps.

'The scientists of today are paving the way for a new and exciting future,' said an odiously mature young man with compassion stamped on every wrinkle of his well-fed face. 'Better schools.' We saw the photograph of a large, modern building.

'Better hospitals' – the same building from another angle. 'More leisure' – two male models drove a speedboat in front of a female model on water skis. 'Better pensions' – a grinning old age pensioner drew an enormous bundle of notes through a post-office grille. 'Better housing' – the original building, photographed from the bottom. 'And more opportunities for the young' – a succession of shots, including a teenager scoring a goal at Rugby football, and dancing to the gramophone in a room furnished in Scandinavian taste with wall-to-wall carpeting. 'This is the future,' said the mealy-mouthed cretin earnestly. 'And these are the men who are working to bring it about – men like Kurt Friesinger' – we saw a pair of eyes staring through thick spectacles which merged into untidy black hair starting almost at the eyebrows; 'Ron Capelby' – another, similar. 'Terence Freeth, from Newark' – Newark, wherever that might be, had not produced a beautiful son in Terence Freeth. He was hideous. If I looked like that, I should refuse to appear on television. 'And William Cunliffe, from Leicester.' We saw a young man running slowly in a tracksuit, his eyes fixed ahead as if he were mesmerised. Probably it was a mistake, intended to illustrate the leisure facilities which awaited us. But would the name of Nicholas Trumpeter never appear on the roll of honour, as someone who was struggling to shape the future of the community? Would everything I had worked for be lost from sight as soon as I died? No future generations of kiddies would bless me for their extra iced lolly, no merry old age pensioner would buy an extra ounce of bulls' eyes. I had a fight, and I knew where I was going, but I was completely alone in my campaign and in that dismal, lonely moment I craved recognition. The applause of listening senates to command my lot forbade. I knew that 20,000 Anglican clergymen were in competition with each other for the opportunity to appear on 'Epilogue'. Had I no place in the future? I switched off the set, feeling rather hurt.

The silence surrounded me again. Half of my conscious mind thought it heard the noise of somebody walking around upstairs, and it was not until a few minutes later that I realised there was no one in the house and I grew frightened. Gillian's stories returned to me as I walked up the stairs. Every creak in the huge house made me stand still, aware only of my terror and the fact that my heart was beating faster than usual. Why did nobody come and discuss their problems with me? In the village families often moved into their neighbours' house when somebody died. Suddenly, I remembered I had an appointment. It was eight o'clock and I was already late.

Mrs Hallowes' house was warm as toast. All the White Circle were there, drinking tea. 'We hardly knew whether to expect you this evening, dear Brother Peter, so soon after your bereavement.'

'I hope you're not shocked,' I said, 'but I was feeling lonely, and the house is rather unpleasant at the moment.'

'Of course we're not shocked,' said Mrs Hallowes. 'Nearly all of us have suffered a bereavement at one time or another. It doesn't do to sit around moping. Surely Mrs Trumpeter wouldn't expect you to be miserable. She was such a fun-loving lady.'

'So full of life,' said Mrs Tartfoot. 'It's hard to imagine she's gone.'

'She was the sweetest lady you ever could hope for,' said Mrs Morelli, entering into the spirit of it all.

'We must hope she has found fresh fields and pastures new,' said Mrs Hallowes.

'I am sure she has,' said Miss Honeycomb and Mrs Lackie together.

'Was she just looking out of the window, then?' said Mrs Allsopp.

'No, no. She was climbing on the roof.'

'Why should she be doing that? It wasn't what Miss Cornhouse said.'

'Miss Cornhouse wasn't there,' I said.

'Nobody was there,' agreed Mrs Allsopp. 'Just the two of you.'

'And the Archdeacon,' I said.

'He wasn't there,' said Mrs Allsopp. 'He just heard about it afterwards. Nobody really knows what happened. I don't suppose they ever will.'

Everybody regarded me with a new interest. I wished to change the subject.

'Weren't you going to do something about Mr Mandarill tonight?'

Nobody wanted to move from the warmth. 'In the light of the day's events, we thought we might give it a miss,' said Mrs Allsopp. 'In fact we were about to go home.'

I had no wish to return to my empty house. 'His spirit was very active tonight,' I said.

'We should go along now,' said Mrs Hallowes. 'It is a full moon, and we have no excuse, really. Come on, Sisters. Bring your wrappings. We will need to borrow a surplice and stole, Brother Peter.'

'Nothing easier. What are we going to do, put a stake through his coffin?'

'It may not be necessary.' Mrs Hallowes had obviously not thought of that.

No genuine ghosts could possibly have looked more ghostly than the eight of us when we were assembled round my predecessor's grave.

'Hold hands,' whispered Mrs Hallowes. 'It concentrates the Laife Force.' We shuffled round tile grave a few times, while Mrs Hallowes stood in the centre, listening. The night was cold and unfriendly, but anything was better than solitude.

'We are calling you. We are calling you. Percy Mandarill, can you hear me? We command you to be at rest,' said Mrs Hallowes, in a ghostly voice. In spite of myself, I shivered. 'You must obey our commands. Can you hear me? Can you hear me?'

We all listened in silence. Suddenly, unmistakably, there was a rustling noise from under a yew tree not three yards from where we stood. Mrs Allsopp screamed. Miss Honeycomb picked up her nightdress and ran like a hare. Mrs Hallowes clung to me like a limpet and twisted me round until I was between her and the source of the noise.

A figure emerged from the gloom.

'Can you please tell me exactly what is going on here, Mr Trumpeter?' said Police Constable Terence Winner.

Mrs Hallowes was the first to recover her poise. Dressed in a white surplice with my purple stole around her neck, she presented a formidable picture of outraged dignity.

'And what are you doing here, officer? Are you aware that you are standing on private property? I suppose you think that now you are a policeman you can get away with anything. I could tell the police force a few things about our Terry Winner, before he became Police Constable Terence Winner, which would make them think twice about employing you at all! And about your younger sister. I suppose you're going to pretend that she has never been near Mr Flitcroft's barn? That's the place you should be keeping your eye on, but I expect the police are in on it, too. I should definitely take his number, Mr Trumpeter, and report him for trespassing. If he has anything to say, we'll have him up for molesting and corruption. They'd never believe his word against yours, particularly when they hear what I've got to say about him.'

It was a gallant effort, but she put her case too strongly. If she had been less aggressive, we might have laughed the whole thing off over a glass of Cyprus sherry.

'Acting upon complaints received and following the discovery of certain articles in this churchyard around the vicinity of where we are now standing, I took up watch on this churchyard following the request of the incumbent transmitted to me by the Vicar's Warden, Mr George Swinger. The discoveries, which were of a certain nature, led me to believe that the said churchyard was being used as the scene of certain irregularities. During the month that this area has been under intermittent surveillance, nothing out of the ordinary was observed. However, on the present night of the sixteenth of December, 1967, I have observed certain happenings which will require to be the subject of a report, and I must ask you to accompany me to the station for the purpose of making a statement.'

'Certainly not,' said Mrs Hallowes. 'Terence Winner, you must be out of your mind.'

'I think we should go along,' I said.

'And be assaulted,' said Mrs Hallowes, but her indignation lacked conviction. 'I know all about the police and what they get up to. None of us is going anywhere near the police station tonight. You can come and take statements tomorrow morning if you like.'

'When you have all had time to confer,' said PC Winner unpleasantly.

'Under the circumstances, I think it would be better if I went to the police station and explained everything,' I said. 'PC Winner is only doing his job.'

At the police station I was given a cup of tea and everybody was most helpful. The Station Sergeant clearly thought that Winner had been over zealous. I explained that it was a perfectly ordinary service of exorcism which had been held, and that we understandably had no wish to attract publicity.

'Trust Winner to put his foot in it,' said the Sergeant sympathetically. This stung the Constable to reply.

'What about the filthy things which were found lying around in the churchyard after these religious ceremonies? And what was Mrs Hallowes doing, dressed up as a priest?' I explained patiently that the nuisance of which I had previously complained was never repeated and that it had no connection with the exorcism. Although opinion in the Church of England was divided on the subject of female ordination, one could never stand in the way of progress and someone had to give a lead. But he had won the Sergeant's attention.

'Furthermore I have been asked to keep an eye on Mr Trumpeter by his Archdeacon, the Reverend Good-Buller. We was both worried about Mr Trumpeter's state of health following the tragedy at the Rectory this afternoon.'

The Inspector came to join us.

'You misunderstood the whole thing,' I said to Winner. 'Father Good-Buller was just discussing a campaign which we are both going to run against the anal orientation of modern society. It is highly complicated, and it would be a waste of time for me to explain it to you, but you should be interested as the law is liable to become involved. You see many people in the complex and problematic world we know, are allowing themselves to be persuaded that psychological and motivational impetus comes from the bowel function, which we know to be absurd, and which when stated as baldly as that, can be seen to be absurd. But its advocates are seldom so explicit, so that you have a state of muddle among otherwise healthy minds which can lead, on occasion, to sexual perversion and ill-health. That is what we are up against. As soon as the enemy comes into the open, we can shoot him down, but it is against the unseen enemy we must be on our guard. None of us, I imagine, is totally unaffected, but until we have achieved some measure of awareness our vulnerability is bound to increase in exact proportion to the amount that our willingness to resist is sapped.'

'Yes, I see what you mean,' said the Inspector. 'Tell me, Mr Trumpeter, do you often suffer from headaches?'

'Most infrequently. But the chief danger is that unless we can create an awareness of the situation, society will no longer be in a position to purge itself, and we shall all rush headlong over the cliff like Gadarene swine.'

PC Winner muttered something about offensive language, but the Inspector said: 'Fainting fits or nervous depression?'

'Never. If we can persuade the police to work with us, that will of course be a tremendous advantage. I have never been prepared to join the general denigration of the police force. Of course there are bound to be a few unfortunate exceptions, as you have in every community of people, but for the most part they seem a very decent body of men,'

'I think we may ask the doctor round to have a look at you, sir,' said the Inspector. 'You say you suffer from occasional headaches, but have you any other physical symptoms – loss of memory, singing in the ears, abdominal pains, anaemia, infrequent or irregular motions…?'

'What's that?' I asked.

'Constipation or diarrhoea,' explained the Inspector.

'You see what I mean?' I shouted. 'There we go again.' But even as I spoke, I realised that the cause was lost. If the law provided no refuge, where could one turn? Everything which had been happening in England since the war – welfare, penal taxation, teenage sexuality, proletarian enrichment, the flight from religion – all led by inexorable logical progressions to the final collapse of the Rule of Law, and this had now happened.

'The person to see him is the Reverend Good-Buller,' said PC Terence Winner.

'Father Coughing will put a few things in the suitcase for you,' said the Archdeacon. 'You must wait in the car with me.'

'Who is Father Coughing?'

'He is the Bishop's Chaplain, as a matter of fact.'

'And is he in the plot, too?' I had seen through Father Good-Buller.

'I am afraid so. Or if that is what you would like to believe, you are at liberty to do so. The most important thing is that you should not excite yourself.'

'Where are we going?'

'To the Holy Fathers' centre at Fyfield. There you will be properly looked after, and you will be able to take a rest. I do not think you are at all well, Nicholas.'

'I am perfectly well. I suppose that in a few minutes time you will start asking how many times I go to the toilet?'

'That will not be necessary. You have been under great strain, and with so many things happening on top of each other, your resistance has cracked. Try not to worry about anything.'

He was quite wrong, of course. My resistance was very far from being exhausted, but it might not be prudent to let him see this. In any case, I had no wish to return to the solitude of the Rectory. It was quite amusing for the moment to be so much more intelligent than anyone else, so many steps ahead.

CHAPTER ELEVEN

Christmas with the Holy Fathers was something which had been dangled in front of our eyes for days. If we did not behave ourselves and drink up our medicine, we were told, it could not occur.

On Christmas Eve we decorated the communal rooms with coloured pieces of paper. I later learned that they had been supplied by the Government, like all the good things of life. In the morning, at breakfast, we all sang 'Happy Birthday to you' to Mr Tuck, which caused him great pleasure. A dance had been arranged for the evening, which made me wish that the ordination of women could be speeded up. There was something a little sad about the sight of twenty clergymen dancing around the dining hall in dressing gowns. Of course everyone was very kind, but it seemed unfair on them that they should have to dance together to be cheerful. After a while, I began to cry, and then it was medicine time.

'Come on, drink it up,' said Staff Nurse Mackie.

'I wouldn't touch it,' said one of my new friends, Mr Ramp. 'It's called Largactil. The Germans used to use it in the war.'

'You shut up, or I'll send you to bed,' said Staff Nurse Mackie.

'No, but seriously, Staff Nurse. Isn't it true that the Germans used to use it?'

'I wouldn't know. Your turn is coming next, Mr Ramp. Now the pills, Mr Trumpeter. All eight of them. Did you swallow that last one? All right.'

'Of course they used to use it,' said Mr Ramp, 'in some of their camps. The Germans found it very effective.'

'Stop talking for a minute and drink it up.'

'You know there's nothing wrong with any of us here,' said Mr Ramp. 'It's just the drugs they give you. Of course one has no option. That's how these places stay in business.'

'Now your pills. Come on, I've got to stay here until I've seen you take them.'

'There's no question that you've got to stay here. Nobody is compelling you. Dr Hyssop would never hear about it if you left. What you mean is that you *wish* to see me eat my pills. Isn't that what you mean?'

'Possibly,' said Staff Nurse Mackie.

'In that case, you should say so,' said Mr Ramp.

Later, we all sang carols as we drank our Ovaltine or Horlicks.

> *We three Kings of Orient are*
> *Bearing gifts we travel afar*
> *Field and fountain, moor and mountain*
> *Following yonder star.*

We sang from duplicated sheets which were circulated in the ward. Afterwards, Mr Ramp said: 'Of course, those weren't the right words. They were something made up specially for the inmates here. The idea is that we should have no contact with the outside.'

'Aren't they the right words?' I asked.

'Don't be absurd. Of course they're not. Look at this: "We three Kings of Orient are" – what on earth does that mean?'

'It is supposed to represent the three Magi. The singers are enacting their journey to Bethlehem for Epiphany. In the first line we announce our identity.'

'You mean to say you swallow that? If you are just announcing your identity, you could say: "We are three Kings from the Orient." Why do you say: "We three Kings from Orient are"?'

'To make it rhyme with "far" and "star".'

'Nonsense. The idea is to mystify us until we think we're loonie. In any case, it doesn't make sense to say we three kings from orient are. You'd never get people outside this place to sing it – they'd want to know what it meant. Of course it doesn't mean anything. Then here they've put: "bearing gifts we travel afar". Is it likely that anyone would go round singing that? They'd be locked up in no time. In any case, the whole idea of these presents was that they were supposed to be a surprise. If you saw three foreign-looking people singing that they were bearing gifts, you'd think they were loonie. Of course you would, and of course that's the whole idea. They want to confuse us.'

'Not only the Three Wise Men,' said Mr Tuck. 'What do you suppose they would do if Jesus happened to be born nowadays? They'd put him in a mental hospital.'

'Of course they would,' said Mr Ramp. 'The whole thing is self-perpetuating. They build all these hospitals and then they have to find people to fill them. So if they can't find enough real-life loonies they have to get hold of people like us and turn them into loonies. The Germans did the same sort of thing during the war.'

At the beginning I had been fairly susceptible to these arguments. I was certainly not prepared to place any credence in Dr Hyssop's denials of them. He was a most indifferent man and, in any case, as Mr Ramp pointed out, he had a vested interest in keeping us misinformed. But twice a week I saw the specialist, who came all the way from Devizes and pointed out that he had nothing to gain by misinforming me, as he was paid a lump sum by the Health Service every year, which was not tied to productivity in any way. He said that the medicines we took actually were helpful, and that they had been scientifically proved.

He thought that I had been suffering from strain due to overwork, and he said that my fears about the anus were all a delusion. Nobody else was worried by the subject at all, he claimed, and it was only I who was obsessed. He may have been right, but I was only partially convinced, realising that he would be bound to take the opposing view. On the other hand, he was most sympathetic when I told him how terrible Gillian had been to me, particularly in the matter of giving me food I disliked and insisting that I should keep my clothes clean. He seemed a much more sensible man than most of these so-called psychologists.

'And look at the next line,' said Mr Ramp. ' "Field and fountain, moor and mountain" – what is all this about fountains? Have you ever seen a fountain in a field? Of course you haven't. And, in any case, if you did, you would probably walk round it, not straight through the middle. That would be silly. The only reason they make us sing these songs is to make us forget about normality. They want us, when we receive a visitor, to say something in conversation like this: "Oh hullo, Aunt Myrtle. I saw a most interesting fountain in a field the other day and I decided to walk through it because you see I was following this star of royal beauty." Then Aunt Myrtle will go away and say to all her friends: "Of course poor Cuthbert really isn't quite up to it yet. He keeps seeing stars which make him want to go paddling." That's the way they keep us here.'

After Christmas depression set in. The patients – for such we had been told to call ourselves – divided sharply into those who sat around all day engrossed in their own thoughts and those who were eager to make friends and swap ideas. The first category included most of the older clergymen, who were extremely surly when approached and took no interest in communal activities. Among the second, there was a recognisable jet-set which included myself, Mr Ramp, Mr Tuck and two or three others. Between moments after medication, when we sat like a row of boiled beetroots staring at each other, we held energetic meetings at which many important topics were discussed. We saw little of the Holy Fathers who ran the establishment. The original idea had been that they should look after the patients, but when the science of mental health made greater strides than they were prepared to follow, the Government took over, and the Holy

Fathers devoted their life anew to prayer and meditation. Occasionally during their recreation hour we heard the noise of a ping-pong game, and the Prior conducted all our religious services in the chapel, but otherwise there was no contact. A few cassocked figures worked in the kitchens, but they were called 'Brothers' and were presumably less holy than the Fathers.

'The reason that nobody comes to church nowadays is that they are bored. The services make no appeal to the imagination,' said Mr Tewny, a deeply serious biblical scholar from Margate.

'I don't think it can be boredom which drives people away,' I said. 'They are prepared to put up with any amount of boredom on television, and if ever they are shown something which isn't boring they complain bitterly. The reason must go deeper.'

'Yes,' said Mr Ramp. 'On television they at least feel that they are being bored in a worthy cause, whereas religion nowadays has disreputable associations.'

'If I appeared on television they would listen to me,' said Mr Tuck.

'Or to any of us,' agreed Mr Ramp. 'That is why we are locked away here. We are too dangerous. If religion became more like television we would be in direct competition with all the huge vested interests of monopoly capitalism.'

'Of course television is a drug,' said Mr O'Queen. 'And that is what we are up against. Many people have found that some of the mind-expanding drugs are an enormous aid to religion. If the Established Church was made the only official agent for the distribution of LSD we would have all the young people flocking in. I tried that in my parish with pep pills, and the results were spectacular. Then the police raided us and the Bishop sent me here. We can't expect any help.'

'But apart from the young people we must try to bring in the Mums and Dads,' I said. 'What they like about television is the advertisements. I know that is true. If they have a choice of two programmes, they will always turn to the one with advertisements in preference to the other, however much worse it is. The television people know it, of course. Have you noticed that during religious programmes on independent television, they never have advertisements? That is because they want people to turn to the other channel. People like advertisements because they are a form of flattery, reminding them that the gift of free will still operates to the extent of allowing them to choose between two brands of dog food. Even if they haven't got a dog, they'll always watch the advertisements. If we were allowed three-minute breaks for commercials during our services, people would be much more interested.'

'It would also be a useful source of additional revenue,' said Mr Ramp. 'It is scandalous the way they under-pay the clergy. If we conducted a market research into regular church attendance, one would certainly find an enormous preponderance of people in the AB groups. That is where we have the edge over the Methodists, who are mostly CD, and the Catholics, who are almost entirely D. It would be a tremendous extension of the Church's function, and a fascinating new medium for advertisers.'

'The Press wouldn't stand for it,' said Mr O'Queen. 'It would put most of the newspapers out of business. Perhaps that is why they are always on the look-out for attempts to revitalise the Church. My youth club was made the subject of an *exposé* in *The People*.'

'I was exposed by the *Sunday Express*,' said Mr Tewny mournfully.

'The reason why all the newspapers and television programmes are so interested in us is because they are scared,' said Mr Ramp.

Television reached us in the smoking-room on a set which had no controls. Mr Ramp was convinced that all the programmes were specially made to confuse us, just as the newspapers were specially printed to keep us in ignorance of outside events and undermine our sanity. The specialist assured me that this was not so, and that the cost of such measures would in any case be prohibitive, but Mr Ramp was not to be persuaded. He produced a copy of the *Daily Mirror* and started reading out the headlines: ' "Cup-crazy Peter's green and yellow hairdo"; "An air girl's bosom grew until it burst"; "Pushchair Mum is turned off bus" – do you think that's what people seriously put in newspapers? Here's another one: "Me Old China. That's how Tizzi, the clown, angered the Chinese waiter." What does that mean, may I ask? Look at this one, down column on an inside page: "Wilson to end pay inequality". Now is that likely? And if it were true, wouldn't it be on the front page instead of all this stuff about "My bride-to-be, by a Catholic priest"?'

'That's just the *Daily Mirror*,' someone said.

'All right, we'll look at the *Daily Telegraph*. Here we are. "No Bonn Pressure for British Six Entry". What is that supposed to mean, may I ask?' The note of triumph in his voice was unmistakable, and I found it hard to defend the specialist's case. 'Who are the British Six and what sort of pressure is referred to? The gas pressure, the pressure of population, or does it mean some of the pressures the Germans used to use during the war? It may be a coincidence, but I can't help noticing there are six of us here in this room.' He was quite right, of course. There was myself, Mr Tuck, Mr Tewny, Mr O'Queen, Mr Ramp and an old fool whose name I never learned sitting in the corner. 'Look at the next line of the heading: "Tactful moves in Paris". Of course that is nonsense. The first line is supposed to reassure us – there is no Bonn pressure for any of us to enter, even if we wished to. The second line seems to hint that if we make trouble we will be put into Plaster of Paris. Of course, it's all bluff. In any case, they're not allowed to. But they print these things to keep us worried.'

Six ordained priests of the Church of England stared at each other in alarm. I happened to know that Mr Ramp was wrong. The specialist had told me, and he was certainly not a fool. But it was one of the conventions that one had to respect other people's obsessions.

'I shouldn't think they have them specially printed, as it would be too expensive, but I think all the newspapers are in this thing to try and confuse everybody. You see they print absolute rubbish day after day until everybody accepts it, and then the rubbish gets worse and worse until it doesn't make any sense at all. People still read it through force of habit, and they gradually convince themselves that it makes sense, so that anyone who announces that it is nonsense can be put in a home like this one. That way they manage to keep these places full while simultaneously ensuring that the advertising revenue is safeguarded.'

Most of them accepted this explanation readily enough. Only Mr Ramp demurred: 'They are all watching us, you see. They want to know our reactions, because they are frightened. If we expose what is going on, they will all fall from power. Especially Mr Wilson. I don't trust him. He says one thing and means another. He sees the Church as the only thing standing between himself and supreme power. That's why he's got us in here. He wants to declare war against Vietnam so that he can announce a State of Emergency and then use his emergency powers to put us into this Bonn pressure. I'm not sure what it is, but I don't like the sound of it at all. Before coming in here I was reading a book about some of the methods which the Germans used during the war. We've been learning a lot from them, in one way or another.'

'Time for medicine,' called Staff Nurse Mackie in the sing-song voice he affected on these occasions. Meekly, we all shuffled down the corridor. On the way, Mr Tuck drew me aside: 'Do you think they all know who I am?' he whispered.

'I expect so,' I whispered back.

'It's my dressing gown,' he said. 'They can't expect to recognise me in this dressing gown.'

'I should keep quiet about it,' I whispered. 'People will only be jealous.'

'That's what the specialist said. But when people know who I am they will realise that I am really a very good mixer.'

Poor Mr Tuck. I noticed that he was rather left out of the conversation. He could only bear to talk about himself and was out of depth in our abstract discussions. But I was interested and disturbed by some of the points we had covered. When I raised them with the specialist, he did not seem too pleased.

'Of course none of us can know what is in Mr Wilson's mind, but I do assure you that he has no sinister intentions so far as you are concerned. He probably doesn't know you exist. Even if Mr Ramp claims he saw it in the *Daily Telegraph* you should let him sort out his own problems. Quite frankly, I am worried about him. He does not listen to other people and refuses to give his confidence to anyone. I am not sure that it is doing you much good to stay here any longer. If you can promise to take your medication, there is no reason why you shouldn't be out and about. The great thing is not to worry too much. If something is upsetting you, or looming very large in your life, come and talk to me about it and we'll see if we can straighten it out. One can't go and check up with Mr Wilson because, obviously, the Prime Minister is a very busy man. All these things are looked after by the Minister of Health and quite honestly I am not even sure who he is, at the moment. They change so quickly. This place doesn't even come under the Ministry of Health altogether, as it is only assisted. I think the Church Commissioners pay for the upkeep. Now you're making very good progress, Mr Trumpeter, and the most important thing is not to worry.'

I pretended to be meek and amenable. Afterwards I explained to Mr Ramp what he had said: 'He doesn't know what is in Mr Wilson's mind. Honestly, Cuthbert, I don't know how we can be expected to.'

'I do,' said Mr Ramp. 'I know exactly what the blighter's thinking.'

Tea was enlivened for us by Mr Tuck. He arrived late, when we were all sitting down, and stood on the small stage at the end of the hall smiling beatifically around. Then he removed his dressing gown and revealed himself as naked underneath. Still smiling like an angel, he was removed immediately by the two staff nurses.

'I am sorry about that, gentlemen,' said Staff Nurse Mackie when he returned. 'You mustn't let it upset you. Mr Tuck is perfectly all right now.'

'Not at all. It was quite a little cabaret,' said Mr O'Queen. 'That is the sort of thing we need in church to make the congregation sit up. It will be better, of course, when we have women priests.'

Poor Mr Tuck did not emerge from his bedroom for two days, and then his dose had been increased so much that he spent the time in a daze and talked to no one. I believe they may have been giving him the shock treatment. They could be extremely tough on people who stepped out of line.

Father Good-Buller visited me on the Monday within the octave of Christmas. He did not enquire after Mr Tuck, and seemed ill at ease.

'They tell me you will be out of here soon, Nicholas. I must say, we can't wait to have you back. The Chapter is in a very poor state. I discovered that Mr Plimsoll had not conducted a single religious service for over two months. He said that as nobody ever bothers to turn up, it seemed a waste of time. And Mr Jackson insists on serving lemonade at all services nowadays because he says they used to do so in early Christian times. The Bishop wants me to organise a diocesan rally in the summer where he can preach the Gospel of Love, but I keep telling him that everyone will be on holiday then. How are they treating you?'

'Very well.'

'Good, I am so glad. I wouldn't mind coming in here for a rest myself, one of these days. Your mother-in-law has been in touch with me and says she'll be delighted to have you come and stay when you are out. She came down for the funeral, which went off very well. I must say, I thought she was a most charming woman. She told me how she always prepared special dishes for you when you used to visit her with your late wife.'

'I don't want to see her.'

'But is there anywhere else you can go? You have no people, I understand, and I think it would be a little gloomy going back to the Rectory all alone.'

'I am not going back to the Rectory. I want to stay here.'

'So do we all, my dear Nicholas,' said Father Good-Buller. 'Ever since the medical profession has abandoned its more unpleasant methods of treating – ah – people who have had nervous breakdowns, I have often thought how pleasant it would be to retire to one of these institutions. I don't suppose there would be much point in appealing to your sense of duty, although if your ailment were being cured by the traditional, well-tried methods of flogging and cold baths, no doubt the call of duty would be stronger. They were probably neither more nor less effective than the present psycho-analysis and drug treatment. But unfortunately we are much too short of priests in the diocese to keep you here in idleness much longer.'

'You propose to drag me out before I am cured.'

'Kicking and screaming into the twentieth century. The dividing line between those who are mentally ill and those who are in perfect health is extremely ill-defined. One can only judge these matters by accepted canons of eccentricity. Many people would think it eccentric to become a priest. Accepting, as we do, only those candidates for the priesthood who offer themselves, we are bound to overlook a certain range of foibles which might prejudice our candidates' chances in less vocational employment.'

'You mean that all clergymen are mad.'

'By certain standards. And we, in the clerical profession, have other standards by which the vast majority of laymen would be declared insane. For instance if you were to announce from the pulpit that you no longer believed in the divinity of Christ, or in the objective existence of a Deity, or in the immortality of the soul, we should decide that you were suffering from a nervous breakdown; whereas that is the considered opinion of most thinking people in England.'

I was profoundly shocked to hear the Archdeacon talking in this way. In my mind, he represented the full horror of organised religion: an unthinking dogmatism sadistically applied; ancient and inane rituals performed in the dark; a cast-iron logic which neither reason nor compassion could ever assail. I had always resented his presence, regarding Good-Bullerism as the natural enemy of true religion, whatever this might be, but I had also felt strangely protected by it. His was the blind orthodoxy by which my own unorthodoxy could be examined and found intelligent, daring and likeable.

'Do you believe in God?' I asked.

'What an extraordinary question,' said Father Good-Buller. 'I am not sure that I am going to answer it. You are being highly personal. Of course it depends what you mean by believe. I can say that I believe that this table is made of wood, because my senses of touching, smelling and seeing indicate that this is the case. I can say that I believe in the brotherhood of man, but what on earth do I mean by that? Merely, of course, that such a Brotherhood, if it existed or could be made to exist, would in my opinion be desirable. You will have noticed that in its original Latin, the Nicene Creed uses the preposition "in" followed by the accusative case, suggesting destination, rather than the ablative, suggesting a permanent state. Belief, in its theological sense, is a creative activity requiring constant exercise of the imagination and the will, rather than a conclusion based on deductive reasoning. Alternatively, if you like, it is a supernatural gift of God, unevenly bestowed at the best of times and in ever diminishing quantities nowadays, which can only be combated by the deliberate activity of the Devil working through our pride. But I tend towards the first explanation. I am glad you raised the point – one has so few opportunities for discussion of what might be called our first principles.'

'Do you believe in God?' I asked.

The Archdeacon thought for a moment. 'Perhaps not entirely,' he said.

'Then why do you pretend to do so?'

'Come, come. That is a most unfair question. Do you suppose that all the eager, idealistic young men who work in advertisement offices believe that their brand of soap is so much superior to any other? The Church of England is my life, and the purpose of religion is to survive. The whole of human life and endeavour is a process of self-perpetuation. In order to survive, one must find out what people want to hear, and tell it to them. Unfortunately, our function has been usurped to a very large extent nowadays by newspapers and television, with which we can't satisfactorily compete on their own terms.'

'Funnily enough, that is just what Mr Ramp was saying.'

'No doubt. My difference with the Jacksons of this world is a difference of means, rather than ends. He thinks that the way to bring people into church is to give them lemonade and assure them that every time they sit down to family lunch they are receiving Communion, whether they like it or not. I believe that you must create an atmosphere of mystery. People appreciate much more what they imperfectly understand, which accounts for the enormous market in every kind of artistic gibberish. But it is only a question of survival. And we can't survive without priests. When do you think you will be able to resume your duties?'

'Never. I don't think I wish to continue as a priest.'

'Don't be so silly. You are over-wrought. What else do you suppose you could do – become a school-teacher? Nobody would apply for ordination in the first place if he had been prepared to do anything else. Have you ever tried life in an office? The frightful, undignified sublimation of one's personality in the herd? When you speak to people in the outside world, delivering an opinion or expressing a hope, they answer back, you know, and every moment of self-expression has to be paid for a hundred times over by listening to other people's fatuous and boring and uninformed comments, which they expect to be treated on a par with one's own. Religious life is the only place for a civilised, articulate person nowadays. One could try journalism, but think of the other journalists. In politics you must work twice as hard to ingratiate yourself and you don't have the same security. Any employment involves acquiescence in lies. There is no truth to proclaim nowadays – it is all a question of viewpoint or mood.'

'Father Good-Buller, I believe you are mad.'

He was quite unperturbed.

'No doubt there is an element of truth in what you say. I have often wondered. Now, I think the Bishop is mad. Whenever Dr Toplass speaks, I wonder what freak of fancy can suppose that there is any logical pattern of thought or connection of ideas behind his utterances, but I have seen rows of people listening happily for hours. Give them properly constructed sentences and a coherent train of thought and they will go to sleep. But if you are adamant in your refusal to return to Middlewalk, we will have to find another job for you. Mr Tuck is more of a problem. We would not like to lose a man so easily, but I can see that his own particular foibles do not make him a suitable candidate for normal parochial duties. We thought that his appointment to the rural diaconate would settle him. Both his self-identification with Christ, and his obsession with animals seem to indicate a lack of self-confidence. No doubt something will be found.'

'But why is it so important that the Church of England – or any other religion – should survive, if it has nothing to teach?'

'I did not say that we have nothing to teach; merely that we have not discovered it yet. Various interesting suggestions have been put forward. No doubt something will be found. Adherence to any church is a question of faith. You have got to believe that there is a need. We know that people have television sets, motor-cars, central heating in their homes, endless entertainment of every sort, but you have got to believe that there is a need for something else. If you haven't that belief, you are lost. Once the belief is established, it only remains to discover what the demand is, and how best we can supply it. I believe they like real-life mystery, something they can participate in themselves, but I may be wrong. Perhaps you believe that people are simply happy with their television sets and bingo and central heating.'

'Yes, certainly,' I said. 'Most of them, anyway.'

'That is exactly what everyone believed before they invented ten-pin bowling,' said Father Good-Buller. 'You see what I mean? People like you were sitting back complacently, letting a fortune slip through their hands. I believe that there is a whole range of experience – and highly pleasurable experience – which only religion can supply. The important thing is that we are not in *opposition* to bingo, drink, sex, drugs, central heating or anything else. We are in *addition* to them. That is the mistake which so many good and sincere men in the Christian Church have made. You should never knock your competitors – it only draws attention and does them good through free publicity. Of course religion fills a need, or it wouldn't exist. If we are to secure a wider market, we must find out what the wider need is and exploit it. Religion can add pleasure to sex, point to drug-taking, make central heating doubly enjoyable by training us to reflect on all the poor wretches in Tibet and other Asian countries who have none, turn bingo into a holy crusade. That is a counsel of perfection, of course. Until then, we must keep religion going as another side-show at the fairground of life, no less enjoyable or diverting because it is unlike the others.'

'Medicine time! Medicine time,' called Staff Nurse Mackie.

'Ah well, I have talked far too long. I wonder what employment would most suit you in a few weeks' time. No doubt something will be found.'

CHAPTER TWELVE

My duties as chaplain were heavier than I had been led to suppose. For the first three weeks I merely held two non-denominational services every Sunday. These were poorly attended, until I suggested to Mr Grizard, the entertainments manager and my direct superior in Kaptain's Sunshine Holiday Camp, that we should change their name to Weekly Oecumenical Fun Sessions. This was a great success, and before long I had a thousand campers a week. We sang 'Daisy, Daisy, Give me your answer do', and 'I'm for ever Blowing Bubbles' to warm up beforehand, although I rejected a suggestion from Bluecoat Brian that the men should be persuaded to sing falsetto.

'They always like that. It helps to break the ice,' he said, but I thought it would be undignified. The Archdeacon visited me in the first week, and settled my qualms about holding non-denominational services.

'The Church of England is essentially non-denominational,' he said.

It was in the fourth week that the rot set in. Mr Grizard had been impressed by my earlier suggestion, and it led him to suppose that he could make greater use of his chaplain. I had no objection to wearing a blue coat over my black shirt and clerical collar – it involved no extra expense – but when he asked me to judge the baby competition I correctly recognised it as the thin end of the wedge. Before long, I presented the prizes at each weekly Kaptain's Princess of the Week tournament, I judged the

Glamorous Grandmother and King Knobbly Knee of the Week competitions and I was one of three judges at the Tiny Tots all-in wrestling and the Junior Lads' Boxing Tournament. This last responsibility was no great strain as a directive from the main office of Mr Delano Kaptain himself had insisted that all competitions should be declared a draw, unless in the case of an obvious foul, when the offender's entire family should be removed from the camp immediately.

None of which I really minded. Nor did I mind being asked for my autograph every time I stepped outside the chaplaincy. Bluecoat Brian, who was a vacationing theological student from Keble College, Oxford, told me that he always signed his autographs: 'With best wishes from Bertrand Russell'. Once, in a spirit of levity, I signed myself: 'Yours in sympathy, Jesus Christ'; but I regretted it immediately afterwards, and spent several days in anguish until it was apparent that nobody had noticed.

What I did resent was a second directive from Mr Grizard to the effect that as I had been promoted from staff status to being a Blue coat, I could no longer talk to members of the staff. I was only allowed to talk to campers. For my guidance, he indicated that they were especially interested in discussions about the other Kaptain camps, and in order to stimulate these conversations I was equipped with five badges, testifying that I had attended Kaptain camps in Exeter, Merioneth, Carlisle, Blackpool and Cyprus. In fact, the campers had no conversation at all on any subject, and were always mystified by my lies about the superior facilities available in Carlisle.

The isolation imposed by my new dignity came as a severe blow. The other Bluecoats were usually too much exhausted after their day's work to communicate in anything except grunts. They resented my presence in the Bluecoats' Mess, and on the few occasions I could persuade them to talk they evinced a misanthropy so profound that even I was appalled. Many of them were students, the rest were ship's stewards on shore leave, who detested students.

'If you had got up at six o'clock this morning, supervised fun and games in the Regency Ballroom, led the Kiddies' Treasure Hunt in a Batman suit, called Bingo numbers all afternoon and danced with all the ugliest women in the Old Time Dancing Hall until eleven o'clock at night, you wouldn't feel like bright conversation,' said Bluecoat Peter. He was a ship's steward whose wife had run away with the man from Kleeneze brushes.

'The trouble with these people is that if you tell them loud enough and long enough that they're having a good time they will believe you. Otherwise they would never know, and their holiday would be wasted,' said Bluecoat Brian.

'I would like to poison them all on the first night,' said Bluecoat Peter. 'Nobody would ever notice the difference, least of all them. It would do the country a lot of good, too. All these so-called workers are just battening off the salary earners, and those with unearned income. They are not an economic proposition in England, any more.'

'Come, come,' said Bluecoat Brian earnestly. 'With redeployment of labour many of them could make a positive contribution.'

'Who's going to redeploy this shower? In England you can't even redeploy a mouse without having the whole trade union movement down your throat. The English working class have battened off the productive efforts of the bourgeoisie for too long. When I come to power, these places are going to be converted into Kaptain's Sunshine Extermination Camps. All the lads and lasses will be given a little pill when they arrive, and on the first night we'll show them how to swallow their sunshine pills, all together in one big gulp. What does the Chaplain think?'

'I can't go all the way with you there, Peter. One must try to remember against all the evidence that these people are our fellow-human beings. And the camps already fill a very useful role in keeping them off the roads at holiday time.'

'Listen to him. The campers are not human bloody beings, they are campers. Just try treating them like human beings and see how far it gets you. In any case, my solution keeps them off the roads, too. The working classes are a mill-stone round our neck in the struggle for national survival. If by any chance some of them are doing a useful job of work, all the money has to be taken away, and given to those who aren't. Abolish the lot, that's what I say.'

These conversations might have been quite stimulating if there had been the faintest suggestion of humour in Bluecoat Peter's manner. But his opinions were so violent, and any opposition was treated with such contempt that it was a pain to be involved.

Perhaps in reaction to his violence, I would have been driven to a sympathetic study of the campers, who wandered between entertainments with their mouths hanging open and their faces set in the vacant expression of people whom other people are trying to make happy. But all my affections were tied up in Trixie Patman, who ran the doughnut stall next to the sundae bar in the Don Quixote Modern Dancing Ballroom. Trixie was studying marine biology at the Wolverhampton Institute of Further Education. She let me make love to her once in the chalet she shared with Pat Bunce, from the Bedford College of Art, and Susan Thumble, who was engaged to a trainee executive in central heating. But after my official appointment as a Bluecoat we both agreed that the risks were too great, and I could only talk to her when buying a doughnut. This was very expensive and my health began to suffer.

'Man doth not live by doughnuts alone,' I whispered to her once, but she replied: 'That will be a shilling, sir' and continued to smile inanely at a grandmother from Fulham who could not find the right change. She now spent her evenings with Terry Hope, a most unprepossessing young man who emptied the dustbins on the York and Gloucester lines. He had won a good BSc degree at Southampton, and could not make up his mind whether to become a poet, and apply for a Government grant, or emigrate to Toronto, where he had a good job lined up with a firm which manufactured bulk liquid transporters. He had a mad scheme by which everyone would be obliged to live in precincts, according to their occupation, and was a convinced Socialist of the authoritarian, neo-feudalist variety. He spoke of the Community as twentieth-century theologians tend to speak about God, as a mysterious entity whose existence is apparent only to themselves and whose purpose is able to be manipulated in conformity with any idea which may enter their heads. In the winter he conducted sociological surveys or drew National Assistance, and my own guess was that he would return to empty the dustbins on the York and Gloucester lines for many summers. Once a person had known this life, anything else seemed dull. His chalet-mate was a despondent individual who claimed that he had once read Kierkegaard in French and the shock had been so great that he had never read another printed word, but devoted his life to maintaining the electrical plant in the kitchens. Both were passionate advocates of enlarging the mind through drugs, and greedily ate any pills which came their way – cough preparations, aspirins, glucose derivatives, aperients, iron pills and others designed to reduce a mother's milk in cases where she had made the decision to bottle-feed.

'This is the grass roots,' said Terry once, before my elevation put a stop to our intercourse. 'This is what life is all about. This is the promised land of the big Rock Candy mountain. They don't realise, of course, that somebody must still empty the dustbins. That is the function of the intelligentsia in our sick, materialist society. These people have no need to die. They are already in Heaven.'

I must say we give the campers quite a good time. In my own small way, I think I make a contribution. Our guests have no moral problems, and their medical problems are adequately catered for in the camp hospital, but I think they like seeing me around, and they nearly always give me a cheery wave. My old friend Mr Tuck has been appointed the Bishop of Leisure, and calls on us every year to judge the finalists in the Holiday

Housewife Competition. Last year he brought the Dairy Queen of the Commonwealth with him in a helicopter and we arranged all the children in a huge 'W' for Welcome. I am not allowed to walk around in the evenings, because Mr Grizard heard complaints that I was inhibiting people's enjoyment. I try to accept this and other restraints as humbly as I can. Baby competitions are the most trying, but Mr Grizard says that even famous actresses have been assaulted when they tried to judge a baby competition, and mothers will only take it from a parson. Personally, I think they are a great mistake, and only cause bad blood, but Mr Grizard says that many families would not come at all if their babies were left out of the fun.

Once Mr Ramp visited us, on a day's outing with his Mothers' Union, paid for by the sale of home-made cakes and jam. They had a most enjoyable time, and one of his mothers was sick on the big dipper.

'This is where we should all be,' he said to me. 'We're wasting our time in the parishes. Annual outings simply aren't good enough if the Church is to survive in the modern world. This is what people like, and they even pay to come here.'

We wandered around the camp together: music blared from loudspeakers every twenty yards; a few people jumped in and out of the swimming pool with loud cries of delight at their own daring; an invalid was wheeled past, and everyone moved out of the way with gentle clucking noises; a few teenagers threw a beach ball at each other rebelliously; others sat in the sun with their mouths open and blinked.

'Many of these people have been working at the factory bench all the year, and this is their one chance to get away from it all,' I said.

'Nonsense.' said Mr Ramp. 'Nobody in England does anything he doesn't want to do nowadays. Unless, perhaps, he is too lazy to do anything else, in which case you might say he has chosen the lesser evil. There are a few things which their limited imaginations suggest as enjoyable. Here they try them out, and return to their normal occupations telling each other that they have experienced enjoyment.'

'Ah, but they need something else,' I said. 'And that is what I am here to supply.'

'Of course they don't need anything else. You are merely here in case they think they do. Mr Kaptain would not like them to think that they were missing anything.'

So it turns out that my good friend Mr Ramp is just another atheist, after all. I am disappointed in him. He refuses to recognise the immense amount of good one does simply by existing. If the people don't need me, Mr Kaptain will hardly waste a lot of money hiring me to walk around waving and smiling to passers-by. As it is I do nothing but add to other people's happiness. In my own way, I think I have become rather a saintly person.

Auberon Waugh

A Bed of Flowers

John Robinson, chairman of the $1,000 million Robinson Securities, is one of the richest men in Britain, but is more interested in establishing an alternative community in the Somerset countryside than pursuing power. After he is framed with a lump of cannabis resin he embarks on his new lifestyle at Williams Farm and invites like-minded souls to join him. In this idyllic backwater Rosalind and Orlando start a love affair, while others take up drugs or religion. As the community is cultivating its bed of flowers, a sinister crime is planned in Whitehall...

The Foxglove Saga

Auberon Waugh's first novel, *The Foxglove Saga*, is an imaginative and savage satire. Its hero, Martin Foxglove, is a golden boy. In the eyes of his devout and beautiful mother, Lady Foxglove, he can do no wrong. Despite her unceasing, protective care, Martin chooses a set of wholly unsuitable friends and abandons his Christian faith. He is hell bent on making a bid for freedom, and he holds all the cards, playing them one by one.

Auberon Waugh

Path of Dalliance

The Honourable Guy Frazer-Morrison and Jamey Sligger have come up to Godolphin Hall, Oxford from their Roman Catholic school, Cleeve. Rumours concerning their sexuality start when they share a college room. Waugh expertly describes the dons, the students, the relationships, intrigues, snobbery, politics – and Guy and Jamey's desire to get laid and get on in life.

Who Are the Violets Now?

Arthur Friendship earns his living writing advice columns for *Woman's Dream*, a woman's magazine. To offset this depressing and dreary activity he works for a peace organization and idolises the lovely – yet unattainable – Elizabeth Pedal. Arthur's plans do not turn out as he wishes them however, in this tragi-comedy.

'Most satire is concerned with knocking the Establishment and criticizing the forces of reaction. The refreshing thing about Auberon Waugh's waspish wit is that he sees just as much to laugh at among…liberals of the Left' – *The Express*

'*Who Are the Violets Now?* Reminded me of the clown's antics; never still, always amusing, sometimes hilarious, sizzling with speed, filled with panache and sangfroid' – *Punch*

AUBERON WAUGH

WILL THIS DO?

'The only question left hanging in the air is the one which every journalist asks himself on submitting an article. It is also the one with which we may all eventually, in trembling hope, face our Maker: Will this do?'

The question should rather be: How does one cope with being the son of a father as famous as Evelyn Waugh? From this side-splittingly funny autobiography it is clear to see that the young Auberon more than managed. A privileged background, unusual childhood and public school education are followed by Oxford and a career as a writer and columnist. Waugh's portrait of his father is affectionate yet droll, his tone self-deprecating, and his stories entertaining and sad by turns. The biting wit is addictive.

'Both an exuberant chronicle of English literary life and a very funny sendup.' – James Atlas, *The New Yorker*

'Terrifically entertaining…funny, acerbic, and a little sad.' – Michiko Kahutani, *The New York Times*

OTHER TITLES BY AUBERON WAUGH AVAILABLE DIRECT
FROM HOUSE OF STRATUS

Quantity	£	$(US)	$(CAN)	€
FICTION				
A BED OF FLOWERS	7.99	12.99	19.95	13.00
THE FOXGLOVE SAGA	7.99	12.99	19.95	13.00
PATH OF DALLIANCE	7.99	12.99	19.95	13.00
WHO ARE THE VIOLETS NOW?	7.99	12.99	19.95	13.00
AUTOBIOGRAPHY				
WILL THIS DO?	9.99	16.50	24.95	16.50

ALL HOUSE OF STRATUS BOOKS ARE AVAILABLE FROM GOOD BOOKSHOPS
OR DIRECT FROM THE PUBLISHER:

Internet: www.houseofstratus.com including author interviews, reviews, features.

Email: sales@houseofstratus.com please quote author, title and credit card details.

Hotline: UK ONLY: 0800 169 1780, please quote author, title and credit card details.
INTERNATIONAL: +44 (0) 20 7494 6400, please quote author, title and credit card details.

Send to: House of Stratus Sales Department
24c Old Burlington Street
London
W1X 1RL
UK

Please allow for postage costs charged per order plus an amount per book as set out in the tables below:

	£(Sterling)	$(US)	$(CAN)	€(Euros)
Cost per order				
UK	2.00	3.00	4.50	3.30
Europe	3.00	4.50	6.75	5.00
North America	3.00	4.50	6.75	5.00
Rest of World	3.00	4.50	6.75	5.00
Additional cost per book				
UK	0.50	0.75	1.15	0.85
Europe	1.00	1.50	2.30	1.70
North America	2.00	3.00	4.60	3.40
Rest of World	2.50	3.75	5.75	4.25

PLEASE SEND CHEQUE, POSTAL ORDER (STERLING ONLY), EUROCHEQUE, OR INTERNATIONAL MONEY ORDER (PLEASE CIRCLE METHOD OF PAYMENT YOU WISH TO USE)
MAKE PAYABLE TO: STRATUS HOLDINGS plc

Cost of book(s):————————— Example: 3 x books at £6.99 each: £20.97

Cost of order:————————— Example: £2.00 (Delivery to UK address)

Additional cost per book:——————— Example: 3 x £0.50: £1.50

Order total including postage:——— Example: £24.47

Please tick currency you wish to use and add total amount of order:

☐ £ (Sterling)   ☐ $ (US)   ☐ $ (CAN)   ☐ € (EUROS)

VISA, MASTERCARD, SWITCH, AMEX, SOLO, JCB:

☐☐☐☐☐☐☐☐☐☐☐☐☐☐☐☐☐☐☐☐

Issue number (Switch only):

☐☐☐

Start Date: **Expiry Date:**

☐☐/☐☐   ☐☐/☐☐

Signature: ————————————

NAME: ——————————————————————

ADDRESS: ——————————————————————

——————————————————————

POSTCODE: ——————————

Please allow 28 days for delivery.

Prices subject to change without notice.
Please tick box if you do not wish to receive any additional information. ☐

House of Stratus publishes many other titles in this genre; please check our website (**www.houseofstratus.com**) for more details.